KU-439-941

PROPHECY AND PEOPLE IN RENAISSANCE ITALY

PROPHECY AND PEOPLE IN RENAISSANCE ITALY

Ottavia Niccoli

translated by

Lydia G. Cochrane

PRINCETON UNIVERSITY PRESS

PRINCETON, NEW JERSEY

TRANSLATED FROM *PROFETI E POPOLO NELL'ITALIA DEL RINASCIMENTO*

PUBLISHED BY PRINCETON UNIVERSITY PRESS, 41 WILLIAM STREET,
PRINCETON, NEW JERSEY 08540

LIBRARY OF CONGRESS CATALOGING-IN-PUBLICATION DATA

NICCOLI, OTTAVIA.
[PROFETI E POPOLO NELL'ITALIA DEL RINASCIMENTO. ENGLISH]
PROPHECY AND PEOPLE IN RENAISSANCE ITALY / OTTAVIA NICCOLI ;
TRANSLATED BY LYDIA G. COCHRANE.
P. CM.
TRANSLATION OF: PROFETI E POPOLO NELL'ITALIA DEL RINASCIMENTO.
INCLUDES BIBLIOGRAPHICAL REFERENCES.
ISBN 0-691-05568-8 (ALK. PAPER) — ISBN 0-691-00835-3
(PBK. : ALK. PAPER)
1. PROPHECIES (OCCULTISM)—ITALY—HISTORY—16TH CENTURY.
2. OCCULTISM—ITALY—HISTORY—16TH CENTURY. 3. ITALY—
HISTORY—1492–1559. I. TITLE.
BF1812.I88N53213 1990 133.3'0945'09031—DC20 90-31111

WE ARE GRATEFUL TO THE ITALIAN MINISTRY OF FOREIGN AFFAIRS FOR ITS SUPPORT

PUBLICATION OF THIS BOOK HAS BEEN AIDED BY A GRANT FROM THE PAUL MELLON FUND OF PRINCETON UNIVERSITY PRESS

THIS BOOK HAS BEEN COMPOSED IN LINOTRON GALLIARD

PRINCETON UNIVERSITY PRESS BOOKS ARE PRINTED ON ACID-FREE PAPER, AND MEET THE GUIDELINES FOR PERMANENCE AND DURABILITY OF THE COMMITTEE ON PRODUCTION GUIDELINES FOR BOOK LONGEVITY OF THE COUNCIL ON LIBRARY RESOURCES

PRINTED IN THE UNITED STATES OF AMERICA BY PRINCETON UNIVERSITY PRESS, PRINCETON, NEW JERSEY

1 3 5 7 9 10 8 6 4 2

1 3 5 7 9 10 8 6 4 2
(PBK)

CONTENTS

EPILOGUE

ILLUSTRATIONS

INTRODUCTION

THIS STUDY was conceived many years ago, the offspring of a headlong reading of an extraordinary volume, the British Museum Library catalog of sixteenth-century Italian books. Reading this volume was not only fascinating ("je ne sais pas de lecture plus facile, plus attrayante, plus douce, que celle d'un catalogue," as Sylvestre Bonnard said) but fruitful. Although my scrutiny was guided by no preordained criteria, it produced (among many other things) a good many prophetic print pieces of a "popular" sort (popular according to the criteria established by Francesco Novati, to be treated in chapter 1 of this book) published between the end of the fifteenth century and about 1530. Since I was fortunate enough to be in London where I could immediately get my hands on the texts whose titles had piqued my curiosity and peruse them, scrutiny of the catalog gave rise to more methodical study as I attempted to comprehend both the vast success of this publishing genre and the nature of its public. At the same time, going through the stacks of the Warburg Institute library, I occasionally came across traces—marginalia in books, extracts, *plaquettes*—of studies that the institute's creator had begun but never completed that also led me back to the theme of the dissemination of prophecy and divination and their significance in the early modern era. In short, from an awareness that materials existed grew a realization of the full-blown phenomenon that lay behind them: the extraordinary dissemination of prophetic tensions among vast but socially and culturally varied milieus in Italy during the *guerre horrende* from the invasion of Charles VIII to that of Charles V. The dates are significant and suggest at least a partial interpretation of the phenomenon, which clearly appears to be linked to the political instability of those years. Prophecy during the Renaissance and, even more, during the Middle Ages, is well known and has been widely studied. The picture that emerges here, however, is at least partially new: A generalized culture that had profound ties to the political and religious events of the period was disseminated very broadly through many different channels. In other words, it was a different aspect of the Renaissance.

In their first phase, my labors took the form of a study of early sixteenth-century popular prophecy as it was transmitted orally from high culture and as a divinatory science autonomous from high culture that even reached the illiterate through itinerant preachers and tale singers, or *cantastorie*. As my research broadened, my perspective to some extent shifted. I shall attempt to describe that change in perspective in these introductory remarks, leaving full discussion to the chapters that follow.

First, the adjective "popular" (an ambiguous term laden with echoes of diatribes that I do not intend to go into here) will, I hope, acquire greater precision by reference to a precise category: the "people" of cities and towns. I have preferred the terms "folk" or "folklore" when the oral transmission of residual pre-Christian elements or elements extraneous to official culture were involved.[1] The prophetic phenomena studied here seem, in fact, to be genuinely urban. Prophecy was a living experience communicated from a portable platform to listeners in the town square, from the pulpit to the nave, in the workshops and the markets, where print pieces and broadsheets were displayed, sold, and discussed. It was an important part of townspeople's practical knowledge. Machiavelli and Guicciardini, Leo X and the Venetian ambassadors will also be heard from in these pages, but only from time to time, when they came into contact with that knowledge. Otherwise the elites of the courts and the universities are excluded from the picture. Nonetheless, the cultural domain that I have attempted to analyze appears extraordinarily varied and composite. It includes "donazole e poltronaglia" (silly womenfolk and common good-for-nothings), as one Milanese chronicler wrote, but also artisans, merchants, and notaries. One should also keep in mind the infinite gradations between illiteracy and fluent reading and writing ability in the period. I have done my best to respect the irreducible individuality of each case while seeking out the characteristics that unify them.

Willem Frijhoff, speaking about the ambiguity of the adjective "popular" (also in a prophetic context), offers this advice: "It is better to attempt first to determine with as much precision as possible . . . the lines of transmission and the circulation groups for texts [and] to examine the nature of the changes that occurred during this process."[2]

This is precisely what can be done for the aspects of sixteenth-century prophecy that will be examined here. In point of fact, it has gradually become clear that the most outstanding characteristic of that phenomenon is not its location within a specific cultural and social milieu but rather an exceptionally open circulation and exchange of its content through different social and cultural strata. Such transfers did not occur only from high to low; quite the contrary. Fragments of a system of prophetic signs that clearly pertained to popular culture appeared, taken out of context, within a higher culture, finally to be used even for political ends—as can be seen repeatedly in Rome under Leo X. More generally speaking, we might say

[1] I concur here with the anthropological viewpoint of Jean-Claude Schmitt, *The Holy Greyhound: Guinefort, Healer of Children since the Thirteenth Century*, tr. Martin Thom (Cambridge and New York: Cambridge University Press, 1983), p. 7.

[2] Willem Frijhoff, "Prophétie et société dans les Provinces Unies au XVIIe et XVIIIe siècles," in Marie-Sylvie Dupont-Bouchat, Willem Frijhoff, and Robert Muchembled, *Prophètes et sorciers dans les Pays Bas. XVIe–XVIIIe siècle* (Paris: Hachette, 1978), p. 360.

that until about 1530 ecclesiastical high culture accepted and freely manipulated materials from folklore. Peter Burke, borrowing the term from Claude Lévi-Strauss, speaks of a *bricolage* in which low culture reassembled and reorganized elements from high culture;[3] the present work will furnish full testimony to the fact that in the time span studied here, that phenomenon operated in the opposite direction as well. Moreover, these transfers of cultural content through various strata of society were usually accompanied by a change in their social and political function. This is an observation that Jean-Claude Schmitt makes concerning medieval culture,[4] but it is certainly valid for the beginning of the modern era as well. The present work exemplifies this hypothesis.

The picture can become even more complicated, however. At times one has an impression of parallel traditions, analogous in content but on different cultural levels; not truly independent of one another but with points of coincidence and reciprocal encroachment. This is the case of the *monstra*—a term that designated the abnormal and the monstrous, but also the marvelous, the prodigious, or the portentous—to which the present work gives particular attention. In the early sixteenth century a fascination with portents doubtlessly reflected the renewed interest in classical culture (in particular, in Cicero's *De divinatione*); at the same time, however, strange occurrences were part of the system of signs of the culture that came to be called *divinatio popularis*. The humanists' interests were not limited to classical texts but ranged from antiquity to their own day, creating a system of interconnected references. As Machiavelli said in a well-known passage of his *Discourses*:

> How it comes about I know not, but it is clear both from ancient and modern cases that no serious misfortune ever befalls a city or a province that has not been predicted either by divination or revelation or by prodigies or by other heavenly signs.[5]

Guicciardini also declared it believable "that now is like the past [and] that great things have been signified ahead of time by great prodigies."[6]

[3] Peter Burke, *Popular Culture in Early Modern Europe* (New York: New York University Press, 1978), p. 123.

[4] Jean-Claude Schmitt, "Les Traditions folkloriques dans la culture médiévale. Quelques réflexions de méthode," *Archives de sciences sociales des religions* 52, no. 1 (1981): 5–20. See also a somewhat analogous point of view in Manuel Martín Serrano, *Sociología del milagro. Las caras de Bélmez* (Barcelona: Barral Editores, 1972), p. 13.

[5] Niccolò Machiavelli, *Discorsi sopra la prima deca di Tito Livio*, ed. Corrado Vivanti (Turin: G. Einaudi, 1972), I, 56, pp. 194–95; quoted here from *The Discourses*, tr. Leslie J. Walker, revised by Brian Richardson; ed. Bernard Crick (Harmondsworth: Penguin Books, 1970), p. 249.

[6] Francesco Guicciardini to Goro Gheri, 19 January 1518, in Guicciardini, *Carteggi*, ed. Roberto Palmarocchi, 17 vols. (Bologna: Nicola Zanichelli, 1938–1955), vol. 2, p. 240.

"Both ancient and modern cases"; "now is like the past": For men of the Renaissance, the classical world was not closed tight, nor was it an object of mere archaeological investigation. It became more comprehensible with the aid of signs manifested even in latter times that repeated their ancient predecessors. Thus the monsters represented both an element from classical tradition and a part of folklore. Nor did these two different aspects necessarily signify independent and separate levels of culture, particularly since even in the ancient world interest in prodigies was considered part of popular superstition.[7]

All these considerations enter into my reasons for emphasizing the channels of transmission for prophecy and the people who served to spread its message. As a contribution to the history of communication, the present work will speak at length of broadsheets, drawings, and letters, of preachers and of *cantastorie*, the professional tale tellers. It will also touch on the more general problems of the transmission of information and of what defined culture in Italy in the period under discussion. Indeed, if the distinctive sign of the culture that I have sought to reconstruct was exchange; if it lay at the intersection of different cultural and social strata and was imbued with motivations and meanings that varied underneath a certain number of consistent and stereotyped formulas (and all the materials presented here may at times seem even monotonous), then studying the means, the techniques, and the go-betweens that assured those transfers is indispensable. This explains the type of sources used. They tend to be printed rather than manuscript because print pieces are more likely to provide a good grasp of the problems involved in the distribution of a text, of its public, and of the uses to which it was put. They are iconographic because images had a great importance within a culture that was in great part oral. Finally, they are city chronicles which, because they offer an extremely rich variety of information on all aspects of urban life, in particular on those that concern us, bear the direct imprint of urban culture. I have used (and cited on almost every page) one chronicle that stands out from all the rest, the journals of Marin Sanudo.[8] In my opinion, this extraordinarily valuable source has not yet been utilized as much as it deserves. More than a chronicle, Sanudo's *Diarii* are a true archive in book form, and at times in more than book form, given their compiler's singular talent for gathering, sifting through, and transcribing materials of every sort. It would be extremely useful, even from the bibliographical point of view, to draw up a catalog of the pamphlets, broadsheets, drawings, and other materials that Sanudo inserted into the original manuscript of his chronicle. It gives sin-

[7] Raymond Bloch, *Prodigi e divinazione nel mondo antico* (Rome: Newton Compton, 1981), pp. 36–40.

[8] Marino Sanuto, *Diarii*, 58 vols. (Venice: R. Deputazione Veneta di storia patria, 1879–1903).

gular testimony to its compiler's omnivorous appetite for news. Not only does it furnish a mass of all manner of information on the greatest imaginable range of social, religious, cultural, and, of course, political topics in contemporary life over a thirty-year period; it also provides a view, albeit through a privileged observer, of the dynamics of the circulation of information within Italy and between Italy and Europe (as Pierre Sardella realized forty years ago).[9] The *Diarii* have, of course, been heavily used and much cited, especially in studies of ecclesiastical history in the Veneto, but close scrutiny shows that they contain a wealth of still largely unexplored material.

One of the ways to study prophecy is to examine it as an instrument of propaganda. There have been a number of studies (largely but not exclusively regarding England) that emphasize the relationships between prophecy and political propaganda, such, for example, as the works of G. R. Elton, Katharine Firth, B. S. Capp, Jean Céard, and Elisabeth Labrousse.[10] Investigation of this sort usually proves fruitful, in the sense that prophecy in the early modern era was an undeniable part of the arsenal of power (as festivities were another), and the propagandistic use of prophecies will arise often in these pages. In my opinion, however, too exclusive an emphasis on propaganda is in some measure insufficient. First, the very variability in the function of prophetic material makes it evident that propaganda was not its only purpose. But that is not all. Thomas A. Kselman's study of miracles, prophecies, and visions in nineteenth-century France has shown that a purely political approach to these problems, analyzing them in terms of instruments for and symptoms of the conflicts between church and state, is deceiving and reductive, just as any study of "mentality" that neglects the political, institutional, and intellectual context represents a distorted reflection of reality.[11] Like other phenomena that served to bind together or patch up connections between the popular world and ecclesiastical and, on occasion, political institutions, prophecy was a unified and complex entity requiring evaluation both for its specificity and for the re-

[9] Pierre Sardella, *Nouvelles et spéculations à Venise au début du XVIe siècle* (Paris: Armand Colin: [1948]).

[10] B. S. Capp, *The Fifth Monarchy Men: A Study in Seventeenth-Century English Millenarianism* (London and Totawa, N.J.: Rowman and Littlefield, 1972); Jean Céard, "P. A. de Chavigny: le premier commentateur de Nostradamus," in *Scienze, credenze occulte, livelli di cultura: Convegno internazionale di studi (Firenze, 26–30 giugno 1980)* (Florence: L. S. Olschki, 1982), pp. 427–42; G. R. Elton, *Policy and Police: The Enforcement of Reformation in the Age of Thomas Cromwell* (Cambridge: Cambridge University Press, 1972); Katharine R. Firth, *The Apocalyptic Tradition in Reformation Britain, 1530–1645* (Oxford and New York: Oxford University Press, 1979); Elisabeth Labrousse, *L'Entrée de Saturne au lion. L'éclipse de soleil du 12 août 1654* (The Hague: Martinus Nijhoff, 1974).

[11] Thomas A. Kselman, *Miracles and Prophecies in Nineteenth-Century France* (New Brunswick, N.J.: Rutgers University Press, 1983), pp. 5–7.

lational networks that it created. In point of fact, during the years in question, prophecy seems to have constituted a unifying sign connecting nature to religion and religion to politics and coordinating all the scattered shreds of a culture that in the end turned out to be an integral way of knowing embracing observation of nature, political analysis, and religious reflection. If God is the lord of history and of the cosmos, to seek in the *orribeli segnali* of nature and in the voices of the prophets signs of his judgment of human history becomes at once a scientific, political, and religious process. Tzvetan Todorov gives an analogous interpretation of Aztec culture, in which, as he observes, the most urgent problem seems not to have been communication between one person and another, but communication between the person and the world, or, as he puts it,

> between the person and his social group, the person and the natural world, the person and the religious universe. And it is this second type of communication that plays a predominant part in the life of Aztec man, who *interprets the divine, the natural, and the social through indices and omens*.[12]

Todorov was probably suggesting too rigid a contrast between Western culture and Aztec culture in this domain. I might in fact note, without any desire to propose superfluous comparisons, that an attitude analogous to the one that Todorov describes was doubtless true of many of Montezuma's Italian contemporaries. It was a *mens* that did not last long in Italy, however. By about 1530, tacit acceptance of prophecy on the part of large sectors of the ecclesiastical world came to an end, and even the urban population seems to have acquiesced without protest. Even in the present study, the years immediately following the sack of Rome emerge as a fundamental turning point in both the religious and the political history of Italy. The spread in Italy of Reformed preaching—hence of militant opposition to it—doubtlessly played an important part in this shift. As the Counter-Reformation progressed, the unity of prophetic knowledge was destroyed and divinatory science was degraded into a negative body of knowledge possessed by the negative—the female—part of society. Thus the end of prophecy was connected with the revival of misogyny that swept through Europe between the latter half of the sixteenth century and the seventeenth century.

This book will thus seek to pass in review the paraphernalia of a culture—visions, signs, monstrous events, prophecies, and prognostications—viewed not in the abstract but in their concrete operation. It will consider their expression in print works and pictures, in the songs of tale singers, and in ephemeral works, personal colloquies, and sermons in an

[12] Tzvetan Todorov, *The Conquest of America: The Question of the Other*, tr. Richard Howard (New York: Harper and Row, 1983), p. 69 (emphasis mine).

attempt, often arduous and certainly not always successful, to reach down to their specific users. This study makes no claims to be exhaustive; in fact it is highly selective (some will find it arbitrarily so) in that for the most part I have chosen to discuss the cases and specific events that seemed to me the most significant. Following this method has meant that some of my research has already been published, albeit in partial form.[13] Working out those essays and writing them down gradually opened my eyes to their common grounding in the Italy of the *guerre horrende* and of the first stirrings of the Reformation, much as if the events I had been following with my magnifying glass were caterpillars or beetles in a total ecosystem.

It may be useful to add a word on the method I have used to reconstruct those events. In a research field in which many fragments of the culture one seeks to reconstruct have been lost, either because they were transmitted orally or because they had been entrusted to ephemeral media (and popular print pieces are eminently perishable), any attempt to recuperate them has to be based, first, on a reading as thorough and as scrupulous as possible—an intensive reading—of apparently irrelevant sources containing indirect information; and, second, it has to be based on a wide use of the category of the plausible. Alessandro Manzoni wrote, with surprising modernity (and we Italians may have to admit that Manzoni is our Michelet), that historians must do their best to cultivate an "art of unhesitatingly seizing upon the most important revelations, [which have] escaped the writer who was not thinking of giving information, and of extending a few positive cognitive acquisitions by means of well-founded deductions."[14] Elsewhere, in a passage also cited by Carlo Ginzburg, Manzoni appeals to verisimilitude:

> It will not be inappropriate to observe that history can even, on occasion, make use of verisimilitude, and without impropriety, because it does so in the right manner; that is, exposing it in its own guise and thus distinguishing it from the real. . . . It is part of man's miserable lot to know only some of what has been, even in his small world; and it is a part of his nobility and his strength

[13] Ottavia Niccoli, "Profezie in piazza. Note sul profetismo popolare nell'Italia del primo Cinquecento," *Quaderni storici* 41 (1979): 500–539; Niccoli, "Il diluvio del 1524 fra panico collettivo e irrisione carnevalesca," in *Scienze, credenze occulte, livelli di cultura*, pp. 369–92; Niccoli, "I re dei morti sul campo di Agnadello," *Quaderni storici* 51 (1982): 929–58; Niccoli, "Il mostro di Sassonia. Conoscenza e non conoscenza di Lutero in Italia nel Cinquecento (1520–1530 ca.)," in *Lutero in Italia. Studi storici nel V centenario della nascita* (Casale Monferrato, 1983), pp. 3–25; Niccoli, "Il mostro di Ravenna: teratologia e propaganda nei fogli volanti del primo Cinquecento," in Dante Bolognesi, ed., *Ravenna in età veneziana* (Ravenna: Longo, 1986), pp. 245–77. Editorial requirements have necessitated limiting the bibliographical apparatus in the present volume; bibliography on all questions considered here can be found in these essays.

[14] Alessandro Manzoni, *Saggi storici e politici*, ed. F. Ghisalberti (Milan: Mondadori, 1963), p. 39.

> to conjecture beyond what he can know. History, when it has recourse to the likely, simply seconds or excites such a tendency. . . . Conjecturing, like narrating, always aims at the real: that is where its unity lies.[15]

Elsewhere, to tell the truth, Manzoni was moved to call the term "verisimilitude" "a terrible word." He did so in his best-known work of history, the *Storia della colonna infame*, a book in which the word *verosimile* returns time and again with an ambiguous and sinister meaning, since for the judges in a trial involving alleged plague spreaders, verisimilitude was a quite different matter than it is (or should be) for historians. When I have spoken of plausible hypotheses (as indeed I have on many occasions), however, I am speaking of a supposition that seems to me not only likely but also the most likely, the most convincing, and the best adapted to the data we possess, even if it is not ascertainable, certain, or positively provable. In short, I have acted like an archaeologist restoring an artifact: It is not indispensable to have all its fragments in order to reconstruct a vase or a statue. The ones we possess can, after attentive examination, be placed into the form held to be most acceptable for them, and the voids filled with clearly distinguishable neutral material. This is what I have sought to do in another discipline. Of course, one runs the risk of imitating the Renaissance restorers of the Laocoön, who erroneously extended an arm that has now once again been returned to its correct bent position. Perhaps it is better to have a statue with a wrongly placed arm than a pile of fragments waiting to be swept away by some impatient historian intent on tidying up.

Many friends have generously discussed all or part of this work with me, helping me to improve it by their criticisms, remarks, and suggestions. I thank them all, and in particular Pier Cesare Bori, Massimo Firpo, Carlo Ginzburg, Alessandro Pastore, Adriano Prosperi, and Roberto Rusconi. I also owe much to my long epistolary friendship with William Christian.

A large part of the research for the present work was aided by a grant from the Ministry of Public Instruction for "Aspetti della comunicazione dei contenuti culturali nell'Italia del primo Cinquecento."

O.N.

[15] Alessandro Manzoni, *Scritti di teoria letteraria*, ed. A. Sozzi Casanova (Milan: Rizzoli, 1981), pp. 213–14; cited in Carlo Ginzburg, "Prove e possibilità," in Natalie Zemon Davis, *Il ritorno di Martin Guerre. Un caso di doppia identità nella Francia del Cinquecento* (Turin: G. Einaudi, 1984), pp. 146–47, the Italian edition of her *The Return of Martin Guerre* (London and Cambridge, Mass.: Harvard University Press, 1983).

PROPHECY AND PEOPLE IN RENAISSANCE ITALY

PROPHECIES AND THE ITALIAN WARS

Prophecy and History

WHEN CHARLES VIII invaded Italy in 1494 the Tuscans found him short and extremely ugly; it was even said that he was more a monster than a man. Surprise soon gave way to acknowledgement of a reality that must in some way have been predicted, for, as Francesco Matarazzo of Perugia wrote in his chronicle, "he was found so by prophecies and signs." There followed a frantic search for other instruments for reading and interpreting the current "novelties," if not future events. Matarazzo continues: "And in these times prophecies without end were found and published anew, as you might think, all of Italy having been peaceful up to this time, because in these times new things began to happen all over Italy."[1]

The "prophecies without end" that became popular toward the end of the forty-year period of peace that followed the Treaty of Lodi would continue to be published, circulated, and used to take the pulse of political and religious trauma for yet another forty years. On 19 May 1527, a few days after the sack of Rome, the Modenese notary Tommasino Lancellotti noted in his journal that he had been shown "a prophecy of St. Bridget that speaks of the deaths in Rome, so that at present it is said that they happen to the pope."[2] There are a number of texts that might fit this description. This prophecy may indeed have been an edition of the *Revelationes* of St. Bridget of Sweden; it may have been the *Pronosticatio* of the German monk and astrologer Johannes Lichtenberger, which was published in many different editions and contained several predictions credited to St. Bridget that could have been interpreted in Lancellotti's sense; it might have been a manuscript transcription of all or part of one of these

[1] Francesco Matarazzo (called Maturanzio), *Cronaca della città di Perugia dal 1492 al 1503*, ed. Ariodante Fabretti, *Archivio storico italiano* 16, pt. 2 (1851): 1–243; p. 16. See Carlo De Frede, " 'Più simile a mostro che a uomo.' La bruttezza e l'incultura di Carlo VIII nella rappresentazione degli italiani del Rinascimento," *Bibliothèque d'humanisme et renaissance* 44 (1982): 545–85.

[2] Tommasino Lancellotti, *Cronaca modenese*, ed. Carlo Borghi, 12 vols. (Parma: F. Fiaccadori, 1863), vol. 2, p. 224. On prophecy in Modena, see Susanna Peyronel Rambaldi, *Speranze e crisi nel Cinquecento modenese. Tensioni religiose e vita cittadina ai tempi di Giovanni Morone* (Milan: Franco Angeli, 1979), pp. 51–59.

texts. The similarity in their titles, however, suggests instead a small book entitled *Prophetia de santa Brigida con alcune altre Prophetie*, published in Venice by Francesco Bindoni only two years earlier. In reality, we know of two different verse compositions published under the approximate title of *Profezie di santa Brigida*, one from the end of the fourteenth century, the other from the early fifteenth century, that went through a dozen editions, nearly all of them printed between 1478 and about 1525.[3] Comparison of the two texts is of little help because both are a jumbled, confused mass in which a modern reader has difficulty finding allusions to the sack of Rome. It is clear, however, that a severely distorted, partial reading was possible for the "book consumer" of the sixteenth century. The discrepancy between books someone read and the interpretation of those same books could be great; furthermore, the recent invention of printing, which threw on the market a mass of texts composed in very different epochs, had suddenly torn texts out of their cultural and historical contexts.[4] For the reader who did not belong within high culture, the book was simply what it was declared to be at that time. That is, readers lacked the instinctive ability of their modern counterparts to mentally locate works of the past, according to their age, on the various shelves of an imaginary bookcase. Furthermore, the literary genre of "prophecy," at least in its specific manifestation under discussion here, was for the most part deciphered under the pressure of present events. Present concerns invaded a text (that was usually deliberately ambiguous), overwhelmed it, and constrained the reader to a noticeably distorted reading of what it contained. Thus Tommasino Lancellotti read St. Bridget uniquely in order to find the sack that in those very days was devastating Rome, not for some echo of far-off events or any admonitions applicable to a distant future. Thus also the Florentines examined and reprinted prophecies in order to grasp the meaning of the arrival of short, ugly King Charles VIII. Such texts, then, cannot be read or understood historically apart from the medium that diffused them, the milieus in which they circulated, and the political context in which they were used.

Popular Print Prophecies

The literary genre of vernacular verse prophecy seems to have met with great favor at the end of the fifteenth century and in the first decades of the

[3] See Ottavia Niccoli, "Profezie in piazza. Note sul profetismo popolare nell'Italia del primo Cinquecento," *Quaderni storici* 41 (1979): 500–539, "Appendice," pp. 535–36 (hereafter cited as "Appendice").

[4] Carlo Ginzburg, *The Cheese and the Worms: The Cosmos of a Sixteenth-Century Miller*, tr. John and Anne Tedeschi (Baltimore: Johns Hopkins University Press, 1980; New York: Penguin Books, 1982), p. 32; Ginzburg, "Folklore, magia, religione," in *Storia d'Italia*, 6 vols. (Turin: G. Einaudi, 1972–1977), vol. 1, pp. 636–37.

sixteenth century.[5] The list of print pieces concerning prophecy that I have attempted to draw up elsewhere, and which is certainly not complete, includes more than fifty items pertaining to twenty or so texts printed and reprinted in a fifty-year period ranging from 1480 to about 1530, with a handful of editions published later than that date.[6] The number of editions, in itself already high, becomes truly extraordinary when the physical specifications of these publications are taken into account. They were small in format (octavo- or, at the most, quarto-sized volumes), of few leaves (two or four, less often eight, at the most twelve), poorly printed with no indication of place, date, or printer, often printed in two columns with antiquated and worn type, using poor-quality ink that has bled into the porous paper. In all cases, they fit into what scholars from Francesco Novati to today have agreed to call "popular literature."[7] These texts were not only "popular" in the sense of aiming at a wide audience; they also enjoyed a large distribution thanks to their low price and their low technical demands. They were subject to rapid deterioration, however, so that they are now quite rare. Entire editions must certainly have disappeared, and the better part of those of which some trace remains exist in at most one copy or extremely few copies.

These limitations explain why the ascertainable existence of more than fifty different works of vernacular prophecies classifiable as "popular" according to the criteria stated above, nearly all in verse, and published within a fifty-year period can be considered a homogeneous and consistent

[5] See Angelo Messini, *Profetismo e profezie ritmiche italiane d'ispirazione gioachimito-francescana nei secoli XIII, XIV e XV* (Rome, 1939), pp. 54–56, 91; Giuseppe Mazzatinti, "Una profezia attribuita al b. Tomassuccio da Foligno," *Miscellanea francescana* 2, no. 1 (1887): 1–7; Enrico Filippini, *La "Prophetia fratris Mucii de Perusio" estratta da un cod. napoletano del sec. XV* (Fabriano, 1892); Francesco Novati, "I codici Trivulzio-Trotti," *Giornale storico della letteratura italiana* 9 (1887): 137–85; p. 182; Alfons Hilka, "Randglossen zu mittelalterliche Handschriften," *Beiträge zur Forschung: Studien und mitteilungen aus dem antiquariat Jacques Rosenthal, München* (Munich: J. Rosenthal, 1915–), 1st ser., no. 6 (1915): 171–75; Hilka, "Über einige italienischen Prophezeiungen des XIV. und XV. Jahrhunderts, vornehmlich über einem deutschen Friedenkaiser," *Schlesische Gesellschaft fur Vaterlandische Cultur* 66 (1917): 11–12; Roberto Rusconi, *L'attesa della fine. Crisi della società, profezia e Apocalisse in Italia al tempo del grande scisma d'Occidente (1378–1417)* (Rome: Istituto storico italiano per il Medio Evo, 1979), pp. 111–20, 158–63. All these studies concern manuscripts on prophecy, not print pieces.

[6] See Niccoli, "Appendice."

[7] Francesco Novati, *La storia e la stampa nella produzione popolare italiana* . . . (Bergamo: n.p., 1907); Arnaldo Segarizzi, *Bibliografia delle stampe popolari italiane della R. Biblioteca nazionale di S. Marco di Venezia* (Bergamo: Istituto italiano d'arti grafiche, 1913–), vol. 1; Carlo Angeleri, *Bibliografia delle stampe popolari a carattere profano dei secoli XVI e XVII conservate nella Biblioteca Nazionale di Firenze* (Florence: Sansoni, 1953); Caterina Santoro, ed., *Mostra di libri di profezie, astrologia, chiromanzia, alchimia* (Milan: Edizioni dell'ente Manifestazioni Milanesi, 1953); Armando Petrucci, "Introduzione," *Libri, editori e pubblico nell'Europa moderna. Guida storica e critica* (Rome and Bari: Laterza, 1977), pp. ix–xxix.

literary current. The real dimensions of this current must have been a great deal larger than the materials presented here, and their distribution was surely much wider, as they were addressed to a public much less select and cultivated than was the case with more refined publications. In short, although up to now they have been little studied, they represent an important aspect, both qualitatively and quantitatively, of the broader phenomenon of prophecy in the sixteenth century.[8]

To return for a moment to the problem of the sort of reading that these texts solicited from less sophisticated readers, I might note that so-called popular publications were addressed to a completely new public that had never before had relations with the written word and was just then making its entry into the "Gutenberg galaxy." The impact of these texts was thus all the more intense. Naturally, their potential and actual purchasers did not belong exclusively to the underclasses. The case of a refined bibliophile like Fernando Colombo, who acquired and catalogued many publications of this sort during his voyages in Italy, among them a good number of books of prophecies now conserved in the Biblioteca Capitular y Colombina of Seville, is sufficient proof of this.[9] It is undeniable, however, that the artisan or the worker who came into contact with the written word did so through this type of publication.

Most of these print pieces omitted information judged irrelevant for the readers targeted but necessary in other instances, such as the printer's name and the place and date of publication. This was true of our prophetic pieces as well. They were almost always presented anonymously or with false attributions to give them greater prestige and authority. Aside from the two often reprinted works known by the name of St. Bridget that have already been mentioned, the names of the thirteenth-century physician and astrologer Pietro d'Abano of Padua and St. Anselmus (probably Anselmus, bishop of Marisco Nuovo, credited with the amplification of the *Vaticinia pontificum*, also falsely attributed to Joachim of Fiore) were attached to two other frequently reprinted texts.[10] Another prophecy was published under the name of St. Angelus of Jerusalem, but in reality, as we shall see, it was an anonymous and interpolated biography of that figure.[11] Very few texts

[8] As a minimum, see Marjorie Reeves, *The Influence of Prophecy in the Late Middle Ages. A Study in Joachimism* (Oxford: Clarendon Press, 1969); "Ricerche sull'influenza della profezia nel basso medioevo," *Bullettino dell'Istituto storico italiano per il Medioevo* 82 (1970) [1974]: 1–158; Rusconi, *L'attesa della fine*.

[9] See Niccoli, "Appendice," nos. 28, 29, 36, 43, 44.

[10] *Questa è la vera prophetia prophetizata dal glorioso santo Anselmo* (n.p., n.d.); *Questa sie la profetia composta per el reverendissimo negromante Piero dabano* (n.p., n.d.). For other editions, see Niccoli, "Appendice," p. 536.

[11] *Vita de santo Angelo carmelitano martyre con la prophetia data a lui per el nostro signor Jesu Christo de tutto quello che e advenuto e advegnira alla christianitade per infedeli et della setta et leze falsa luterina* (n.p., n.d.).

bear the name of their true authors. There is the *Del diluvio di Roma del MCCCCLXXXXV* of Giuliano Dati, a canon from Florence who lived in Rome; there are the *Proffetia de Nocturno* and the *Iuditio sopra tutta la Italia* of the prolific *cantastorie* Notturno Napolitano;[12] there are three publications that bear the name of Tommasuccio da Foligno, the authorship of which is impossible to confirm.[13]

In a literary genre in which anonymity was generally the rule, the formulation of a work's title took on particular importance. Among other things, we know that itinerant vendors customarily hawked their wares. Furthermore, because these publications represented an advantageous commercial operation for the printer, who on occasion could use them to finance more refined works,[14] we can suppose that their titles were contrived with a view to stimulating the public's curiosity and to placing the merchandise that was being offered in a category known to be popular. As is obvious, the word *profezia* recurs in most of the titles, but it is also interesting to note the frequent use of the terms *pronostico*, *pronosticatione*, and *iuditio*, references to the more "official" level of astrology that seem to underscore a desire to give a scientific cast to the predictions contained in the text.[15] In short, there seems to be an intent to lend nobility to these little works by suggesting references to aspects of a higher culture. Another way to lend prestige to titles was by referring to epigraphs and monuments of classical and Oriental antiquity. Thus there is a *Prophetia trovata in Roma intagliata in marmoro in versi latini tratta in vulghar sentimento*; there is the *Iuditio sopra tutta la Italia quale è stato trovato nella città di Roma in una pirramida* already referred to (and which, in another edition, becomes *Profetia over Pronosticatione trovata in Roma in una piramide in versi latini tradotti in vulgare*). There is, finally, a *Profetia nuovamente trovata sotto la torre di Nembrot, dove s'intende tutta la renovatione del mondo*. Reference to the antiquity of the texts must have been thought to guarantee their authenticity (another publication bears the title *Profetie antiche*).[16] At the same time, however, references to epigraphs, pyramids, and towers return us to Renaissance Italy's lively taste for archaeology and antiquarianism sensed and represented in these modest compositions with the evident aim of giving

[12] Giuliano Dati, *Del diluvio di Roma del MCCCCLXXXXV adi iiii di dicembre et daltre cose di gran meraviglia* (n.p., n.d.); Notturno Napolitano, *Proffetia de Nocturno* in his *Opera nova amorosa* (n.p., n.d.); *Iuditio sopra tutta la Italia quale e stato trovato nella citta di Roma* (n.p., n.d.).

[13] Published in Vicenza, 1510; Fano, n.d.; Foligno, 1566.

[14] See Rosanna Alhaique Pettinelli, "Elementi culturali e fattori socio-economici della produzione libraria a Roma nel '400," in Walter Binni et al., eds, *Letteratura e critica. Studi in onore di Natalino Sapegno*, 5 vols. (Rome: Bulzoni, 1976), vol. 3, pp. 101–43.

[15] See Niccoli, "Appendice."

[16] Ibid., nos. 18, 34, 35, 37, 46, 47, 51.

them luster, just as other prophecies gained prestige by being attributed to famous persons.

The vast circulation of these prophetic publications and their success among the public for whom they were designed are attested in many ways. The genre must have been one of the first to be exploited by printers, if we remember that the presses of San Iacopo a Ripoli, one of the first print shops to operate in Tuscany, had already published two different works of prophecy by 1479. One was a *Profezia di santa Brigida*, listed in the print shop's register, under the date of 25 January 1479, as sold to one Giovanni Michele, presumably at the price of one *soldo*; the second was another *Profezie* not further identified, printed before 28 June 1479 together with other works (the *Confessioni di santa Maria Maddalena*, *Le sette allegrezze*, and *Il lamento di Giuliano*) for Giovanni di Nato, stationer at the Porto al Prato.[17] Stationers (*cartolari*), together with tale singers (*cantambanchi*), were frequent customers of the Ripoli print shop, from which they ordered the texts that they thought they could sell most easily. Until the end of the fifteenth century, Florence was undoubtedly the most important center for the distribution of popular print publications on prophecy, with at least six works published there before 1500.[18] Tuscany during the years when Savonarola was preaching and veneration of St. Bridget was well entrenched must have provided a particularly receptive market for this sort of publication.[19]

The Circulation of Prophecy in Manuscript

These first printed works on prophecy, Florentine for the most part and dated or datable between the late fifteenth century and the first years of the sixteenth century, showed several consistent characteristics. They offered one, but more often two, three, or even four compositions not written for the occasion but already known in manuscript form at least since the beginning of the fifteenth century; works laden with Joachimite echoes and that often had been written originally to fulfill various tasks of political propaganda.[20] Thus we find in them the two prophecies of St. Bridget that have already been mentioned, a satirical poem entitled *El se movera un gato*, the *Prophetia de uno sancto homo*, the *Prophetia de Santo Severo* (later repub-

[17] Emilia Nesi, *Il diario della stamperia di Ripoli* (Florence: B. Seeber, 1903), pp. 20, 41–42, 115.

[18] Niccoli, "Appendice," nos 1, 2, 4, 17, 19.

[19] See Roberto Rusconi, "Note sulla predicazione di Manfredi da Vercelli O.P. e il movimento penitenziale dei terziari manfredini," *Archivum fratrum praedicatorum* 48 (1978): 99.

[20] See Rusconi, *L'attesa della fine*.

lished in the works of Galatino and Postel),[21] the so-called "Prophecy of the second Charlemagne," written around 1380 to apply to Charles VI of France and subsequently adapted to fit Charles VIII and Charles V,[22] and others.

These publications were the direct heirs of the many manuscript anthologies of prophecies in circulation in the fourteenth and the fifteenth centuries.[23] In more general terms, they represent the final outcome of an intense circulation of this sort of material in manuscript—a phenomenon not difficult to explain when we recall that after the invention of print, works composed in every epoch, presented as current, suddenly appeared on the market. Before we can compare the audience for these publications with the users of printed prophecies, we need to reach a better understanding (and in some cases this is possible) of the social group to which the transcribers of prophecies belonged and of the use they made of them.

Transcribers were often jurists, like Tibaldo Civeri of Lombardy (possibly of Piedmont), who copied prophecies indefatigably for nearly fifty years (at least from 1327 to 1481) until he had a volume of some two hundred fifty leaves. He copied "ex quodam antiquo libelleto, et satis vetusto scriptura" that belonged to a schoolmaster who lived in Vercelli, or from a *scriptura* owned by a goldsmith in Asti, or from pages lent to him by another jurist.[24] It was another jurist—in fact, a "doctor *in utroque*

[21] See Niccoli, "Appendice," nos. 7–11, 14, 15, 18, 22. See also Guillaume Postel, *Le Thresor des prophéties de l'univers*, ed. François Secret (The Hague: Martinus Nijhoff, 1969), pp. 165–66; Arduinus Kleinhans, "De vita et operibus Petri Galatini O.F.M. scientiarum biblicarum cultoris (c. 1460–1540)," *Antonianum* 1 (1926): 154–79.

[22] Niccoli, "Appendice," nos. 20, 21, 22. No. 22 clearly refers to Charles V. On the fortunes and origins of this text, see Reeves, *The Influence of Prophecy*, pp. 328–29 and 359; Maurice Chaume, "Une prophétie relative à Charles VI," *Revue du Moyen Age latin* 3 (1947): 27–42. On prophecies concerning Charles VIII, see also Donald Weinstein, *Savonarola and Florence: Prophecy and Patriotism in the Renaissance* (Princeton: Princeton University Press, 1970), p. 242.

[23] See Reeves, *The Influence of Prophecy*, pp. 534–40.

[24] See Gustavo Vinay, "Riflessi culturali sconosciuti del minoritismo subalpino," *Bollettino storico bibliografico subalpino* 37 (1935): 136–49, which examines the MS K^2.IV.13 of the Biblioteca Nazionale di Torino. Information on the source of the prophecies can be found on pp. 139–40 and 146. Vinay does not seem to have remarked, however, that he might also have considered MS K^2.V.8 of the same library, which is quite evidently part of the same manuscript, restored and erroneously bound separately after a disastrous fire in the library in 1904. Both manuscripts, in fact, begin with a folio that belongs to the same series of the *Vaticinia Pontificum*. They contain, respectively, 185 and 58 folios, and they belonged to a manuscript of 244 folios. In fact 185 plus 58 equals 243, plus one extra, probably the back flyleaf, which would make 244, the number written on the back flyleaf in an eighteenth-century hand. Because the two remaining folios of the *Vaticinia Pontificum* contain only sixteen pictures of popes, it is presumable that two others have been lost and were already missing in the eighteenth century, when the existing folios were counted and the sum written on the back flyleaf. For his help with these problems, I am indebted to Dr. Angelo Giaccaria.

iure"—Marco Amaseo of Udine, whose nephew Gregorio found among his papers, after his death, two prophecies "written on parchment in handsome letters" (from what I can gather, the *Prophetia de Santo Severo* and the prophecy of the second Charlemagne) "to which then in my hand [Gregorio is speaking] I added others given me from time to time by diverse [persons]."[25] Another transcriber was a notary, thus someone of a lower social and cultural level, Marco Antonio Gatti from Piacenza. Between 1473 and 1501, following a custom common in his profession, he inserted a number of historical notations and moralistic and political poems into the pages of his notarial records, among them an extract of the prophecy of St. Cataldo. For Gatti, then, this prophecy was as noteworthy as a poetic dialogue of Antonio Cammelli, known as Il Pistoia, "with the Turk's brother . . . asking him about the powers of Italy" that he also noted down, or as historical notations and verse compositions about Charles VIII's arrival in Italy and his death.[26] Another notary, Gaspare Marri of Cesena, transcribed a prediction of the cataclysmic end of the world on the back of an act that he drew up on 25 September 1472;[27] while in 1536 we find among the acts of yet another notary, Antonio Belloni of Udine, a copy of the well-known Latin prophecy *Gallorum levitas*.[28]

On other occasions it was chroniclers who acquired prophecies and recopied them into their journals. To take just one example, the verses of the prophecy known by its incipit, *Gallorum levitas*, mentioned above (never printed in the works under consideration here, however), were inserted in a number of chronicles in Bologna as early as the mid-fourteenth century. They appear in 1461 in the *Notabilia temporum* of Angelo Tummulilli; in 1495 in the *Annali* of Domenico Malipiero; in 1509 in the journal of Canon Tommaso di Silvestro of Orvieto; in 1527 (probably, as we shall see) in the papers of Leonello Beliardi of Modena; and again in 1552 in the chronicle of another Modenese, Tommasino Lancellotti, who states that he had found them in another compilation of forty years earlier.[29]

[25] Leonardo and Gregorio Amaseo and Gio. Antonio Azio, *Diarii udinesi, dall'anno 1508 al 1541*, Monumenti Storici ser. 3, vol. 1, (Venice: R. Deputazione di storia patria per le Venezie, 1884), p. 388.

[26] A. G. Tononi, "Note storiche e rime politiche e morali tra gli atti di un notaio piacentino del secolo XV," *Strenna piacentina* 18 (1892): 28–44, esp. p. 37. On the prophecy of St. Cataldo, see Giampaolo Tognetti, "Le fortune della pretesa profezia di san Cataldo," *Bullettino dell'Istituto storico italiano per il Medioevo* 80 (1968): 273–317.

[27] Carlo Grigioni, "Una tradizione del finimondo nel 1472," *Arte e storia* 27 (1908): 154–55.

[28] Antonio Medin, "La battaglia di Pavia. Profeti e poeti italiani," *Archivio storico lombardo* 52 (1925): 252–90; p. 255.

[29] Rusconi, *L'attesa della fine*, p. 143; Angelo de Tummulillis, *Notabilia temporum*, ed. Costantino Corvisieri (Livorno: Tip. F. Vigo, 1890), p. 112; Domenico Malipiero, *Annali veneti dall'anno 1457 al 1500*, *Archivio storico italiano* 7 (1843–44): 5–586; p. 372; Tommaso di

Even before they appeared in urban chronicles, however, these texts were copied for personal use, lent, and read aloud in public within a given social group until the paper was worn to shreds, as with the *Gallorum levitas* in verse, which was transcribed in 1495 by ser Tommaso di Silvestro and later, in 1509, copied into his journal. Tommaso tells us that he "kept them tacked up in the bedroom. They broke into pieces because I wanted everyone to read them."[30] This literature was a true consumer product, then, and the object of impassioned and voracious circulation.

Some of these collections or transcriptions give texts in Latin or in a mixture of Latin and the vernacular; others contain only texts in the vernacular, giving us a glimpse of the continuity that must have existed in certain cases (allowing for some disparity in the readers' social level, however) between the manuscript anthologies of prophecies and the printed versions of the same. One example of apparent continuity emerges in an unassuming small paper codex of twenty-four leaves—a true fifteenth-century *libro da bisaccia*.[31] It contains four prophecies in vernacular, three of which are in verse and at least two of which—the so-called prophecy of St. Bridget and the one known by its incipit, *El se movera un gato*—were among those most often republished. In any event, manuscript compilations of this sort were made for political purposes with the aim of comparing predictions with events in course and preparing oneself to face the future that they foretold. Leone Cobelli, a painter from Forlì, had a "little book of prophecies" provided him by a Third Order Franciscan friar in 1480. From that time on, Cobelli compared the tumultuous political scene in Forlì with his book of prophecies and transcribed long passages from them into his chronicles. In particular, after April 1488, when Count Girolamo Riario, lord of the city, lost his life in an attempted coup (which was, however, soon foiled by the widowed Caterina Sforza), Cobelli's citations become continuous, accompanied by such admiring comments as

Silvestro, *Diario*, ed. Luigi Fumi, in *Rerum italicarum scriptores* (hereafter cited as RIS) 15, pt. 5 (Bologna: Nicola Zanichelli, 1923), vol. 2, p. 410; Lancellotti, *Cronaca modenese*, vol. 11, p. 156; Leonello Beliardi, *Cronaca della città di Modena (1512–1518)*, ed. Alberto Biondi and Michele Oppi (Modena: Panini, 1981), p. 150.

30 Tommaso di Silvestro, *Diario*, p. 410. It is probable that his first transcription of the prophecy in 1495 was prompted by the battle of Fornovo.

31 See Novati, "I codici Trivulzio-Trotti"; Hilka, "Randglossen"; Hilka, "Über einige italienischen Prophezeiungen." My description of the codex is based on information given by Novati and Hilka. The location of the manuscript is unknown; it is reported to have been sold in the United States, but it does not appear in Seymour De Ricci and W. J. Wilson, eds, *Census of Medieval and Renaissance Manuscripts in the United States and Canada*, 4 vols. (New York: H. W. Wilson Co., 1935–1962). In 1916 it belonged to an antique dealer in Monaco. The expression *libro da bisaccia*, "saddlebag book or haversack book," has been borrowed from Armando Petrucci, "Alle origini del libro moderno: libri da banco, libri da bisaccia, libretti da mano," in his *Libri, scrittura e pubblico nel Rinascimento: Guida storica e critica* (Rome and Bari: Laterza, 1979), pp. 139–56.

"note, reader, [how] perfectly"; "here again it follows the prophecy"; "now note, reader, whether this prophecy seems true or not to you."[32] What strikes the modern reader is the contrast between Cobelli's passion as he identifies events with predictions and the extreme obscurity of the prophetic book, a work in tercets full of reminiscences of Dante that must have been extremely long, given that the chronicler quotes over two hundred lines of verse and the last page he cites is page 136. Cobelli's notations provide us with a useful example because they allow us to grasp directly, step by step, the strength of the tension that urged readers of prophecies to consider them realized in events that bore only a vague resemblance to them.

Cobelli's case is paradigmatic but it is by no means unique. Periodically, in moments of political tension, Gregorio Amaseo went back to the collection of prophecies that he and his uncle had compiled. He comments on one work of prophecy (the prognostications of Antonio Arquato) that "there having occurred things that vary marvelously little from that time to this, we can presume that the rest will follow, since they were true for all the past."[33] The chronicler Leonello Beliardi also collected a handful of prophecies, Latin and vernacular (probably immediately after the sack of Rome, hence they range from 1519 to 1528), which he quite obviously regarded as a description of Emperor Charles V and a tribute to his sacred and redemptory role.[34]

In comparison to the large number of manuscripts that circulated, however, the brief print pieces that interest us here represent merely a selection. Except in a few isolated cases, the texts chosen for publication were all in the vernacular. Furthermore, their low price and small size guaranteed that they would be accessible to a broader public than those—for the most part jurists, as we have seen—who collected such texts and copied them by hand.

The Role of the *Cantastorie*

At the same time, however, starting at the very end of the fifteenth century, new prophecies were composed and published, more often in Venice or other cities of north-central Italy like Ferrara and Bologna. These were sim-

[32] Leone Cobelli, *Cronache forlivesi dalla fondazione della città all'anno 1498*, ed. Giosuè Carducci and Enrico Frati (Bologna: Regia tipografia, 1874), pp. 282, 302, 326, and elsewhere (information on the book of prophecies, p. 458). See also Andrea Bernardi (called Novacula), *Cronache forlivesi . . . dal 1476 al 1517*, ed. Giuseppe Mazzatinti, 2 vols. (Bologna: R. Deputazione di storia patria, 1895–1897), vol. 1, pt. 1, p. 272; pt. 2, p. 105.

[33] Amaseo, Amaseo, and Azio, *Diarii udinesi*, p. 412.

[34] Beliardi, *Cronaca della città di Modena*, pp. 144–55 and 166–68. See below, pp. 177–81, however.

ple texts with a schematic syntax, an elementary vocabulary, and none of the complicated symbolism of the older publications. The rhyming lines punctuated with facile refrains used sure signs sent by God to predict suffering and pain, famine, pestilence, and marauding armies, but they also foretold final victory over the infidels, their conversion, and an eventual age of universal peace under an *imperator iocondo*. One of the earliest, perhaps the very first, of these new prophecies is the short poem entitled *Del diluvio di Roma del MCCCCLXXXXV adi iii di dicembre et daltre cose di gran meraviglia*, unusual in that it was published under the name of its actual author, the canon Giuliano Dati. Dati had also written a number of short verse works on subjects ranging from the recent discovery of America to Prester John and the Holy House of Loreto. I shall return to Dati's cultural function.[35] The title, *Del diluvio di Roma*, might not seem appropriate for a prophetic text (although we shall return in chapter 6 to a particular and quite popular verse genre on floods that usually included both prophetic and meteorological elements). The colophon describes the work's contents a good deal better. It reads:

> End of the treatise on celestial signs and on modern tribulations and on the recent waters that inundated the ancient and holy city of Rome in our iron and last age collected and put in verse by messer Iuliano de Dati in praise of the celestial Court. M. CCCC. LXXXXV. Finis.

The Roman Deluge (that is, the flooding of the Tiber in December 1495) was, Dati tells us, simply the most recent of many signs that God had sent to Italy:

> voltata tutta in ira e furore
> certo mi pare la divina clementia,
> per tanti segni grandi e smisurati
> che sono a nostri die e de' passati.
>
> (divine clemency seems to me completely turned to anger and fury, [made] clear by many great signs beyond measure that are in our day and in days past.)

Among these "segni grandi e smisurati" the canon poet placed all the political and military disasters on the Italian peninsula, from Turkish forays

[35] On Dati, see Achille Neri, "La gran magnificenza del Prete Janni. Poemetto di Giuliano Dati e quattro lettere inedite di Carlo Roberto Dati," *Il Propugnatore* 9 (1876): 138–72; Leonardo Olschki, "I 'Cantàri dell'India' di Giuliano Dati," *La bibliofilia* 40 (1938): 289–316; Renato Lefevre, "Fiorentini a Roma nel '400. I Dati," *Studi romani* 20 (1972): 187–97; Antonio M. Adorisio, "Cultura in lingua volgare a Roma fra Quattro e Cinquecento," in Giorgio De Gregori, Maria Valenti, and Giovanna Merola, eds., *Studi di biblioteconomia e storia del libro in onore di Francesco Barberi* (Rome: Associazione italiana biblioteche, 1976), pp. 20–24.

to the invasions of "men from beyond the mountains [the Alps] who have turned all Italy upside down." Italy, however, had refused to believe in either signs or prophets sent by God; thus God had sent a last warning, the great flood that in this "nostra ferrea et ultima etade" (the eschatological allusion is noteworthy) was to lead men to penitence, to righteous acts, and to life eternal:

> là ci conduca l'alto Iddio di gloria,
> al cui onor fo fine alla mia storia.
>
> (that is where the highest God of glory is leading us, to whose honor I put an end to my story.)

Thus this was a *story*, and a story to be *sung* ("perhaps I have bored you, O hearer, by making my singing so prolix"), and to be sung to an audience accustomed to listening sitting down:

> bench'io voglia il mio dire abreviare,
> perché non sia la storia a 'lcun noiosa;
> so che chi si diletta d'ascoltare
> non si cura star rito o se si posa,
> ma pur lo star posato al auditore
> fa molte volte grate el parlatore.
>
> (although I want to shorten my tale so that it will not bore anyone, I know that whoever loves to listen does not care whether he is standing or seated, but still, by allowing him to sit the speaker often pleases the listener.)[36]

We can easily imagine the stage, the singer, and the public. We are in a square, and the person declaiming the poem and talking so familiarly with his *auditore* is certainly the *cantastorie*, or professional tale singer. The allusion to the possibility for the listener to be "posato," seated, contains an indirect request that he or she pay for that comfort, and in fact the *cantastorie*, between the fifteenth and the sixteenth centuries, owned and brought along with them both the platform on which they stood to declaim their repertory and benches for the audience.[37] The singer interrupted the reci-

[36] *Del diluvio di Roma*, fols. a vi*v*, a i*v*, a iii*v*, a vi*v*, a iii*r*, a iv*r*.

[37] See Guido Fusinato, "Un cantastorie chioggiotto," *Giornale di filologia romanza* 4 (1880): 170–83; Francesco Flamini, *La lirica toscana del Rinascimento anteriore ai tempi del Magnifico* (Pisa: Tip. T. Nistri, 1891), p. 152; Francesco Novati, "La poesia sulla natura delle frutta e i canterini del comune di Firenze," in his *Attraverso il Medio Evo: Studi e ricerche* (Bari: G. Laterza e figli, 1905), pp. 327–65; Benedetto Soldati, "Improvvisatori, canterini e buffoni in un dialogo del Pontano," in Arnaldo della Torre and Pier Liberale Rambaldi, eds., *Miscellanea di studi critici, pubblicati in onore di Guido Mazzoni*, 2 vols. (Florence: Successori B. Seeber, 1907), vol. 1, pp. 321–42, esp. p. 328; Ezio Levi, *I cantari leggendari del popolo italiano nei secoli XIV–XV* (Turin: Loescher, 1914), pp. 5–19. On professional entertainers in

tation from time to time to pass the hat among the seated listeners, and in fact the verses I have cited represent a transitional moment in the poem that could easily have been followed by such a pause. With *Del diluvio*, then, prophecy entered into the repertory of the bench singers, the *cantambanchi*, hence into the patrimony of urban oral culture. It was to remain there.

That Giuliano Dati, the polygraph to whom we owe this "treatise on celestial signs and on modern tribulations," wrote for the professional tale singers was established by Leonardo Olschki, who deduced from a study of the texts themselves that the singers used to illustrate the verse tales written by the canon of Santa Maria Maggiore with schematic drawings or pictures,[38] following a custom that professional street singers were to continue up to modern times. Moreover, it is known that the tale singers enjoyed a preferential relationship with printers, in particular the printers who specialized in "prognostications, histories, songs, letters, and other similar things," as the Council of Ten in Venice expressed it in a decree of 10 February 1542.[39] The category of *historiari* was defined in similar terms more than a century later in the statutes of the printers' trade association of Rome, the "Venerabile Compagnia et Università de' Librai di Roma," as those who printed and sold "short histories, prayer books, almanacs, and other small books usually paper bound or center-sewn, not frame-sewn on their spines, provided they not exceed 10 sheets each."[40] The tale singers placed orders with these printer-booksellers, even with printers who published both popular texts and more demanding works.

The registers of the Ripoli print shop, which published two different works of prophecy, offer an interesting example of this special relationship. Fra Domenico, the manager of the print shop, wrote in his account book, "Bernardino who sings on a bench took, on the 16th day of November 1482, one hundred of the *Bellezze di Firenze*; we agreed that he must give venti *soldi* for them. And he left me a tablecloth as a gage. He paid on the 18th day and took back the said tablecloth."[41]

Bernardino the *cantambanco* continued to buy from the Ripoli print shop. On eleven occasions between 1483 and 1485 he took a total of 495 copies of *Sale di Malagigi* and fifty copies of *Pistole della domenica*, each time

general, see also Peter Burke, *Popular Culture in Early Modern Europe* (New York: New York University Press, 1978), pp. 92–102.

38 Olschki, "I 'Cantàri dell'India,' " p. 292.

39 Giuliano Pesenti, "Libri censurati a Venezia nei secoli XVI–XVII," *La bibliofilia* 58 (1956): 15–30; p. 16.

40 Francesco Lumachi, *Nella repubblica del libro . . . Bibliomani celebri, librai d'altri tempi, spigolature e curiosità bibliografiche* (Florence: F. Lumachi, 1907), p. 97.

41 Nesi, *Il diario della stamperia di Ripoli*, p. 80.

paying after a few days.[42] Other names of "cerretani e ciurmatori" (sharpers and pitchmen) appear in Fra Domenico's journal, but the name of "Bernardino who sings on a bench" is the most significant example of the singular economic exchange that Fra Domenico describes: The tale singer commissions a text from the printer, takes delivery without payment, at least for the first few times, but leaves a personal possession as a gage (one Florentine named Giovanni sent in his young son with "a small sheet [as] security"),[43] then recites and sells the printed verses in the town square and, with the profits, pays off the printer. The introduction of printing had thus helped the tale singers to keep up and broaden their repertories and to raise their revenues by selling printed works. In only a few years, Bernardino the *cantambanco* had the Ripoli press print more than six hundred copies of these slim works, a figure that obviously implies a higher number of listeners. We find another proof of the wide diffusion of this practice in a Lombard chronicle that reports "many laments" in the vernacular on the destruction of Otranto by the Turks in 1480, "sung everywhere in the squares before people and offered for sale."[44]

Before the advent of print, a manuscript copy of the work recited was probably posted to make it available to anyone who wanted to copy it, as the final lines of a song on a historical topic from Genoa, dated 1467, seem to indicate:

> Chi me leze me lassa stare
> aziò che possa essere exemplata.
>
> (May he who reads me let me be so that I can be copied.)[45]

When already reproduced texts could be distributed, this custom was no longer needed and disappeared. This worked to the economic advantage of the tale singers, some of whom used printing as a base for new and

[42] Ibid., pp. 97–113. Bernardino of Florence was the author of a short poem in Italian in ten cantos or chapters of tercets, *De laudibus clarissime familie Vendramine ad Magnificum et generosum D. Lodovicum Vendraminum Tarvisii potestatem et capitanum benemeritum* (Biblioteca Marciana di Venezia, MS Marc. it. IX.370 [=6762]), composed for the triumphal entry into Treviso in 1481 of the *podestà* Luigi Vendramin (about which, see Giovanni Bonifaccio, *Historia Trivigiana* [Treviso: D. Amici, 1591], pp. 647–48, available in reproduction of the Venice 1744 edition as *Istoria di Trivigi* [Bologna: Forni, 1968]); as well as the *Bellezze e casati di Firenze*, just mentioned (on which, see Carlo Dionisotti, *Machiavellerie. Storia e fortuna di Machiavelli* [Turin: G. Einaudi, 1980], p. 20).

[43] Nesi, *Il diario della stamperia di Ripoli*, p. 86.

[44] "Multae lamentationes . . . ubique per plateas cantatur coram populum et vendunter": *Cronica gestorum in partibus Lombardie et reliquis Italie (aa. 1476–1482)*, ed. Giuliano Bonazzi, RIS, new ed., vol. 22, pt. 3 (Città di Castello: S. Lapi, 1904), p. 84.

[45] Cornelio Desimoni, "Tre cantari dei secoli XV e XVI concernenti fatti di storia genovese," *Atti della società ligure di storia patria* 10 (1876): 610–82; p. 643.

broader activities. Paolo Danza, born in Florence but active in Venice, was both a printer and a seller of poems of his own composition, which he probably also sang. We owe to him at least one prophetic publication (the *Prophetia de uno imperatore*) and possibly another work that uses the same text but with a different title and showing a few variants (*Profecia de santo Anselmo*)—a shrewd commercial operation aimed at selling the same merchandise twice to a public seemingly eager to purchase such merchandise.[46] Often the process was more complex, involving at least the tale singer and the printer. At times, as in the case of Giuliano Dati, a third person was involved—the "poet," who composed the verse tales and poems that were declaimed and offered for sale. (He probably worked on commission too.) We should thus link Dati's name with those of Giovan Battista Verini and Eustachio Celebrino, whose roles as "cultural operators" and "professionals, albeit humble and part-time, of the pen" merits further investigation, as has been suggested.[47]

We can postulate that in many cases prophecies were composed with recitation, even declamation, in mind. Particularly in their introductory and final passages, they frequently refer to listening rather than reading:

Ascoltati, mortali,
li orribeli segnali
che annuntiano gran mali
alla età nostra

Vo' far fine al mio cantare
excellente auditore,
. . .
questa nobil prophetia
è finita al vostro onore

O auditor iocondo
qui fo fine al mio trattato.

[46] An earlier edition bore the title *La vera prophetia prophetizata dal glorioso Santo Anselmo la quale declara la venuta de uno imperatore: el qual mettera pace fra li christiani e conquistara infideli trovata in Roma*, "stampata in Collicuti per Maestro Francesco da Udine." On this printer and his activities as a publisher of prophecies, see Giovanni Comelli, "Francesco da Udine tipografo a Roma nel primo Cinquecento," in *Studi forogiuliesi in onore di Carlo Guido Mor* (Udine: Deputazione di storia patria per il Friuli, 1984), pp. 163–69. The two editions to which I refer appeared around 1520; the one entitled *Profecia de santo Anselmo* lacked the refrain ("Vegnirà uno imperatore") and the opening stanza ("Vegnirà uno imperatore / tutto il mondo meterà in pace / mai fu homo sì verace / poi che nacque el Salvatore"). Carlo Dionisotti has used the edition entitled *Prophetia de uno imperatore* in "La guerra d'Oriente nella letteratura veneziana del Cinquecento," in his *Geografia e storia della letteratura italiana* (2nd ed.; Turin: G. Einaudi, 1971), p. 210.

[47] Petrucci, "Introduzione," in his *Libri, editori e pubblico*, pp. xxv–xxvii.

(Listen, mortals, to the horrible signs that announce great trials to our age; I wish to bring an end to my song, excellent listener, . . . this noble prophecy is ended, to your honor; O merry listener, here I make an end to my discourse.)[48]

These allusions to the relationship between recitation and listening rather than to the one between writing and reading signify that not only were these texts recited but they had been composed expressly to be recited. Interestingly enough, the compositions that contain these passages had all gone through several printings (at least three or four each) in editions that often consistently reproduced the same variants and additions. We might deduce that the compositions were part of the repertory of a number of tale singers, each one of whom introduced additions or what he felt to be improvements.

One specific testimony that prophecies were recited and spoken rather than merely put into books can be drawn from a notation in the journal of ser Tommaso di Silvestro. He wrote, early in 1504:

> Jaco de Colavabbo, a man of seventy-five years of age, a jocular man, died today, which was Monday, first day of January of the year 1504. He was at home after dinner by the fireside; he was singing to himself the prophecy of St. Bridget with great festivity and joy. He felt a sudden pain and suffered a stroke and he died of it.[49]

Neither of the two prophecies of St. Bridget known to us seems to lend itself to being sung merrily of an evening by the fireside, and certainly it was important to our chronicler to emphasize Jaco di Colavabbo's serenity before his sudden death. The fact remains, however, that Jaco was reciting or singing the text, not reading it, so that the text was considered in some way separable from the written or printed word.

At this point, then, we can state that in the early sixteenth century manifestations of prophecy connected with the expectation of catastrophe and with a subsequent regeneration were not restricted to narrow or esoteric groups,[50] but existed and circulated even among the underclasses and

[48] *Memoria delli novi segni et spaventevoli prodigii comparsi in piu loci de Italia et in varie parte del mondo lanno mille cinquecento undese* (n.p., n.d.), fol. 1*r*; *Questa è la vera Profecia de santo Anselmo*, fol. 2*v*; *Prophetia trovata in Roma / Intagliata in marmoro in versi latini / Tratta in vulghar sentimento*, "Stampata in Roma per Maestro Francesco da Udine" (n.d.), fol. 2*v*.

[49] Tommaso di Silvestro, *Diario*, p. 241.

[50] Maria Pia Billanovich, "Una miniera di epigrafi e di antichità. Il Chiostro Maggiore di S. Giustina a Padova," *Italia medioevale e umanistica* 12 (1969): 197–293; Billanovich, "Bernardino da Parenzo pittore e Bernardino (Lorenzo) da Parenzo eremita," *Italia medioevale e umanistica* 24 (1981): 385–404; Maria Teresa Binaghi, "L'immagine sacra in Luini e il Circolo di Santa Marta," in *Sacro e profano nella pittura di Bernardino Luini* (Milan: Silvana,

among people who could not read (let alone write, an ability that reflects a higher degree of instruction than minimal reading literacy). There was, in short, a notable qualitative change from the milieus of notaries, priests, schoolmasters, and jurists among whom, as we have seen, manuscript prophecies circulated. The "Gutenberg effect" applies even to this literary and publishing genre.

Italian Wars from the Descent of Charles VIII to Agnadello in Popular Prophecy

Printed prophecies circulated widely and in large numbers, as we have seen, until about 1530, after which the phenomenon seems to have died out suddenly. This rise and fall probably has a complex explanation, but a first hypothesis would certainly connect prophecy, in the manifestations that concern us here, with the political and religious disintegration that occurred during the first decades of the sixteenth century—with the *guerre horrende de Italia* and the continual passage of troops that brought with it the scourges of pestilence, famine, and devastation that gave credibility to the catastrophes predicted by the preachers and the tale singers. After 1530, however, that period seemed to be coming to an end, and Italy enjoyed a phase of greater tranquillity, which caused prophecies to lose their interest and topicality and to disappear from circulation.

In point of fact, the connection between prophecy and the political disintegration of the peninsula was clear in the minds of contemporaries. Both Francesco Matarazzo in Perugia and Andrea Bernardi, the barber-surgeon from Forlì, acknowledge this relationship explicitly.[51] It is also clearly perceptible in our publications, even when they contain texts that had been written more than a century earlier. Prophecy, as we have seen, was read with immediate reference to current events, whatever they might be. Thus even the prophecy of St. Bridget into which Tommasino Lancellotti read a prediction of the sack of Rome came to be considered an account of the Italian wars in one piece published at the end of the fifteenth

1975), pp. 49–76; Bernard McGinn, "Circoli gioachimiti veneziani (1450–1530)," *Cristianesimo nella storia* 7 (1986): 19–39; Anna Morisi, *Apocalypsis nova. Ricerche sull'origine e la formazione del testo dello pseudo-Amadeo* (Rome: Istituto storico italiano per il Medio Evo, 1970); Giampaolo Tognetti, "Note sul profetismo nel Rinascimento e la letteratura relativa," *Bullettino dell'Istituto storico italiano per il Medioevo* 82 (1970) [1974]: 129–57; Cesare Vasoli, *Profezia e ragione. Studi sulla cultura del Cinquecento e del Seicento* (Naples: Morano, 1974); Vasoli, *I miti e gli astri* (Naples: Guida, 1977); Vasoli, *La cultura delle corti* (Bologna: Cappelli, 1980), esp. pp. 129–218.

[51] Matarazzo, *Cronaca*, p. 16; Bernardi, *Cronache forlivesi*, vol. 1, pt. 2, p. 72.

century.[52] The versatility of these texts rendered them capable of illustrating whatever political trauma came along, with no need for modifications, which allows us to make reasonable inductions concerning the sort of reading that could be made of them in other cases as well. Thus when in 1495 the printer Angelo Ugoletti published separately the prophecy *El se movera un gato*, a text that had first appeared early in the century and that two years before had been printed in an appendix to the *Libro de Santo Iusto paladino de Franza*,[53] it is not difficult to suppose that this republication was prompted by an updated reading, in particular of the final lines:

O Italia piange, disse
—ube ube ube bis bis Italia—
che li stranieri e stracie
guarderà el vostro paese;
e queste seran l'imprese
che ferà di voi li vostri signori.
E picoli e mazori
se graterà la rogna
più che non bisogna
e con gran sangue.

(O Italy, weep, he said—sob, sob, sob, gasp, gasp; Italy!—for your land will see foreigners and disasters, and these will be enterprises that your lords will involve you in. And great and small will be troubled out of measure and with great bloodshed.)[54]

In a few cases (actually, very few), reprinting led to modifications in the text in the interest of adapting it better to a specific situation. One example of this is the prophecy of the second Charlemagne that was written for Charles VI of France and printed in Italy at the end of the fifteenth century on the occasion of the French invasion. When it was later attributed to Emperor Charles V, he was no longer called "fiol de Caroli" (Charles' son) but "Philippi filius" to recall his descent from Philip the Handsome. In other cases, the texts were expressly written to fit a specific context. Certain titles indicate this clearly, such as the *Imminente flagello de Italia*, or *Queste sono quattro prophetie novamente cavate le qual narra le grandissime guerre che ha da occorrere in la Italia et fora d'Italia*, or, again, *Pronostico e profecia de le cose debeno succedere generalmente maxime dele guere comenziate per magni*

[52] *Queste sono quattro prophetie novamente cavate le qual narra le grandissime guerre che a da occorrere in la Italia et fora ditalia* (n.p., n.d.).

[53] Published in Parma, 1493.

[54] *El se movera un gato*, fol. 2*v*.

potentati contra venetiani.[55] The texts themselves present allusions to current happenings, in particular to wars and battles. Giuliano Dati had already referred directly to the invasion of Charles VIII, presenting it as a sign of divine wrath and a portent of further afflictions to come;[56] later, even the battle of Agnadello and the events of the War of the League of Cambrai would find strong echoes in verse prophecies to testify to prophecy's role as a sounding board for political events.

In reality, the battle of Agnadello, in which the Venetian troops under Bartolomeo Alviano were routed by the French cavalry and the Swiss infantry, making the collapse of the power of the Serenissima in north-central Italy inevitable, almost immediately gave rise to a prophetic myth that long remained as alive among the Venetian patriciate as it was in folklore and that was clearly symptomatic of the political importance of that event. Some days before the battle a strange old man clothed in a bearskin had appeared before Alviano and, showing him "a long pike with a bent point," warned him that, like that weapon, the Venetians would have to bend in order not to break. He was later reported to have come back to scatter flaming embers and give out "writings of various predictions."[57] He was Francesco da Bergamo, Luigi da Porto tells us, a former mason "who, no longer exercising his craft, gave himself over exclusively to divination and philosophy, for which everyone thought him mad." The picture Da Porto presents of him has indeed something ludicrous about it, recalling a well-known theatrical tradition. This *om salvadegh* (wild man) who spoke only Bergamo dialect seems to us today more like a Carnival Zanni (the "mask" or stock character of a peasant from the mountains of Bergamo) than like St. John the Baptist, the prototype and model of the prophet in Italy of that period.[58] Within a few days, however, Venice lent a more attentive ear to prognostications. "Prodigious happenings and signs" had multiplied, Luigi da Porto tells us: "Already many people are afflicted. Even the comets seen these past days and the birth of several small monsters, and the entrance of wolves into many cities have disturbed many people."[59]

After the battle of Agnadello, prophetic tension seems to have increased further, becoming more contradictory, however. Since the catastrophe had

[55] The three publications bear no indication of place or date.

[56] *Del diluvio di Roma*, fol. a iii*v*.

[57] Luigi da Porto, *Lettere storiche di Luigi da Porto vicentino dall'anno 1509 al 1528*, ed. Bartolommeo Bressan (Florence: Felice Le Monnier, 1857), pp. 38–40. See also Innocenzo Cervelli, *Machiavelli e la crisi dello stato veneziano* (Naples: Guida, 1974), pp. 150–57, 215–16.

[58] See Domenico Merlini, *Saggio di ricerche sulla satira contro il villano* (Turin: E. Loescher, 1894), pp. 120–48; Lucia Lazzerini, "Preistoria degli zanni: mito e spettacolo nella coscienza populare," in *Scienze, credenze occulte, livelli di cultura. Convegno internazionale di studi (Firenze, 26–30 giugno 1980)*, 445–76, esp. pp. 465–74.

[59] Da Porto, *Lettere storiche*, p. 52. For monstrous births, see chap. 2 of this book.

now occurred, prediction of its immediate consequences was mingled with more consoling forecasts. In the weeks following Agnadello, Marin Sanudo included in his journals notes on astrological prognostications and celestial signs and even a report of a supernatural vision: On 19 June a woman dressed in white—the Virgin—had appeared to a widowed wool spinner and charged her to demand processions "so that this land may have victory against its enemies." As early as the end of May, however, Sanudo tells us that "*la brigà* [the throng] at present expects much from prophecies." He himself had been to the island of San Clemente to consult an old friar, Don Piero Nani, "a gentleman of our own, of ninety years of age, who says many things, such as drawing prophecies . . . of which he has a great store." Thus Don Piero was another collector of prophecies (in manuscript, we may suppose), a noble, consulted by other nobles ("he has a great following of patricians"). Nani stated that Venice would lose all its mainland empire, but would win back its territories at a later date; that the emperor would go to Rome, where he would cut the pope's head off; that later he would be chased out of Rome and replaced by another monarch, whom Nani "thinks is Duke Charles of Burgundy, who is rumored to be alive and in a hermitage," and who would assure the election of "a good pope." Finally, the Turk would be converted to Christianity.[60]

Identifying the various predictions on which Nani founded his meditations is an impossible task. Certainly in 1509 many prophecies circulated on the fall (definitive or temporary) of Venice and its state, as is clear even from a contemporary French source, the *Legende des Venitiens* of Jean Lemaire de Belges.[61] There was also a *Prophetia beati fratris Bartholomaei de Vincentia ordinis predicatorum*, conserved in a codex in the Biblioteca Marciana in Venice, which predicted a great war in 1509 "in quo Veneti in terra et in mari quicquid habent perdent, Venetiis exceptis."[62] The most interesting aspects of Sanudo's remarks lie elsewhere, however. First, he points to a clear social distinction in the circulation of the prophecies that centered on Nani: Nobles had recourse to the hidden wisdom of another noble to receive the same sort of comfort that other milieus and cultural and social levels would obtain, only a few weeks later, through the direct mediation of a visionary experience (or at least a visual experience, as we

[60] Sanuto, *Diarii*, vol. 8, cols. 419, 326.

[61] Jean Lemaire de Belges, *Le traicté nommé la legende des Venitiens, ou leur Chronique abregée*, in his *Oeuvres*, ed. J. Stecher, 4 vols. (Louvain: Imp. de J. Le Fever, 1882–1891), vol. 3 (1885), pp. 361–63, 409. On Lemaire, see Jennifer Britnell, "Jean Lemaire de Belges and prophecy," *Journal of the Warburg and Courtauld Institutes* 42 (1979): 144–66, esp. pp. 144–46; the article, however, does not mention the *Legende des Venitiens*.

[62] Biblioteca Marciana di Venezia, MS Marc, it. XI. 66 (=6730), fol. 119*v*. See also a *Prophetia abbatis Joachim Astrologi summi (re vera prophetia de civitate Venetiarum)*, Biblioteca Apostolica Vaticana, Vat. lat. 6085, fols. 195*r*.–196*v*.

shall see). Also, Nani proposes that the emperor of peace who was to create an angelic pope was Charles the Bold, duke of Burgundy, "who is reputed to be alive and living in a hermitage." This choice can be explained by the hypothesis, first, that Nani owned a copy of the prophecy of the second Charlemagne (perhaps in the version that began with the words, "Carolus Philippi filius," since Charles the Bold was in fact the son of Philip the Good) predicting the advent of a monarch named Charles who would bring peace, and second, that he interpreted it in the sense of the rumors that had spread after the death of Charles the Bold in the battle of Nancy in 1477. As Luca Landucci wrote, "It was never known what became of the duke's body, and it was never found; so that some were of opinion that he was not dead, but had been carried off, and would one day appear again."[63]

What we have here is one more example of the full operation of the mechanisms of prophecy. We have many texts (in this case, probably manuscript), a moment of political crisis, the selection of an appropriate text, the application to it of a rumor spread by word of mouth (there is no evidence that news of the survival of Charles the Bold was transmitted in writing),[64] and, finally, re-elaboration by an exegete for the purpose of comforting members of his own social group.

"Prophecies in Mosaics" in the Basilica of San Marco

Opposed to the *patricij* who consulted Piero Nani stood a broader and less clearly defined category: *la brigà*, the throng. "It is known [that] the throng at present expects much from prophecies, and goes to the church of San Marco seeing prophecies in mosaics, such as the abbot Joachim had made."

Just what were these *prophetie di musaicho* that all could see (rather than being shut up in a monk's cell) we learn from Jean Lemaire de Belges and, later, from Giovanni Stringa, writing at the beginning of the seventeenth century. They were figures that actually existed in the mosaic pavement of the basilica.[65] One was a cock (interpreted as the king of France) who was

[63] Luca Landucci, *Diario fiorentino dal 1450 al 1516*, ed. Iodaco del Badia (Florence: G. C. Sansoni, 1883), p. 15 (quoted from *A Florentine Diary from 1450 to 1516*, tr. Alice de Rosen Jervis [London: J. M. Dent; New York, E. P. Dutton, 1927], p. 13).

[64] In particular, nothing of the sort appears in Reeves, *The Influence of Prophecy*.

[65] See the reproductions in Giuseppe Marino Urbani de Gheltof, "Il pavimento," in Camillo Boito, *La Basilica di San Marco in Venezia illustrata nella storia e nell'arte da scrittori veneziani*, 18 vols. (Venice, F. Ongania, 1878–1893), vol. 15, pt. 3, table 42, fig. 3, and table 43, fig. 12. See also Giovanni Stringa, *La chiesa di S. Marco* (Venice: F. Rampezetto, 1610), fols. 20*r*–*v*.

pecking out the eyes of a fox (Venice); another showed two lions, one fat and sturdy, swimming through the waves, the other, thin and emaciated, on dry land. According to Lemaire, repeating an interpretation he had heard in Venice, the portrayal of the two lions had been ordered by Joachim of Fiore and were to be understood as the Republic, opulent and peaceful so long as Venetians remained lords of the sea, but which would lose power and wealth should it "begin to usurp on the mainland."[66] What Lemaire reports as prognostication was in reality a clearly defined political opinion that sought to acquire a broader hearing and borrow greater authority from prophecy. It was even a broadly held opinion, shared, for example, and expressed well by the anonymous author of a sonnet printed a few months later, which contrasts the noble activity of seafaring with the latest mania of the Venetians for agrarian expansion on the *terraferma* and cultivating fields and crops.

> et mai finisse questa rural fame.
> Uscite di tal trame,
> ché chi si vol far ricco vadi in mare,
> e lassi i buo' al villan per seminare.
>
> (and this rural hunger never ended. Get free of those trammels, and anyone who wants to get rich can go to sea; leave oxen to peasants for sowing.)[67]

To return to the "prophecies in mosaics," their fame was established all the more easily because it was based on a tradition that had arisen in Franciscan circles in the latter half of the fourteenth century, well accepted by the sixteenth century, that not only scattered details of the pavement but the entire plan for the mosaics of San Marco had been drawn up by Joachim of Fiore.[68] Thus the basilica was a precious coffer filled with prophecies to be conserved and investigated, and as late as 1566 its supervisors

[66] Lemaire de Belges, *Le Traicté nommé la legende des Venitiens*, p. 363.

[67] These are the final lines of a sonnet entitled "Ad illustres Venetos dominos ut mare pernavigent," the "inspired opening" of which ("Andate in mar, signori venetiani / che sete i primi marinar del mondo" [Go to sea, Venetian lords, who are the first sailors of the world]) Dionisotti records in his *Geografia e storia*, p. 208. The sonnet appears in the anonymous collection *Laus Venetorum* (Venice, 1509), fol. 3*r*.

[68] On this topic (to which I intend to return on another occasion), see Otto Demus, *The Mosaics of San Marco in Venice*, 2 vols. (Chicago and London: University of Chicago Press, 1984), vol. 1, pp. 256–59. The tradition of prophetic reading of the mosaics of San Marco throws new light on the behavior of the armorer Benedetto, who, around 1560, expounded to a group of followers on his *Espositione nell'Apocalipse*, which he had written (in manuscript form) with the help of the mosaics on that theme, newly mounted on the west face of the west dome by the Zuccato brothers (see Adriano Prosperi, "Intorno a un catechismo figurato del tardo '500," in *Von der Macht der Bilder* (Leipzig: E. A. Seeman; Karl-Marx-Universität, 1983), p. 111.

gave firm orders not to do away with any inscription or mosaic without taking due note of it, "so that those same works and prophecies, which it is said were ordered by St. Joachim, can be worked on and returned."[69] That these prophecies concerned the fortunes of the Serenissima was suggested by the utterly political tone, well attuned to political functions and demands, of all religious practice in the basilica and in Venice.[70] These images, publicly displayed inside the principal temple of the Republic, were thus open to exegesis by the *brigà*, who enjoyed much greater freedom of interpretation than Friar Piero Nani. They even solicited interpretation by the evocation of the glorious name of Abbot Joachim, and they gave efficacious expression to a hard political truth—the collapse of Venetian power—and to proposals for emerging from a difficult situation by abandoning the mainland empire and returning to sea power. The role of such prophecies far surpassed simple consolation: They were an instrument for political analysis and the proposal of political programs—a rough-hewn tool, perhaps, but one with an important impact on public opinion.

The War of Cambrai in Prophetic Publications

The same complex role can be seen in vernacular prophetic print pieces published during the same period. One example of these emerges out of a burlesque anti-Venetian text, the *Iudicio del frate Bechierante da Cervia commissario e studiante*,[71] probably printed in the early months of 1510. This piece is a bizarre mixture of Latin and vernacular, of rhythmic prose and nonsense verse, of anticlerical attitudes and homage to Pope Julius II. It is structured like the traditional prognostications, with an introduction, a dedication, then various chapters: "De Iulio II," "De rege Francorum," "De infirmitate," "De le guerre," "Del ricolto," and so forth. References to political events are frequent. With a good bit of irony and pointed satire, interspersed with street players' gags and macaronic doggerel, Julius II and the other members of the League of Cambrai are promised victory over Venice and, at a later time, over the Turks. Another edition of this strange text bears a more explicit title (already cited): *Pronostico e profecia de le cose debeno succedere maxime dele guere comenziate per magni potentati contra venetiani. Adi XX de zenaro M.V.X.*[72] It was illustrated with a woodcut that

[69] *Documenti per la storia dell'augusta ducale Basilica di San Marco in Venezia dal nono secolo sino alla fine del decimo ottavo* (Venice: Ferdinand Ongania, 1886), p. 80.

[70] Edward Muir, *Civic Ritual in Renaissance Venice* (Princeton: Princeton University Press, 1981).

[71] N.p., n.d.

[72] N.p., n.d.

Fig. 1. Frontispiece to *Pronostico e profecia de le cose debeno succedere* . . . (n.p., 1510).

referred to events concerning the League of Cambrai (see Figure 1). The four principal allies (the pope, the emperor, the kings of France and of Spain), each recognizable by an emblematic element, are seated around a playing field on which there are bowling pins, for the most part knocked down, to symbolize the cities that they threatened to take or had already taken from Venice early in 1510. To one side there is a pin with a joker's head, labeled *Mato*, and a sort of wheel—the *zurlo*—which obviously serves as a bowling ball. A two-line caption explains the rules of the game and warns the allies not to be too sure of their luck:

> Guardate il zurlo non abati il Mato,
> perché, abatendo, nula fia sto tracto.
>
> (Take care that the zurlo does not strike down the Mato because if it does the match is off.)[73]

[73] *Pronostico e profecia de la cose debeno succedere*, fol. 1*r*.

That is, if the ball strikes down the Fool, the turn is invalid and the other pins already knocked down will not count. In nonmetaphorical terms, imponderables can take from the leaders of the League what they think they hold securely. The joking tone of the prophecy is contradicted by this prudent warning.

The dedication of the piece to Julius II is dated, in the author's bizarre style, "de l'anno cinquecento e nove, de dicembre a XX che sempre piove" (in the year five hundred and nine, December 20, and still raining). At precisely the same time (the immediately preceding entry concerns Christmas night, 1509), ser Tommaso di Silvestro in Orvieto transcribed in his journal a "Pater Noster made in tercets signifying what is to be, according to the prophecies."[74] This prayer was a parody of the "Our Father," a literary genre well known and particularly widely practiced in the sixteenth century.[75] Following a *topos* of biblical origin, it predicts "plagues, wars, and famines . . . until the coming of a Christian Lord" who is to defeat and convert the Turks. Wars and tribulations would then continue until the year 1509; then, under the aegis of "a Roman shepherd . . . all the world will be pacified." This was to be the new Golden Age:

> et in tal tempo non varrà né carlino né ducato
> . . .
> multi superbi seranno in basso stato;
> qualunche serrà humile, esaltato,
> non se extimarà né seta, né imbroccato.
>
> (and in that time neither the *carlino* nor the *ducato* will be worth anything. . . . Many of the proud will be in low estate; some of the humble [will be] exalted, neither silk nor brocade will be esteemed.)[76]

To offer a prophecy at the end of 1509, when the war of the League of Cambrai was raging, explicitly dating the defeat of the Venetians in that year and predicting the conversion of the Turks after many wars, to be followed by universal peace and social palingenesis under a "Roman shepherd," was equivalent to implicit support of the current political aims of Julius II. We should keep in mind, among other things, that one of the official reasons for taking up arms against Venice lay in its attitude toward the Turks, which was judged unpropitious to an anti-Ottoman crusade. One logical deduction was that war against Venice was a necessary precon-

74 Tommaso di Silvestro, *Diario*, pp. 415–17.

75 See Francesco Novati, "Una poesia politica del Cinquecento: il Pater Noster dei Lombardi," *Giornale di filologia romanza* 2 (1879): 121–52; Novati, "La parodia sacra nelle letterature moderne," in his *Studi critici e letterari* (Turin, Florence, and Rome: E. Loescher, 1889), pp. 177–310.

76 Tommaso di Silvestro, *Diario*, p. 416.

dition to a crusade against the Turks, hence itself a crusade.[77] Furthermore, the prophecy could very well have been drawn up in Roman circles: Certain grammatical forms (*speramo*, *magnaranno*, *imbroccato*) support this, and we can reasonably hypothesize that Tommaso di Silvestro's usual sources of information were Roman.

These were not the only instances of the appearance, direct or indirect, of the War of Cambrai in prophecies. In 1511 a very short work of only two leaves was put out, probably by Giovanni Antonio Benedetti, a printer in Bologna, containing a narrative ballad entitled *Memoria delli novi segni et spaventevoli prodigii comparsi in piu loci de Italia et in varie parti del mondo lanno mille cinquecento undese*. This is a singular text, fascinating for its lack of polish, to which we shall have frequent occasion to return. It continued to be reprinted, with additions, corrections, and adaptations, past the mid-century. We have already encountered the incipit: "Ascoltati mortali / li orribeli segnali" (Listen, mortals, to the horrible signs). As the title and the opening words tell us, this was a collection of omens, portents, and extraordinary occurrences that foretold of divine wrath directed at the world in general and at Italy in particular. The signs described in greatest detail were "an impious and fierce serpent" sighted in the air on 5 May between Brescia and Cremona, ghostly fires that appeared "where the conflict with the Venetians had been," sounds of mysterious battles between specters in the same area on 7 May (the identity of the ghostly combatants will be revealed in chapter 3), finally, two angels who appeared for three hours with drawn swords "over the territory of Padua."[78] All these prodigies concerned the area involved in the Cambrai War in 1509–1510, which culminated in the battle of Agnadello ("where the conflict with the Venetians had been") and the imperial assault on Padua. In fact, the poet deliberately and erroneously transfers the angels with drawn swords from a bell tower in Udine, where a good number of other contemporary accounts place this apparition, to the skies over Padua.[79] A good fifteen quatrains are devoted to these phenomena, whereas the *cantastorie* used only eight to describe the signs that had appeared in Venice, Rome, and Florence, and seven for those that had occurred in Turkey. Although this disproportionate concentration on prodigies in the war zone cannot be coincidental, here we are not dealing with propagandistic and celebrative demands as in the two texts examined earlier. The *Memoria delli novi segni* is better considered as an echo of the devastation and suffering that the War of the League of Cambrai had brought to the populations of the Veneto and Lombardy. To use places that were, as Ruzante put it, "se no cielo e uossi de morti"

[77] Dionisotti, *Geografia e storia*, pp. 207–208; Cervelli, *Machiavelli*, pp. 160–63.

[78] *Memoria delli novi segni*, fol. 1*r–v*.

[79] Ottavia Niccoli, "Visioni e racconti di visioni nell'Italia del primo Cinquecento," *Società e storia* 28 (1985): 253–73; pp. 262, 264.

("nothing but sky and dead men's bones")[80] as a background for portents and prodigies was to draw upon them for presages of affliction that deeply involved the listeners' emotions. The tale singers' verse shows an unconscious but clear connection between war, political disintegration, and prophecy.

[80] Angelo Beolco, called Ruzante, *Parlamento de Ruzante che iera vegnù dal campo* in his *Teatro*, ed. Ludovico Zorzi (Turin: G. Einaudi, 1967), p. 529.

2

MONSTERS, DIVINATION, AND PROPAGANDA IN BROADSHEETS

Signs and Popular Divination

IN HIS *Del diluvio di Roma del MCCCCLXXXXV* Giuliano Dati declared to his *auditori*, through the voice of a tale singer, that divine castigation was imminent. The announcement was presumably based on incontrovertible indications, on "signs great and immeasurable" clearly of religious origin and pertinence, on which Dati expounded for thirty-five eight-line stanzas:

> Par che 'l Signor tal cosa lui ci mandi
> quel che su nella croce fu defunto;
> per farci più acciepti in ne' sua regni
> ci manda gl'infrascripti e detti segni.
> . . .
> Questi segni ci manda l'alto Idio
> che no' ci prepariamo, al parer mio.
>
> (It seems that the Lord, who died upon the Cross, sends us such a thing; in order that we be made more acceptable in his kingdom he sends us the said signs, written below. . . . These signs almighty God sends us so we will prepare ourselves, it seems to me.)[1]

What exactly did he mean by "infrascripti e detti segni" or by "segni grandi e smisurati"? Precisely what were these signs? In this context, the word obviously has biblical origins, its most explicit utilization being in the Gospel according to St. Luke:

> And there shall be signs in the sun, and in the moon, and in the stars: and upon the earth distress of nations, by reason of the confusion of the roaring of the sea and of the waves. Men withering away for fear, and expectation of what shall come upon the whole world. . . . But when these things begin to come

[1] Giuliano Dati, *Del diluvio di Roma del MCCCCLXXXXV adi iiii di dicembre et daltre cose di gran meraviglia* (n.p., n.d.), fol. a ii*r*.

to pass, look up and lift up your heads: because your redemption is at hand. *(Luke 21:25–28)*

Thus the signs in question were alterations in the stars (and in nature in general) observed attentively and interpreted as portents of imminent and terrible events. The word *segno* or its equivalent occurs with overwhelming frequency in this sense and with these connotations. Signs were not simply extraordinary events, however; taken as a whole, they served as something like an elementary set of orally transmitted techniques common to both the learned and the unlettered and instrumental for predicting the future on the basis of changes in what was considered the natural course of things. As Leone Cobelli, a painter from Forlì, said in 1497, "signs never come without some matter."[2] With the focus on classical divination in humanistic culture and philosophical study of the occult following Pomponazzi (in the *De incantationibus*, for example), an interest in portents and in what came to be defined as *divinatio popularis* even reached learned circles.[3] Still, as we shall see, this relationship worked both ways; if anything, it was a case of reciprocal influence.

Signs and portents could be a generic indication of the wrath of God, as in the verse of Giuliano Dati, or they could have a more carefully worked out political reading, as in a lively passage in Marin Sanudo's journals. Sanudo saw Italy's imminent liberation from the barbarians at the hands of the Republic of Venice in the disastrous effects of the earthquake that struck the city in March 1511:

> First, there fell four marble kings that before had stood over the façade of the church of St. Mark. . . . There fell a woman in marble who represented Prudence, even though she was standing amid other virtues. . . . The upper portion of the decorations over the great balcony of the Great Hall of the Major Council, which was high, fell, [along] with a Justice that was there, but a marble St. Mark held firm and did not fall. . . . A marble merlon decorated with a plaster seal bearing a lily blossom fell, and many held this to be a good sign, because the lily, which is the crest of France, will fall and come to ruin, which is what God wants for the good of Italy, sorely tried by barbarians. . . . And I saw the holy Mark, who remained intact on top of the palace. . . . Thus this city will be the savior of Italy and of the faith of Christ by chasing the barbarians from Italy.[4]

[2] Leone Cobelli, *Cronache forlivesi dalla fondazione della città all'anno 1498*, ed. Giosuè Carducci and Enrico Frati (Bologna: Regia tipografia, 1874), p. 412.

[3] For a definition of *divinatio popularis*, see p. 187.

[4] Marino Sanuto, *Diarii*, 58 vols. (Venice: R. Deputazione veneta di storia patria, 1879–1903), vol. 11, cols. 79–80.

Not only were imposing phenomena such as earthquakes, eclipses of the sun, and comets carefully noted; so were much less clamorous events such as the five meteorites that fell near Forlì on 26 January 1496, the unusual rainbow that appeared in Orvieto on 25 May 1507, and the myriad of red butterflies that invaded Brescia on Friday, 23 May 1522.[5] Monstrous creatures like the strange pig and the four-legged hen recorded in the *Diluvio di Roma* came in for particular attention:

E una troia un porco partorì
col capo tutto d'homo, e poi morì.
Con quattro piedi nacque una gallina,
e sequitò dipoi una gran peste;
d'animal e di gente fu rovina,
e le gente rimasen tutte meste.

(And a sow gave birth to a pig with a man's head, and then died. A hen was born with four feet, and a great pestilence followed; it was the ruination of animals and people, and people were greatly distressed by it.)[6]

On the Meaning of Monsters

Within this system of divination by signs, increasing attention was paid to the birth of malformed infants in the waning Middle Ages and the first decades of the early modern age.[7] It was a phenomenon that differed radically from both the preceding century's interest in fantastic monstrosities and the passion for classification that was to explode after 1550 and provide a precedent and encouragement for the new science. The "monsters" born as the fifteenth moved into the sixteenth century were actual births, and although descriptions of them tended to include some fantastic elements they had little in common with the Oriental monsters that the Indies so generously furnished in the Middle Ages. They often had a purely human fate. First and most obviously, they died, and not only from natural

[5] Cobelli, *Cronache forlivesi*, pp. 398–99; Tommaso di Silvestro, *Diario*, ed. Luigi Fumi, RIS 25, pt. 5 (Bologna: Nicola Zanichelli, 1923), vol. 2, pp. 1–512; p. 340; Paolo Guerrini, ed., *Le cronache bresciane inedite dei secoli XV–XIX*, 5 vols. (Brescia: Editrice Brixia Sacra, 1922–1932), vol. 2, p. 50.

[6] *Del diluvio di Roma*, fol. a ii*r*.

[7] Aby Warburg, *La rinascita del paganesimo antico*, tr. Emma Cantimori Mezzomonti (Florence: La Nuova Italia, 1966), pp. 348–54 (also available in his *Ausgewählte Schriften und Würdigungen*, ed. Dieter Wuttke [Baden-Baden: Verlag Valentin Koerner, 1980]); Jean Céard, *La Nature et les prodiges. L'insolite au XVIe siècle en France* (Geneva: Droz, 1977). In classical antiquity, the word *tératon* originally signified "terrifying prodigy," so by antomasia the monstrous creatures were terrible and prodigious events.

causes, but also from the deliberate withdrawal of care and nourishment. This is what happened in the case of a misbirth in Florence in 1506, who "by order of the Signoria was not fed and died," and to another malformed infant abandoned to the Hospital of the Pietà in Venice in 1513, who "was let die" in like manner.[8] These were patterns of behavior for which there is long-standing testimony and which continued into the eighteenth century and probably longer, as did the custom of displaying malformed babies for money, also well attested in these decades. Such was the case of the female Siamese twins born in 1475 outside Verona, who, as Conrad Wollfhart (Conrad Lycosthenes) recalls, "parentes multum diuque per Italiae urbes quaestus causa circumtulere,"[9] or of the other female misbirth in Ficarolo in the Polesine on 31 December 1531, of whom Tommasino Lancellotti says that she "has a permit from the vicar of the bishop of Ferrara, and whoever wants to see her pays."[10]

The display of abnormal infants hid another, deeper divinatory function. The monstrous creature, alive or embalmed, was shown not only because it was a "cosa spaventevole," a "cossa stupenda," or a "prodigio" but also because it was taken as a portent. As the physician Francesco Bonafede wrote to his father-in-law, Alessandro Pesaro, in March 1514 concerning various monstrous creatures of which he had had recent news, prognostications of the "tumult of wars, killing, [and] destruction" could be drawn from such events. Bonafede did not agree with this divinatory analysis, however, and he offered his father-in-law a detailed naturalistic explanation of abnormalities based on Aristotle. He had his own divinatory system, however, and his letter went on to describe "the revolution of the present year made by the most enlightened astrologer messer Pelegrin di Presciani [Pellegrino Prisciani]."[11] The contrast he sets up between astrology and the analysis of omens thus appears to imply a substantial difference in levels of culture.

The predictions that Bonafede noted were fairly generic, albeit catastrophic in content: *guerre, occisione, stragie*. Similarly, as early as 1489, Luca Landucci, after transcribing in his journal a letter containing a description of monsters that had been sent from Venice to Tanai de' Nerli's bank, concludes that "such signs signify great trouble in the city where they

[8] Sanuto, *Diarii*, vol. 6, col. 390; vol. 17, col. 347.

[9] Conrad Lycosthenes [Conrad Wollfhart], *Prodigiorum ac ostentorum chronicon* (Basel, 1557), p. 490.

[10] Tommasino Lancellotti, *Cronaca modenese*, ed. Carlo Borghi, 12 vols. (Parma: P. Fiaccadori, 1863), vol. 4, p. 23.

[11] Sanuto, *Diarii*, vol. 18, col. 33. On Bonafede, see Valerio Giacomini, "Bonafede, Francesco," in *Dizionario Biografico degli Italiani* (Rome: Istituto della Enciclopedia Italiana, 1960–), hereafter cited as DBI, vol. 11, pp. 491–92.

take place."[12] Aside from this generic prophetic function, however, misbirths had another, more specific function. From the late fifteenth century to 1530, a true literary genre emerged in Germany and Italy in the brief ephemeral works, pamphlets, and broadsheets that, in many cases, strove not only to give a global and cataclysmic prophetic sense to the monstrous creature but also a political-prophetic interpretation, arrived at through analysis of its various deformities.[13] This was what happened in the cases of misbirths in Rome in 1495, in Ravenna in 1512, in Bologna in 1514, in Freiberg in Saxony in 1522, in Castelbaldo in the Polesine in 1525, and so forth. Analysis of the monstrous bodies of these beings seems linked to the specific historical moment. Indeed, interpreters presented their expertise as political knowledge, explicitly contrasting it to that of "these modern sages with their tricks and their con games who advise princes, 'non timentes Deum, sed in sua versutia confisi,' " as one anonymous author wrote concerning the monster born in Bologna in January 1514, or, as another anonymous author said, commenting on a creature born with three legs in the Polesine in 1525, to the "secret cogitation of rulers."[14] Thus what was needed was a different sort of knowledge—a political analysis of the monstrous creatures aimed more at tracing the signs of divine wrath than investigating the maneuvers of men but tied to elements and events also considered by the *savieti* of the anonymous author of 1514, in substance, to use his words, the sorry condition of "misera Italia."

[12] Luca Landucci, *Diario fiorentino dal 1450 al 1516*, ed. Iodaco del Badia (Florence: G. C. Sansoni, 1883), p. 57; quoted from *A Florentine Diary from 1450 to 1516*, tr. Alice de Rosen Jervis (London: J. M. Dent; New York: E. P. Dutton, 1927), p. 47. The same event, reported in a different manner, can be found in Domenico Malipiero, "Annali veneti dall'anno 1457 al 1500," *Archivio storico italiano* 7 (1843–44): 5–586; p. 309, which connects the births to the attempted coup in which Girolamo Riario was killed.

[13] A model for the political interpretation of monstrous births emerged out of humanistic milieus surrounding the emperor Maximilian: See *Varia Sebastiani Brant Carmina* (Basel: [Johan Bergmann de] Olpe, 1498). See also Dieter Wuttke, "Sebastian Brant und Maximilian I. Eine Studie zu Brants Donnerstein-Flugblatt des Jahres 1492," in Otto Herding and Robert Stupperich, eds., *Die Humanisten in ihrer politischen und sozialen Umwelt* (Boppard: Harald Boldt, 1976), pp. 141–76; Wuttke, "Wunderdeutung und Politik. Zu den Auslegung der sogenannten Wormser Zwillinge des Jahres 1495," in Kaspar Elm, Eberhard Gönner, and Engen Hillenbrand, eds., *Landesgeschichte und Geistesgeschichte. Festschrift für Otto Herding zum 65. Geburtstag* (Stuttgart: W. Kohlhammer, 1977), pp. 217–44; Wuttke, "Sebastian Brants Verhältnis zu Wunderdeutung und Astrologie," in *Studien zur deutschen Literatur und Sprache des Mittelalters. Festschrift für Hugo Moser zum 65. Geburtstag* (Berlin: Erich Schmidt, 1974), pp. 272–86. On the Roman monster of 1496, see Konrad von Lange, *Der Papstesel; Ein Beitrage zur Kultur- und Kunstgeschichte des Reformationszeitsalters* (Göttingen: Vandenhoeck and Ruprecht, 1891) and Antonio Rotondò, "Pellegrino Prisciani," *Rinascimento* 11 (1960): 69–110; pp. 106–107. For the monster of Ravenna, see also Rudolf Schenda, "Das Monstrum von Ravenna. Eine Studie zur Prodigienliteratur," in *Zeitschrift für Volkskunde* 56 (1960): 209–225.

[14] Sanuto, *Diarii*, vol. 17, col. 516; vol. 40, col. 652.

The wealth and the polyvalence of prophetic language emerges with particular clarity from the pamphlets, broadsheets (often illustrated), and other written or pictorial descriptions of the monsters. We have already encountered some of these pieces, and others will be taken up, at least in some of their aspects, in a later chapter. Here I shall focus on two such monsters, the creature born in Ravenna in March 1512, best known for foreshadowing the battle of 11 April of that year, in which the French forces inflicted a bloody defeat on the pontifical army,[15] and another, less famous monster born in Bologna in January 1514.

The Monster of Ravenna: How the News Got Around

Information on the monster of Ravenna is plentiful and of various sorts, but deeper understanding of its meaning requires careful analysis. We need first to reconstruct the origin and the circulation of pamphlets and broadsheets, then to pass on to the figures that illustrated these pieces and to investigate their origin, and finally, we need to turn to the texts themselves and to the significance and global function of these materials.

The earliest testimony available to us is that of the Roman chronicler Sebastiano di Branca Tedallini:

> The 8th day of March. How in Ravenna there was born to a nun and a friar an infant such as I shall write to you. It had a big head, with a horn on its forehead and a large mouth; on its chest, three letters, as you see here: YXV, with three [tufts of] hairs on its chest; one leg hairy with a devil's hoof, the other a man's leg with an eye in the middle of the leg; never in memory of man has there been anything like this. The governor of the land sent [information] of it on paper to Pope Julius II.[16]

The news thus arrived in Rome on 8 March: "Lo governatore de la tera [Marco Coccapane] mandàne nella carta a papa Iulio 2o."[17] The phrase suggests fairly swift communication (as we shall see, another source tells us that the monster was born 6 March), according to Tedallini transmitted "nella carta," an expression that probably indicates that a drawing picturing the monster was sent along with the news itself and a description.

15 On the Battle of Ravenna, see Giancarlo Schizzerotto, *Otto poemetti volgari sulla battaglia di Ravenna del 1512* (Ravenna: Edizioni del Girasole, 1968), and the bibliography given in that work.

16 Sebastiano di Branca Tedallini, *Diario romano dal 3 maggio 1485 al 6 giugno 1524*, ed. Paolo Piccolomini, RIS 23, pt. 3, pp. 287–445; p. 327.

17 Silvio Bernicoli, *Governi di Ravenna e di Romagna dalla fine del secolo XII alla fine del secolo XIX. Tavole di cronologia* (Ravenna: tip. Ravegnana, 1898), p. 57. This work is available in reproduction (Bologna: Forni, 1968).

Our next piece of information comes from Luca Landucci in Florence: "11th March. We heard that a monster had been born at Ravenna, of which a drawing was sent here." Landucci continues, after a description much like Branca Tedallini's, "I saw it painted, and anyone who wishes could see this painting in Florence."[18] Landucci was thus aware of a drawing, not a written description: The monster, he says, "venne qui [that is, notice of it arrived in Florence] disegnato" or "dipinto." It must have been a colored drawing, probably with a caption, perhaps reproduced in many copies, and certainly posted in public, as indicated by the notation that "chi lo volle vedere" could do so. There is an ample fund of information on the public posting of pictures, *scartabelli* (pamphlets), and manuscript texts of various sorts, a topic that would repay further reflection. Even infamatory depiction—the judicial penalty of displaying a picture of a condemned criminal in a public place—is attested in Bologna and Venice as late as the end of the 1530s in the modest form of broadsheets and paintings rather than the more usual wall paintings.[19]

But "revenons à nos monstres." With the drawing cited by Landucci we are apparently still in the phase of the circulation of manuscript texts and illustrations, and a brief word on the continuing importance of these two channels of communication in the early sixteenth century might not be amiss. The piece that arrived in Spain and that Pietro Martire d'Anghiera described in a letter to Marchese Pietro Fajardo dated 20 March (however, Anghiera's letters are often misdated) may also have been a captioned drawing or perhaps a broadsheet.[20] Anghiera's description concurs in substance with that of the Spanish historian Andrés Bernáldez, who mentioned the matter a few months later in his *Historia de los reyes católicos* (in particular, both insist on the leonine aspect of the creature's face and hair). Anghiera concludes, "cuius imaginem ab Urbe allatam vidimus"; Bernáldez tells us that the monster "fué llevado al Papa, el cual lo vidó y mandó dibujarle de la manera y forma que era" (was shown to the Pope, who saw

[18] Quoted from Landucci, *A Florentine Diary*, pp. 249–50.

[19] For infamatory paintings, see Gherardo Ortalli, "*. . . Pingatur in palatio. . .*": *La pittura infamante nei secoli XIII–XVI* (Rome: Jouvence 1979). See also cases mentioned in Giuliano Fantaguzzi, *Caos. Cronache cesenati del sec. XV*, ed. Dino Bazzocchi (Cesena: Tip. Arturo Bettini, 1915), pp. 117, 134–35 (for the years 1495 and 1500); Sanuto, *Diarii*, vol. 47, cols. 100, 495–97, 514 (for the year 1528); Jacopo Rainieri, *Diario bolognese*, ed. Olindo Guerrini and Corrado Ricci (Bologna: Deputazione di storia patria per le provincie di Romagna, 1888), pp. 35 and 38 (for the year 1538); Girolamo Bonoli, *Storia di Lugo ed annessi* (Faenza: nella stampa dell'Archi impressor camerale e del S. Ufizio, 1732), p. 495 (for the year 1646).

[20] *Opus epistolarum Petri Martyris Anglerii* (Amsterdam: typis Elzevirianis, 1670), p. 256. On the dating of Anghiera's letters, see L. Gazzero Righi, "L'Opus epistolarum' di Pietro Martire d'Anghiera visto alla luce della critica tedesca della fine del XIX secolo," in *Pietro Martire d'Anghiera nella storia e nella cultura* (Genoa, 1980), pp. 261–85.

it and sent to ask of the manner and form that it was).[21] Both Anghiera and Bernáldez thus stress that the image and the description of the malformed creature originated in Rome and circulated at the pope's initiative. It was also in Rome that versions of the image shifted from largely figurative, hand-done pieces to a greater emphasis on writing and to print. On 22 March 1512 Marin Sanudo notes in his *Diarii*, "Item: There was sent me from Rome a monster born in Ravenna in this year; a horrendous thing, which was put into print there in Rome."[22]

The "monster"—that is, the pamphlet or the broadsheet that depicted and described it, on the identity of which I shall offer a hypothesis below—was enclosed in a letter of 18 March from the Venetian ambassador in Rome, Francesco Foscari. Thus very little time separated the misbirth from its being "butado a stampa": First circulated in largely illustrative manuscript pieces, the news appeared in print within ten days or so. Such dispatch was not unusual, however, nor was the stir that this sort of news created in court circles in Rome, as evidenced by the interest aroused by the so-called pope-ass, by the monster found on the banks of the Tiber after the flood in December 1495 ("sung" by Giuliano Dati), by another Roman monster born in 1513,[23] and by the Bolognese monster of 1514.

The news reached Venice from Ravenna, but via Rome. This is a sign, it seems to me, of Ravenna's passage from Venetian to Roman domination. In early Cinquecento Italy, the circulation of news (important news, at least) inevitably followed the paths of political power.

A Genealogy of Images

From Rome news of the monstrous birth was spread throughout Europe. We have already seen that it arrived in Spain; in France as well, broadsheets were printed on the topic. We have one such piece, or, more accurately, we have it transposed and inserted into a longer text that appeared in Valence on 18 September 1513 entitled *Les Avertissemens es trois estatz du monde selon la signification de ung monstre ne lan mille. v. cens et xij*.[24] The author,

[21] Andrés Bernáldez, *Historia de los reyes católicos, Don Fernando y Doña Isabel*, 2 vols. (Seville: J. M. Geofrin, 1870), vol. 2, p. 373 (available in a modern edition edited by Luciano de la Calzada; Madrid: Aguilar, 1959).

[22] Sanuto, *Diarii*, vol. 14, col. 200.

[23] On which, see a brief publication of four leaves, Ioannis Baptiste Ruberti Pegasei, *Monstrum apud Urbem natum* (n.p., n.d. [Rome, after 11 March 1513]). A broadsheet on the same topic bearing an engraving analogous to the one in this work and a verse caption in German is reproduced in Eugen Holländer, *Wunder, Wundergeburt und Wundergestalt in Einblattdrucken des funfzehnten bis achtzehnten Jahrhunderts* (Stuttgart: F. Enke, 1921), p. 312.

[24] The title continues: *Par lequelz on pourra prendre avis a soy regir a tousioursmais* (Valence: Iehan Belon, 1513).

one François Inoy or Yvoy, succeeded in blending together in this singular work a broadsheet describing the Ravenna monster, a prophetic text that had been immensely popular for more than a quarter century, the *Pronosticatio* of the German astrologer Johannes Lichtenberger (Inoy's principal source),[25] and his own typically medieval erudition. Inoy's *auctoritates* are, first, the Bible, then Albertus Magnus, Albumazar, the glosses of Nicolas de Lyra, Aristotle, the patristic texts, Aratus, Varro, Lucan, and the medieval encyclopedia *Lueur de Philosophie*, written in the early fourteenth century by one Jehan Bonnet and here cited under the better-known title of *Placides et Tymeo*.[26] The print that gave Inoy his point of departure was inserted into the text, and under an engraving portraying the monstrous creature (Figure 2) was a description very similar to the ones we have already seen, in all probability a caption to the broadsheet that Inoy had in hand.[27] It is here, among other places, that we find 6 March given as the monster's date of birth.

The picture illustrating this learned Frenchman's pamphlet seems closely related to one that appeared on a German broadsheet, also printed in 1512 (see Figure 3), referring, however, to another monstrous birth that supposedly occurred in Florence on 27 February (a place and date that will require explanation later).[28] Both presumably derived from a common source, now lost. Another Italian broadsheet, also now lost, was the source of another group of images: the first illustrating a short, four-folio work containing a poem in Latin by Giano Vitale of Palermo entitled *De monstro nato*, published in at least two editions in 1512;[29] the second a German broadsheet of a slightly later date, since it mentions a battle that occurred

[25] On Lichtenberger, see Warburg, *La rinascita del paganesimo antico*, pp. 340–48; Dietrich Kurze, *Johannes Lichtenberger (d. 1503). Eine studie zur Geschichte der Prophetie und Astrologie* (Lübeck and Hamburg: Hattiesen, 1960); Kurze, "Popular Astrology and Prophecy in the fifteenth and sixteenth Centuries: Johannes Lichtenberger," in Paola Zambelli, ed., *"Astrologi hallucinati": Stars and the End of the World in Luther's Time* (Berlin and New York: W. de Gruyter, 1986), pp. 177–93; Marjorie Reeves, *The Influence of Prophecy in the Late Middle Ages: A Study in Joachimism* (Oxford: Clarendon Press, 1969), pp. 347ff.

[26] *Sen suit le Lueur de Philosophie contenant plusieurs demandes et questions proposées par le sage Placides au Philosophe Tymeo et les responses contenues in icelluy*, à Paris par Denis Janot, n.d.

[27] *Les Avertissemens en trois estatz du monde*, fol. 6*v*. The passage in question corresponds to the first chapter of that pamphlet, "De la forme que a le monstre."

[28] See Holländer, *Wunder*, p. 318; Gisela Ecker, *Einblattdrucke von dem Anfänge bis 1555* (Göppingen, 1981), no. 192.

[29] Ioannes Franciscus Vitalis Panormitanus, *De monstro nato* (n.p., n.d.). Another edition, nearly identical to this one except for a few lines of Latin verse, "Ad lectorem," on fol. 4*v*, not present in the preceding copy, appeared in Erfurt in July of that year with the imprint: "Impressum Erfordiae per Mattheum Pictorium Anno novi seculi xij Mensis Iulio." On Vitale, see, above all, Girolamo Tumminello, "Giano Vitale umanista del secolo XVI," *Archivio storico siciliano*, n.s. 8 (1883): 1–94; Fernanda Ascarelli, *Annali tipografici di Giacomo Mazzocchi* (Florence: Sansoni antiquariato, 1961), pp. 68–69.

Fig. 2. The Monster of Ravenna. From François Inoy, *Les Avertissemens es trois estatz du monde* . . . (Valence, 1513).

on 11 April, now preserved in Nuremberg, the only piece extant on the monster of Ravenna.[30] The two illustrations contain a number of features such as the "leonine" face of the creature and a leg terminating in a webbed frog foot rather than birdlike claws. These were also mentioned by Bernáldez, who thus must have seen an image of this group and used it as the basis of his description. Finally, an analogous figure accompanied by a verse description ("cum interpretatione carmine expressa") must have come into the hands of Conrad Wollfhart (Lycosthenes), who used it in his *Prodigiorum ac ostentorum chronicon*, published in Basel in 1557.[31] Ly-

[30] Ecker, *Einblattdrucke*, no. 67.

[31] Lycosthenes, *Prodigiorum ac ostentorum chronicon*, p. 517.

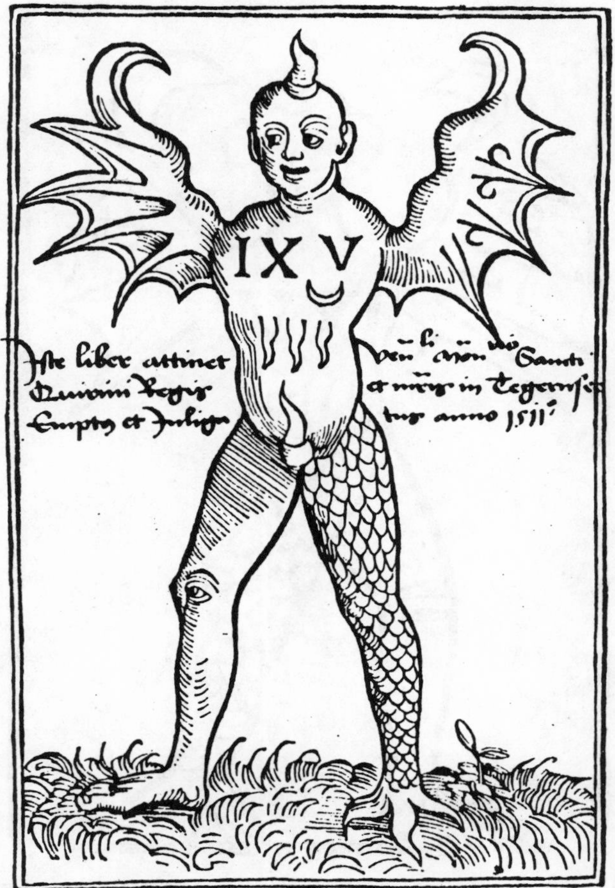

Fig. 3. The Florentine Monster of 1512. German broadsheet, Bayerische Staatsbibliothek, Munich.

costhenes also furnished another and quite different version of the monster, pictured with only one leg with a clawed foot and with bird's wings instead of bat's wings (Figure 4). In his description and explanation of this second image, Lycosthenes made use of additions that Johannes Multivallis of Tournai had made to the *Chronicon* of Eusebius of Caesarea.[32] Thus we have at least two different iconographic models and perhaps three, because in his poem in Latin on the Battle of Ravenna, published in Rome

[32] Eusebii Caesariensis Episcopi, *Chronicon . . . ad quem . . . et Ioannes Multivallis complura quae ad haec usque tempora subsecuta sunt adiecere* (Paris: H. Etienne and J. Bade, 13 June 1512).

Fig. 4. Two versions of the Monster of Ravenna from Conrad Wollfhart, *Prodigiorum ac ostentorum chronicon* (Basel, 1557).

in October 1513, Marcello Palonio, a Roman, describes the monster in a lateral gloss to his verse as having two heads ("gemino capite").[33]

Such details do more than satisfy erudite curiosity, since we can trace the iconographic and other origins of each of these models, thus increasing our understanding of the many and interwoven cultural threads in the network of broadsheets that, as we have seen, extended throughout most of Europe. In fact, although we cannot exclude the possibility that a gravely malformed infant was indeed born in Ravenna on the date indicated, it is nonetheless certain that the various depictions were constructed almost totally from preexisting figurative materials. This is particularly clear in the largest group of images showing the misshapen creature with only one head and two legs, which follow, nearly trait for trait, images of the other monster (mentioned above) that the explanatory caption says was born in July 1506 in Florence. This explains, in particular, the German sheets that, as late as 1512, still place the monstrous birth in Florence, an event that might be deemed the incestuous fruit of a liaison between two already related news items and images. News of this Florentine monster of 1506 also passed beyond the Alps, where it was circulated in various forms. The remaining evidence includes a colored drawing that Marin Sanudo pasted into the manuscript of his *Diarii* in August 1506[34] and a nearly identical German broadsheet,[35] which must thus have been taken from a drawing

[33] Marcello Palonio, *Clades ravennas* (Rome, 1513), fol. F iii*r*.

[34] Biblioteca Marciana di Venezia, MS Marc. it. VII.234 (=9221), fol. 179*v*. In the printed edition, the description of the monster is in Sanuto, *Diarii*, vol. 6, col. 390.

[35] Ecker, *Einblattdrucke*, no. 189.

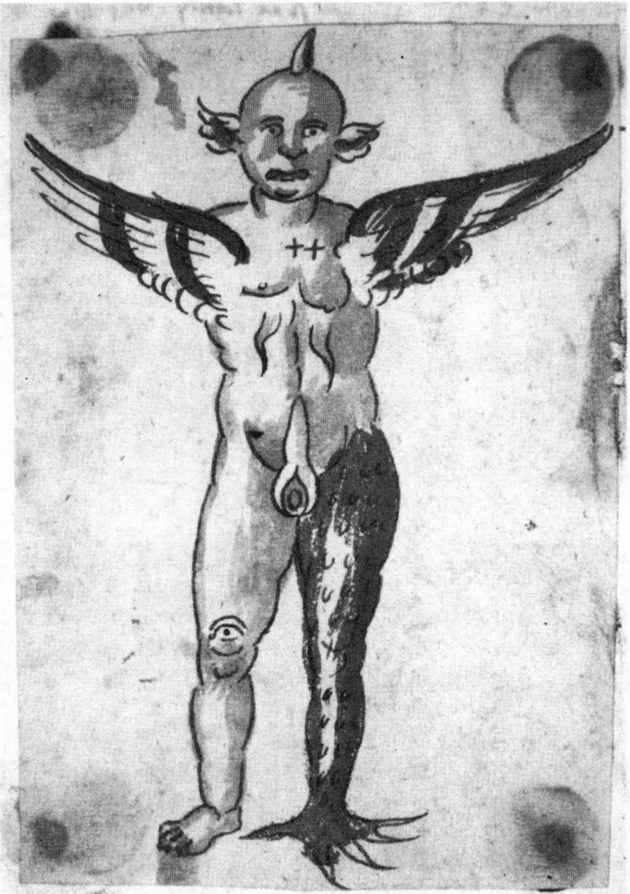

Fig. 5. The Florentine Monster of 1506. Colored drawing, Biblioteca Marciana, Venice.

analogous to the one Sanudo had procured or, more probably, from an Italian broadsheet based on that same drawing (Figures 5 and 6).

The group of images and descriptions representing the monster with only one leg and an avian, clawed foot had a less immediate origin. One likely common source—perhaps not the only source, however—lies in images, fairly common in late medieval German lands, in particular, in the area bounded by Alsace, Switzerland, and Bohemia, which personified the sinful world as Frau Welt.[36] Dame World was portrayed as a woman with

[36] On this iconographical theme, see Wolfgang Stammler, *Frau Welt. Eine mittelalterliche Allegorie* (Fribourg [Switzerland]: Universitätsverlag, 1959); Fritz Saxl, "A Spiritual Ency-

Fig. 6. The Florentine Monster of 1506. German broadside, Bayerische Staatsbibliothek, Munich.

bat's wings, tufts of hair or feathers on her head, standing on her one raptor's leg; the various parts of her body symbolized the seven capital sins. We have a number of depictions of Frau Welt in illuminations or drawings in manuscript encyclopedic miscellanies of a symbolic and spiritual nature. Above all and most appropriate to our interests, we have several engravings of the late fifteenth century from Switzerland and Alsace. One of these (Figure 7), now preserved in the British Library, recalls particularly closely the one-legged version of the monster of Ravenna.[37]

clopedia of the later Middle Ages," *Journal of the Warburg and Courtauld Institutes* 5 (1942): 82–142, esp. 126–28 and figs. 31a, b, c, d.

[37] Saxl, "A Spiritual Encyclopedia." Among the manuscripts Saxl cites, the one owned by the Casanatense Library of Rome has recently been illustrated in Fabio Troncarelli, ed., *La*

Fig. 7. Frau Welt. Alsacian or Swiss engraving (late fifteenth century), British Library, London. Reproduced by Courtesy of the Trustees of the British Museum.

The next problem is whether this was a simple figurative association re-emerging from a common mind-set or a true iconographic source. We should ask first if it is plausible to suppose that a print of this type circulated in early sixteenth-century Italy, in particular, in Ravenna or in Rome, the two possible cultural birthplaces of the monster. The answer for both cities is yes, thanks to relations maintained, for differing reasons, with Ven-

città dei segreti. Magia, astrologia e cultura esoterica a Roma (XV–XVIII secolo), Convegno Roma ermetica (1983: Rome, Italy) (Milan: Franco Angeli, 1985). For the print in the British Museum, see Campbell Dodgson, *Woodcuts of the XV Century in the Department of Prints and Drawings, British Museum*, 2 vols. (London: British Museum, 1935), vol. 2, pp. 20–21, n. 240, table 102.

ice—Rome through a long-standing political and cultural tradition,[38] and Ravenna because until 1509 it was part of the Venetian domain. Venice in the latter half of the Quattrocento and the beginning of the Cinquecento was, in fact, an important center of diffusion for "figure stampide depente," as one contemporary put it, works either engraved in Venice by both local talent and German craftsmen or directly imported from the north.[39] Toward the end of the fifteenth century, a notary from Parma, Jacopo Rubieri, collected a number of print pieces and pasted them into his records as decorations. Several of these were of German origin, and certainly came to him by way of Venice, the great commercial center.[40] The engravings that Rubieri collected nearly all had sacred subject matter, but we know that prints on profane subjects also penetrated into Italy from the north, albeit in lesser numbers, and that their echo is perceptible in Italian images.[41] Thus we cannot exclude the circulation in the Venetian states (hence in Ravenna) during the first decade of the Cinquecento of prints analogous to those conserved in the British Museum, and certainly the iconography of the monster of Ravenna in its monoped version would seem to confirm this. A further sign that prints like those portraying Frau Welt circulated in Venice can be inferred from the iconography of one of the five paintings of the so-called Restello Catena, now in the galleries of the Accademia in Venice, the *Summa Virtus*, formerly attributed to Giovanni Bellini and now to Andrea Previtali, which shows the four cardinal and the three theological virtues represented symbolically concentrated in one figure.[42] In both instances we see a winged female figure with a high headdress or feathers on her head, a cup or goblet in her hand, and her clawed feet or foot affixed onto a globe. Naturally, Previtali's inspiration (or his client's) might be sought elsewhere—for example, in the classical iconography of the Harpies—but it seems to me that we cannot exclude the possibility of contact with the north European print, also because of the close parallel between the theme of the seven sins and that of the seven virtues.

As we have seen, the monster was described in a third fashion (not given pictorial form, however) in Marcello Palonio's poem, where it had two heads ("gemino capite"). When he translated part of the *Historiae* of Gi-

[38] Pierre Sardella, *Nouvelles et spéculations à Venise au début du XVIe siècle* (Paris: Armand Colin, [1948]), esp. pp. 56–57.

[39] Giancarlo Schizzerotto, *Le incisioni quattrocentesche della Classense* (Ravenna: Zaccarini, 1971), pp. 107–8.

[40] Ibid. For biographical information on Rubieri, see pp. 37–69.

[41] See, for example, the well-known Florentine engraving showing twelve women fighting over a pair of trousers, used by Warburg (*La rinascita del paganesimo antico*, pp. 173–75) precisely to illustrate the influence of northern graphics on Italian artistic milieus.

[42] See Gustav Ludwig, "Restello. Spiegel und Toilettenutensilien in Venedig zur Zeit der Renaissance," *Italienischen Forschungen vom Kunsthistorischen Institut in Florenz* 1 (1906): 185–368.

rolamo Rossi in 1826, Jacopo Landoni added a note to a passage in Rossi based on Palonio's poem, offering this explanation:

> Marcello Palonio poetically gave a body and a soul to a marble [statue] in this guise that he had seen fixed to a wall in Ravenna, sculpted in later [Roman] days. Since no written trace of this strange figure in marble had ever existed, that was enough for the fantasy of the people, who loved marvels, to conform to the fantasy of the poet, and, heedless of the signs of antiquity of that marble, to consider the original a copy, and the copy the original.[43]

Attempts at a plausible identification of the late classical marble statue to which Landoni refers have come to naught, but in reality, the solution to the enigma probably lies elsewhere, as we shall see. If there were any truth to it, the notion would be interesting, however, precisely because it would help us to understand the multiple cultural influences—classical forms and medieval symbolic systems, popular prints and learned elaborations—that went into the formation of symbolic figures during that period.

Political Uses of the Monster

Finally, we need to examine the social function and political uses of the monsters. The first broadsheets of which we have a record appear to limit their text to a brief description that usually serves simply as a caption for a preeminent image. The earliest recorded notice, that of the chronicler Sebastiano di Branca Tedallini, contains one detail that deserves to be remarked, however: The deformed creature was born "of a nun and a friar." Moreover, one of his two legs, which in later descriptions was presented as scaly or feathered, like a frog's leg or that of a bird of prey, is called a *zampa di diavolo*, seeming to imply that the corruption of the clergy led ineluctably to demoniacal results. We can perhaps see a trace of this connection between the monster, ecclesiastical corruption, and divine chastisement in an oration given several weeks later (3 May) by Egidio Canisio of Viterbo, general of the Augustinian order, to open the Fifth Lateran Council. After painting a catastrophic picture of the moral decadence of the Church, Canisio exclaims:

> When have there ever appeared so frequently and with such horrible aspect monsters, portents, [and] prodigies, signs of celestial threats and of terror on the earth? When will there ever be a bloodier disaster or battle than that of

[43] Girolamo Rossi, *Ravenna dall'anno 1500 sino all'anno 1513, volgarizzamento dalla latina storia da Jacopo Landoni* (Ravenna: A. Roveri e figli, 1826), p. 112. Landoni was basing his version on the edition with additions published in Venice in 1589.

Brescia or that of Ravenna? . . . This year the earth has been drenched with more blood than rain.[44]

Among the monsters to which Canisio refers, the one born in Ravenna, the city of divine castigation, was certainly the most recent and perhaps to his eyes the most indicative. The connection between the monster and the immorality of the clergy is quite explicit in the brief French work mentioned earlier, the *Avertissemens es trois estatz du monde*, which accompanies its analysis of the various parts of the deformed creature's body with repeated and insistent references to the greed, immorality, and abuses of the clergy, citing the widely known proverb: "Rome is the glory of cardinals and the paradise of whores."[45]

It is interesting that the detail of the nun and friar as parents soon disappears, at least in the texts that we know. We find it again only in the *Historia* of Bernáldez (who speaks only of a *monja*, however) and, in its full form, in the broadsheet that circulated in Germany and is conserved in Nuremberg. Otherwise, reference to a sacrilegious conception for the creature was not only omitted but in some cases even replaced by counterindications, which leads us to suppose a deliberate attempt to annul the anticlerical note. Thus Landucci says simply, "era nato d'una donna un mostro."[46] Pietro Martire d'Anghiera presents the creature's parentage more specifically, informing his correspondent, Marchese Fajardo, that he had received from Rome ("ab urbe allatam") the picture of a monster born in Ravenna to a married woman ("Ravennae ortum ex coniugata").[47] Here there is little doubt that a specific decision must have been made at the source of the news—Rome—to eliminate a clearly anticlerical element from the general picture.

On the whole, then, the moral and religious analysis of the monster sketched out in pamphlets and broadsheets had an anti-Roman cast to it, confutation of which went through the same channels. We also find traces of a more strictly political analysis, however. Almost as soon as news of the

[44] *Oratio Prima Synodi Lateranensis habita per Egidium Viterbiensem Augustiniani Ordinis Generalem* (n.p., n.d. [Rome: Johannes Beplin, 1512]), unnumbered fols 9*v*–10*r*. There is a recent critical edition in Clare O'Reilly, " 'Without Councils we cannot be saved . . .' Giles of Viterbo addresses the Fifth Lateran Council," *Augustiniana* 27 (1977): 166–204; passage cited, pp. 202–3.

[45] "Lon dit par ung proverbe commun a Rome de Rome, que cest la gloire des cardinaulx et le paradis des putains": *Les Avertissemens es trois estatz du monde*, fol. D i*v*. There is a more ample version of the same proverb reported in Francisco Delicado, *Retrato de la loçana andaluza* (1524): "So it is said: Observe Rome, the glory of men of power, a paradise for whores, a purgatory for the young, a fraud for the poor, a drudgery for the beast of burden, a market-place for swindlers and a hell for all": *Portrait of Lozana: The Lusty Andalusian Woman*, tr. Bruno M. Damiani (Potomac Md.: Scripta Humanistica, 1987), p. 63.

[46] Landucci, *Diario fiorentino*, p. 314.

[47] *Opus epistolarum Petri Martyris Anglerii*, p. 256.

monstrous birth reached Rome, Giovan Francesco Vitale of Palermo, a Latin poet connected with the papal court, produced an interpretation of it in Latin verse. The brief work (mentioned earlier) must have been composed rapidly, because in the two printed editions extant it is preceded by a letter from Carlo Pontelli dated 16 March 1512 addressed to Vitale and praising him for the "attentive scrutiny the poet has given to that most deformed monster." Under its burden of incongruous mythological erudition, Vitale's verse offers some interesting insights that appear to be closely related to the contingent political situation, in particular, the crisis opposing Louis XII and Julius II. Lands where the French set their feet, the poet says, bear monsters:

> Gallica monstriferis ornataque terra figuris;
> . . .
> heu pia relligio, monstrum te cernimus atrum!
> nam solum corpus bina cervice retectum
> dicitur.

The French, that is, had reduced the Church itself to a horrible monster, a body with two heads. The lines allude to the pro-French cardinals who had met in schismatic council in Pisa and were at that moment meeting in Milan. But Jove, Vitale continues, will strike the Giants (the French) with his lightning bolts as they attempt to scale Olympus (that is, to defeat the papacy with military and spiritual arms). Why these hopes were well founded becomes clear in the final tercet: Amid fertile fields, shady groves, and fruit orchards lay the city of Ravenna, "sub ingentis pedibus ditissima Iuli"—wondrously wealthy so long as it was under the feet of the great Julius. But in that land, on which the French now marched, a monster had been born:

> Haec pius Omnipotens misit portenta petenti.
> Non te, Roma, suis vexant pia sidera monstris,
> nec vereare: petunt non tua funera Parcae.

To paraphrase: The Omnipotent sends such prodigies to those who invite them. It is not you, Rome, whom the pious stars torment with their monsters; nor should you fear that it is your end that the Fates are seeking. May the stars be favorable to the court of Rome, Vitale goes on to say, and may they proclaim the excellence of the divine Julius even to the new Thule (the Americas).[48]

Thus the monster was useful in encouraging and supporting the policy of Rome against the French and their allies at a moment of serious division in the Roman See in the early months of 1512. Giano Vitale's short poem

[48] Vitalis, *De monstro nato*, fols. 1*v*, 2*r*, 4*r*.

enjoyed a limited circulation and he was sufficiently well known that some of his works fell into the hands of Erasmus.[49] He had important connections in Rome, including the Latin poets attached to the academy of Giovanni Goritz (of which Vitale does not seem to have been a member, although he contributed to their collection *Coryciana*), Giovanni Pierio Valeriano, and above all Egidio da Viterbo, who, as we have seen, was much interested in the *monstra* and their interpretation, took part in the assemblies at the houses of Goritz and Angelo Colocci, and received Vitale as a house guest in 1521.[50] *De monstro nato* had at least two editions, one without indication of place or date, but probably printed in Italy soon after the event, the other printed in Erfurt in July 1512.

The haste with which the brief work was composed and perhaps printed makes it likely that *De monstro nato* was the piece referred to as the *monstro* that ambassador Francesco Foscari sent to Sanudo from Rome. The timing is tight, but in substance the dates mesh (the dedication is dated 16 March). It also seems probable that Vitale's poem was the pamphlet *cum interpretatione carmine expressa* received by Lycosthenes, as we can see by comparing the pictures. Finally, it is possible that Vitale's poem and not a marble statue from Ravenna was the source of Marcello Palonio's verse. Vitale and Palonio frequented the same circles, and ten years later they both contributed to a collection of *Lachrime in M. Antonium Columnam*, for which Palonio wrote a dedicatory letter and Giano Vitale some verse.[51] It would not be surprising that one knew the other's work. This hypothesis would permit us to explain the strange detail of the "gemino capite" attrib-

[49] Fritz Husner, "Die Bibliotek des Erasmus," in *Gedenkschrift zum 400. Todestage des Erasmus von Rotterdam* (Basel: Braus-Riggenback, 1936), p. 239, n. 95. At the death of Erasmus, Vitale composed a somewhat pungent epitaph for him: "Lubrica si tibi mens fuit, et spinosior aequo, / ingenium certe nobile Erasme fuit." See Silvana Seidel Menchi, "Alcuni atteggiamenti della cultura italiana di fronte ad Erasmo (1520–1536)," in *Eresia e Riforma nell'Italia del Cinquecento: Miscellanea I* (Florence: G. C. Sansoni; Chicago: The Newberry Library, 1974), pp. 67–128; p. 109.

[50] Vitale's connections with the Latin poets attached to Goritz and Colocci are demonstrated by his participation in several collective enterprises of this group, such as the collections *In Celsi Archelai Mellini funere amicorum lacrimae* (Rome, 1519), *Lachrime in M. Antonium Columnam* (Rome, 1522), and *Coryciana* (Rome, 1524). Verse of Giovanni Pierio Valeriano, Giovan Battista Sanga, Francesco Maria Grapaldo, and others in praise of Vitale can be found in Iani Vitalis Panormitani, *Teratorizion* (Rome: Mazzocchi, 1514). That Vitale did not take part in the meetings at the homes of Goritz and Colocci is clear from lists of the participants, which do, however, include the name of Egidio da Viterbo. See Federigo Ubaldini, *Vita di Mons. Angelo Colocci. Edizione del testo originale italiano (Barb. Lat. 4882)*, ed. Vittorio Fanelli (Vatican City: Biblioteca apostolica vaticana, 1969), pp. 111, 114–15. On Vitale's visit with Egidio da Viterbo, see Tumminello, "Giano Vitale," p. 43.

[51] See Carlo Dionisotti, "Appunti su Leone Ebreo," *Italia medioevale e umanistica* 2 (1959): 409–28; esp. 425–26; information on Marcello Palonio, p. 426. See also Domenico Gnoli, *La Roma di Leon X* (Milan: Ulrico Hoepli, 1938), pp. 180–84, 300–304. Palonio was still alive in 1541: *Trattato dell'entrar in Milano di Carlo V* (Milan: Andrea Calvo, 1541), fol. 2*r*.

uted to the monster in the lateral gloss to Palonio's verse, since the two heads could result from a hasty reading of the Vitale passage already cited: ". . . monstrum . . . cernimus atrum! / nam solum corpus bina cervice rectum / dicitur."

As we have seen, though, Vitale is referring here not to the monster of Ravenna but to the two Councils of 1511–1512, the schismatic council convoked in Pisa and the Lateran Council in Rome. It is an interesting example of how an error can slip into literary and figurative descriptions.

After the battle of 11 April and the sack of Ravenna that occurred immediately after, a propapal, anti-French interpretation of the monster made little sense, so it acquired the more generic significance of a forewarning of great ills about to fall upon Ravenna and Italy. Egidio da Viterbo's homily is exemplary in this sense, as is Landucci's comment on hearing news of the sack, which seems to express a commonly shared thought, almost an accepted aphorism:

> It was evident what evil the monster had meant for them! It seems as if some great misfortune always befalls the city where such things are born; the same thing happened at Volterra, which was sacked a short time after a similar monster had been born there.[52]

Landucci proposes here the globally prophetic and catastrophic interpretation of the *monstra* discussed above and that he himself had offered twenty-five years earlier when he copied the letter from Venice at Tanai de' Nerli's bank. The German broadsheet follows the same tendency, but extends the threat of divine punishment to all Italy: "Alia denique per Italiam mala plurima et multifaria portenduntur." It is clear from the fact that this sheet addressed a quite different social and cultural public that this type of letter had an extremely broad audience: The text is given in both Latin and German, and the space devoted to the illustration made it at least partly available to the illiterate.[53]

Finally, we need to keep in mind the interpretation of Johannes Multivallis in his continuation of the *Chronicon* of Eusebius of Caesarea to 13 June 1512. In the final page of this work, Multivallis speaks of the Italian

[52] Landucci, *A Florentine Diary*, tr. Jervis, p. 250.

[53] For problems connected with the multiple possible uses of broadsheets, see Ecker, *Einblattdrücke*; Roger Chartier, "L'ancien régime typographique: réflexions sur quelques travaux récents," *Annales E.S.C.* 36 (1981): 191–209, esp. p. 206; Hans-Joachim Köhler, ed., *Flugschriften als Massenmedium der Reformationzeit, Beiträge zum Tübinger Symposium* (Stuttgart: Klett-Cotta, 1981). Köhler has taken up the question of broadsheets elsewhere: "Die Flugschriften. Versuch der Präzisierung eines geläufigen Begriff," in Hansgeorg Molitor and Hans-Christoph Rublack, eds., *Festgabe Ernst Walter Zeeden zum 60. Geburtstag am 14 Mai 1976* (Münster in Westfalen: Aschendorff, 1976), pp. 36–61; "The Flugschriften and their Importance in Religious Debate: A Quantitative Approach," in Zambelli, ed., "*Astrologi hallucinati*," pp. 153–75.

wars. He notes Julius II's preparations for war, describes the sack of Brescia and the taking of Ravenna, and concludes, precisely, with a description of the monster, which in the treatise thus becomes a worthy seal put by God to the history that humankind constructs with its own hands and by its evil deeds. The passage runs thus:

> Ravannae paulo ante natum fuerat monstrum cornu in capite; allas habebat; brachia nulla; pedem unum ut avis rapax; occulum in genu; sexum utrumque; in medio pectore ypsilon et crucis effigiem. Aliqui interpretati sunt: cornu superbiam; allas brevitatem mentis et incostantiam; carentiam brachiorum defectum bonorum operum; pedem rapacem rapinam, usuram et omnimodam avaritiam; oculum in genu solum ad res terrenas mentis deflectionem; utrunque sexum sodomiam. Et propter haec vicia Italiam sic bellicis contritionibus quati; regem autem Franciae non sua virtute id facere, sed solum esse Dei flagellum. Ypsilon vero et + signa esse salutis; nam ypsilon figura est virtutis. Ideo, si ad virtutem recurrant ed ad Christi crucem, ab his pressuris et tribulationibus conveniat respirationem et pacem, conquassationibus desiderabiliorem, quam dare dignetur Christus in omnia saecula benedictus. Amen.[54]

It is difficult to say who are the "aliqui" whose interpretations Multivallis reports here—perhaps a pamphlet or a broadsheet that has not survived. The analysis somewhat resembles that of the *Avertissemens es trois estatz du monde* of Inoy, which appeared the following year, however, and presents several differences of detail. It also recalls the prints of Frau Welt, and in that connection I might add that this text signals the beginning of the model of the monster with a single leg of a bird of prey, which became prevalent in teratological treatises of the latter sixteenth century (Figure 8). One might hypothesize that Multivallis's source made available a print of the Frau Welt sort and made use of it for its interpretation of the monster. What is more interesting to note is the national coloration of the text, which contrasts the Italians, whose sins have brought on the destruction of Brescia and Ravenna, and the king of France, who carried out that destruction not as a political decision but acting as a simple instrument of divine wrath: "regem autem Franciae non sua virtute id facere, sed solum esse Dei flagellum."

The Monster of Bologna: A Different Political Science

The monster and its various body parts thus served as a flexible instrument for a political and religious reading of the War of the Holy League, just as the verse prophecies and interpretation of mosaics had done at the time of

54 Eusebii Caesariensis, *Chronicon*, fols. 175*r–v*.

Fig. 8. The Monster of Ravenna. From Pierre Boaistuau, *Histoires prodigieuses* (Paris, 1560).

Charles VIII's invasion of Italy and the War of Cambrai. Another sort of analysis arose, however, that lent itself particularly well to criticism of ecclesiastical life-styles. Both interpretive formulas seem to have been applied to another deformed infant born near Bologna in January 1514. This time—and the case is exceptional—it was not a semifantastic being but a real human child for whom it is impossible not to feel sympathy. She was the daughter of a man named Domenico Malatendi, who raised vegetables in Marano, not far from the gates of Bologna.[55] The child had two faces

[55] The case is reported in Giovan Francesco Negri, *Annali della patria*, VII, fol. 145*r* (Biblioteca Universitaria di Bologna, hereafter cited as BUB, MS 1107); *Cronica di Friano degli Ubaldini*, fol. 32*v* (BUB, MS 430); *Cronaca della città di Bologna di Nicolò Seccadinari* [Fileno delle Tuate], III, unnumbered (BUB, MS 437); *Cronica Bianchetti*, II, p. 366 (Biblioteca dell'Archiginnasio di Bologna, MS Malvezzi 60).

("as Prudence is figured," one chronicler notes), two mouths, three eyes, and no nose. On the top of her head she had an excrescence defined as "like a red cockscomb" or "a vulva."[56] She was brought to Bologna to be baptized in the cathedral of San Pietro on Sunday, 9 January, probably the day she was born. The bishop himself, Cardinal Achille Grassi, administered the sacrament of baptism, showing by this act the significance he attributed to the person of the infant, whom he named Maria.[57] Maria lived only four days, but her brief life caused a considerable stir, though nothing approaching that caused by the other monstrous creatures. This was particularly because it coincided with other prodigious events: a terrible fire that gutted the quarter of the Rialto in Venice on the night of 10 January and three suns, three moons, and a mysterious light seen in the sky at various times on 11 January.[58] These were "things that gave material to ingenious minds curious to prognosticate."[59] Indeed, as Leonello Beliardi of Modena said concerning the birth of little Maria, "the Bolognese astrologers made a prognostication about this, which was a sign of great pestilence and war."[60] That publication, *Pronostico de Thomaso Philologo Gianotho da Ravenna sopra la significatione del Monstro nato a Bologna: e nel Iudicio suo del presente anno da lui pronosticato*, was a broadsheet printed in Gothic letters in two versions, vernacular and Latin (the version examined here).[61] Tommaso Giannotti, the author, was a figure we shall encounter again. In later years he attempted to increase his repute by adding to his name that of his patron, Guido Rangoni, commander of the pontifical states' military installation in Modena (or, more accurately, by replacing his own name with Rangoni's). Early in 1514, Giannotti seems to have taken steps toward obtaining the patronage of Cardinal Achille Grassi, to whom his prediction is dedicated. It is dated from Bologna, 15 January 1514, and in its Latin version speaks of "strages malignas . . . gravissimam pestem . . . lue . . . terremotus . . . bella," basing these predictions less on the body of the de-

[56] Negri, *Annali*; Leonello Beliardi, *Cronaca della città di Modena (1512–1518)*, ed. Albano Biondi and Michele Oppi (Modena: Panini, 1981), p. 92; Sanuto, *Diarii*, vol. 17, col. 515.

[57] Negri, *Annali*; *Cronaca della città di Bologna*; *Cronica Bianchetti*.

[58] See Sanuto, *Diarii*, vol. 17, cols. 458–61, 506, 530. The connection between Maria's birth and these signs appears also in Negri, *Annali*.

[59] Negri, *Annali*.

[60] Beliardi, *Cronaca della città di Modena*, p. 92.

[61] There is mention of the vernacular edition in Alberto Serra-Zanetti, *L'arte della stampa in Bologna nel primo ventennio del Cinquecento* (Biblioteca de "l'Archiginnasio," n.s. 1; Bologna: Archiginnasio, 1959), pp. 258–59, who cites the *Catalogue de la Bibliothèque de feu le Duc Mario Massimo de Rignano* (Rome, 1909), p. 13, n. 55, and in Carlo Piancastelli, *Pronostici ed Almanacchi. Studio di bibliografia romagnola* (Rome: D. Ripamonti, 1913), pp. 27–28. The Latin edition, which was also printed in Gothic type, is not otherwise noted. Sig. Luciano Borrelli of Trent owns a copy, and I wish to thank him warmly for informing me of it and allowing me to examine it.

formed child than on a conjunction of Saturn and Jupiter that had occurred the previous 29 December, of which Maria was merely the first horrible result. It is interesting to note, in fact, that Beliardi's chronicle fails to place the abnormal birth within the schemes of astrological science. The same sort of hasty interpretation (that is, one that simply establishes a relationship between the monster and the catastrophe, eliminating reference to the conjunction of planets) can probably be seen in the letter of Francesco Bonafede mentioned above, who only a few weeks later deplored that recent "monstrous" births had been misused to predict "tumulti di guerre, occisioni, stragie."[62] As an astrologer, Giannotti had attempted to rely more on the stars than on the monsters, but for much of the public the operation failed, and the tradition of interpretation of *orribeli segnali* had the better of the science of major planetary conjunctions.

The broadsheet concludes with a warm invitation to the pope and the emperor to renew their vigilance against the threat of the Turks and foreigners, "ne Italia reliqueve Christianorum urbes dilapidentur," and with an odd puzzle in Latin verse:

> Fixa manet summo si nunc clementia celo,
> *u* vertant in *o*, *p* ac gemino vel *a* sidera iungant,
> ut sacro una horum is fungi diademate possit:
> aurea tunc aetas; in pace et cuncta regentur.

In that the text speaks, among other things, of *lue*, it is not too farfetched to suppose that the solution to this *Tetrasticon sub enigmate* is *Leo papa*, the pope under whom the star-studded tiara was to ensure the world a new Golden Age. Giannotti's vocation for flattery was to continue to flourish in the years to come, and, as is evident, seems already more than mature here. The myth of a Golden Age under a Medici pope had gained one more proselyte.

A letter on the matter sent from Rome on 25 January to the pontifical ambassador in Venice, Pietro Dovizi of Bibbiena,[63] offers more details. It analyzes little Maria's body in symbolic and political terms, even proposing a specifically political model that differed markedly from the others (which, I might add, enjoyed greater fame and fortune). The writer, whose name is not given in the copy extant, states, "You have seen the figure of the monster of Bologna, with two faces and three eyes, and on its head a woman's open vulva." This means that prints or drawings were in circulation (Giannotti's prognostication was not illustrated). After noting that the news had reached Rome through the governor of Bologna (presumably,

[62] Sanuto, *Diarii*, vol. 18, col. 34.
[63] Ibid., vol. 17, cols. 515–16.

Lorenzo Fieschi),[64] the writer continues, "of which portent, along with the fire that followed in Venice, one could give a wondrous and profound interpretation, two parts of which I will leave out quia non omnia sunt litteris committenda." There follows a brief summary of the two parts left out. The first was

> that of the little church untouched in the middle of much fire, in its ancient foundation and its primitive state; the second part I shall say nothing about, but I think that I apply well that double forehead with three eyes, why two of them are entirely closed, and [why] one cannot discern of the third, which is in the middle, how much sight it has or what it sees, even though it is open.

The second part of this is obscure, only hinting at ambiguity and blindness, but the meaning of the first part is singularly clear and relevant. The little church of San Giacometto in Rialto, which Marin Sanudo tells us, following a widespread tradition,[65] was the first church built in Venice, serves as the symbol and the silent, physical embodiment of the myth of the primitive church.

But "non omnia sunt litteris committenda," and our anonymous Roman prefers not to expatiate on this point. Instead, he continues with a full interpretation of the body of the Bologna monster that merits quotation in full for its stylistic intensity and the interest of its contents:

> I turn to the third figure of the vulva with tears in my eyes: I saw that Italy has become this monster with closed eyes and two faces looking in two different directions because of its divisions; one part looking west to follow its affections and its own convenience; the other [looking] north according to its passions; and thus divided and blinded, O miserable wretch! it has become a monster. The open vulva on its head is that land and province that has so long conserved and defended the beauty, the virginity, and the modesty of calamity-stricken Italy; now, so prostrated and lying with open vulva that many outsiders, whom we have seen before us, have come to luxuriate and run wild. Even in this hour it invites still others even more foreign to us. And note well, that this monster born in the Bolognese has two faces, and by its two mouths—as the governor of that city writes—it takes milk and nourishment, which descends through the same channel to the stomach, because the two faces respond to only one neck, and the rest of the body is made as a female, like poor Italy, of which every man takes his pleasure as of a female and a prostitute. With all my heart I pray to almighty God, and I invite all religious persons and

[64] See Maria Ferretti, "Legati, vicelegati e governatori di Bologna nel sec. XVI," tesi di laurea discussa presso l'Università di Bologna a. a. 1967–1968, relatore Paolo Prodi, pp. 103–105.

[65] Ferdinando Forlati, *La basilica di San Marco attraverso i suoi restauri* (Trieste: Lint, 1975), pp. 53 and 69, n. 13.

true Christians in Italy to pray that he turn the eyes of his mercy upon us, quod solus habet spiritus et ministros et ignem urentem; ipse enim est Dominus exercituum, qui facit mirabilia magna solus; et non respiciat pecata nostra sed fidem et misterium Ecclasiae suae. I am certain that these modern sages with their tricks and their con games who advise princes, non timentes Deum, sed in sua versutia confisi, would laugh at my discourse. And I laugh at theirs, knowing that I communicate and write to a man Catholic and well-mannered, grave, experienced, old, and prudent, and removed from all passion and avarice, as I find myself to be, by divina gratia. Romae 25 Januari 1514.[66]

In explaining this letter we need to keep in mind the political situation in Italy during the winter of 1513–1514. The letter was sent, as we have seen, to the pontifical ambassador, Pietro Dovizi, called Il Bibbiena from his birthplace, as was his better-known younger brother Bernardo. Pietro had received his charge from the new pope, Leo X, on 21 March 1513.[67] The two Bibbienas were close to Leo and the Medici family, but Pietro had for many years lived in Venice, where he had taken a wife and had many close friends (Sanudo calls him "very much my friend").[68] Thus he had particularly high qualifications for his office. In reality, it gave him nothing but trouble, of which, according to his friend Sanudo, he died on 8 February, only a few days after receiving the letter in question.[69] In point of fact, the pope, after an initial show of friendship to the Venetians, had become more ambiguous and hesitant in his attitude toward them. In particular, after the Venetians had been roundly defeated by the Spanish army under Raymond de Cardona near Creazzo, in the territory of Vicenza, Leo X leaned toward the imperial side, partly because of the influence of Cardinal Matthäus Lang, the bishop of Gurk, and encouraged the Venetians to break their alliance with France and move in the direction of an alliance with the emperor.[70] This strategy was by no means clearly defined, however, and in January 1514 the pope spoke with the Venetian ambassador, Pietro Lando, and showed every sign of being open to an agreement with Venice and with France.[71] This situation continued for some time (as much as a year later Niccolò Machiavelli was called upon to give his opinion on

[66] Sanuto, *Diarii*, vol. 17, cols. 515–16.

[67] Ibid., vol. 16, col. 54.

[68] Ibid., vol. 17, col. 533. Information on Bibbiena's stay in Venice can also be found in col. 542.

[69] Sanuto, *Diarii*, vol. 17, cols. 533 and 542.

[70] Vittorio Cian, "A proposito di un'ambascieria di M. Pietro Bembo (dicembre 1514)," *Archivio Veneto* 30 (1885): 355–407, and 31 (1886): 71–128; Franco Gaeta, "Il Bibbiena diplomatico," *Rinascimento* 9 (1969): 69–94. See also Sanuto, *Diarii*, vol. 17, cols. 341–42, 364, 372, and so forth.

[71] Sanuto, *Diarii*, vol. 17, col. 511.

the pope's dilemma),[72] and it prompted discontent even in Roman circles. At the end of November 1513, Marin Sanudo noted that "Romans are complaining that the pope gives his men to Germans and Spaniards, saying that if this were not so, the Spanish would be torn to pieces by our men, and Italy freed from the hands of barbarians."[73]

The letter on the Bologna monster may easily have come from the same Roman circles. The writer identified the monstrous body of Maria Malatendi as Italy, an Italy blinded and divided, turning alternately to the west and the north, toward France or the Holy Roman Empire. Her chief deformity was on her head, where an "open vulva" stood for "quella patria et provintia" that in the past had protected and defended the integrity of Italian soil but that now, prostrate and open to every sort of violence, left free passage to so many foreigners and indeed called others to come from even more distant places. As we now know, the allusion to the monster's two faces referred to the two possible choices in international policy facing the pope (which was the bone of contention between Venice and Rome), while the second part clearly referred to Venice itself. Venice was traditionally considered the "outer bulwark of Italy," but now its territories had been devastated by Spanish and imperial troops and, above all, alarming rumors were circulating that Venice was thinking of calling the Turks into Italy for their aid and support. These rumors, which circulated above all in Rome toward the end of December 1513, were far from unfounded. Early in February 1514 an ambassador from Selim, the Ottoman ruler, came to Venice and was received with the greatest honors. On that occasion a peace treaty between Venice and the Ottoman Turks signed 17 October was made public and several Venetian noblemen of ancient family—a Grimani, a Tron, an Emo—went so far as to state "that there is no other redemption for our affairs than leaguing ourselves with Turks and bringing them into Italy."[74]

[72] Niccolò Machiavelli to Francesco Vettori, Florence, 10 December 1514, in Machiavelli, *Lettere*, ed. Franco Gaeta (Milan: Feltrinelli, 1961), pp. 351–61.

[73] Sanuto, *Diarii*, vol. 17, col. 342.

[74] Ibid., cols. 423–24, 426, 529, 535, 539–40. The mixed expectation and fear deriving from a Venetian appeal to the Turks was already widespread immediately after the battle of Agnadello, as is clear from a verse lament of that period: "Si non vedo pace o tregua / chiamarò in mare in terra / il gran Turcho con sua guerra / como gente disperata" (If I see no peace or truce, I will call, on sea and on land, the Great Turk with his army, as desperate men): [Simone Litta], *Lamento de venetiani novamente composto. Per domino Simeone el quale se contene el paexe che ano perse in Italia he fora de Italia* (Mondovi: Berruero, n. d. [1509]), fol. 4*v*. The same possibility is also clear from an oration of Egidio da Viterbo delivered in the presence of the doge in the Collegio dei Savi on 9 June 1519, referred to by Marin Sanudo thus: "All Christendom was sworn to our ruin . . . in these persecutions [Venice] never agreed to call for aid from infidels, but strove to persevere in the faith of Christ; nevertheless, many expected [that] in order not to perish this state must demand help from those enemies of the

The alarm prompted by a notion of the sort is easy to imagine. The letter cited above is imbued with it, and with a sense of malaise over the slow and painful contacts between Rome and Venice. Who might have written it? Bibbiena clearly was acting with discretion in giving Sanudo a copy lacking the salutation, final greeting, and signature. Although we cannot identify the writer by name, we can nonetheless reconstruct a fairly clear portrait of him. He must have been a person Bibbiena knew directly, as indicated by the last lines of the letter, which presuppose personal acquaintance; he must have been connected with the papal court and with Medici circles, as Bibbiena was; he shows full awareness of the latest political maneuvers, but he was also interested in ecclesiastical reform (as we can gather from his mention of the primitive church). He was, in short, a person of a certain stature.[75]

After displaying his own erudition and invoking divine aid, the writer sets up his ideal opponents; they are "questi savieti moderni, with their tricks and their con games who advise princes, non timentes Deum, sed in sua versutia confisi." This reference can (and perhaps should) be understood in a generic sense. The "savieti" then would be all those involved in politics who rely on their skill alone and pay little attention to the signs that the hand of God places in history to admonish humankind. It is tempting, though, to give a name to at least one of these "savieti," who only recently had finished a work in which, precisely, he proposed to advise princes—or rather, *a* prince—with his "versuzie" (wiles, cunning tricks) while bitterly lamenting the fate of poor Italy, "beaten, despoiled, torn apart, overrun." Is it possible, though, that our anonymous Roman could have had a copy of Machiavelli's *Prince* in his hands and that his quarrel was with that work? Certainly, in the preceding weeks, the treatise had been sent by Machiavelli to Rome, where, as is known, Francesco Vettori had read it, although perhaps not from start to finish.[76] We also know that a few months later Vettori showed to the pope, to Cardinal de' Medici (the future Clement VII), and to Cardinal Bibbiena (the younger brother of

---

Christian faith, which thing God had frowned on" (Sanuto, *Diarii*, vol. 27, col. 367). See also Paolo Preto, *Venezia e i Turchi* (Florence: G. C. Sansoni, 1975), pp. 37–38.

[75] It could not have been Vincenzo Quirini, who otherwise would fulfill all the requirements, because his vernacular letters never show the continual Latin inserts present in this text. Furthermore, it is not certain that Quirini had yet returned to Rome in January 1514, although he was surely there in April of that year. On this period of his life, see Cian, "A proposito di un'ambascieria," and Hubert Jedin, "Vincenzo Quirini und Pietro Bembo," in *Miscellanea Giovanni Mercati*, 6 vols. (Vatican City: Biblioteca Apostolica Vaticana, 1946; 2nd ed., 1973), vol. 4, pp. 407–424 (Jedin, *Kirche des Glaubens, Kirche der Gesehichte: aus gewählte Aufsätze und Vorträge* [Frieberg: Herder, 1966]), also available in Italian translation as *Chiesa della fede, Chiesa della storia* (Brescia: Morcelliana, 1972).

[76] Francesco Vettori to Niccolò Machiavelli, Rome, 18 January 1514, in Machiavelli, *Lettere*, p. 319.

Pietro, who had died by that time) two letters of Machiavelli in which he gave his opinion on pontifical policies, in substance blaming the pope for his indecision.[77] It is not inconceivable that Vettori had shown *The Prince* (which was to be dedicated to the pope's brother), in whole or in part, to some Medici functionaries in Rome, among them the anonymous personage who then wrote to Pietro Bibbiena.

The Roman Career of the *monstra* and the Reasons Thereof

In brief, the prophetic language of signs and, especially, of those signs such as monsters that permitted a more fully developed interpretation could be used not only to express a generic concern for a traumatic situation—as we have seen, in particular, for prophecies connected with the invasion of Charles VIII and the widespread destruction caused by the War of Cambrai—but also, especially on a higher social and cultural level, to formulate a quite specific political analysis or to organize a line of propaganda. The phenomenon of the *monstra* had pan-European dimensions, at least in an area embracing France, Germany, Spain, and central and northern Italy, and it was publicized through an unusually varied set of channels ranging from personal letters to prints and multicopy drawings. The success of these print pieces was also based on the variety of readings that it was possible to give them and on their position at the point of contact between different levels of culture. They thus became a significant element in political debate and in the formation of public opinion, particularly in periods of crisis, and their use was quite consciously contrasted (as we have seen in the anonymous letter from Rome) with other modes of furthering political ends. They had particular success in Rome, and it was in fact in Rome that the "political" description of monsters seems to have evoked the most lively interest, as we have seen for the monster of Ravenna, that of Bologna, and the one born in Rome itself early in March 1513, "sung of" by Giovan Battista Ruberti.[78] It was to Rome that news of misbirths was sent in official communications through the governors of the cities in which the monstrous creatures were born. I might add that teratological subjects had a ready success among Latin poets in Roman circles,[79] a success also to be

[77] Niccolò Machiavelli to Francesco Vettori, Florence, 10 December 1514, in *Lettere*, pp. 351–61; Machiavelli to Vettori, Florence, 20 December 1514, pp. 363–67; Francesco Vettori to Niccolò Machiavelli, Rome, 30 December 1514, p. 369.

[78] See Ruberti, *Monstrum apud Urbem natum*, and Holländer, *Wunder, Wundergeburt und Wundergestalt*, p. 312.

[79] See the works already cited plus Vitalis, *Teratorizion*. The same characteristics of court poetry and antiquarianism (well described in Rotondò, "Pellegrino Prisciani," p. 106) are found in a work that appeared in a quite different context: *Ad illustrissimum ac Excellentissi-*

attributed to the profound influence of the memory of classical divination in such circles. The success and the use of courtly and antiquarian poetry are, in the last analysis, political, but they also arose out of a new interest in the monsters as signs that was present among all levels of the urban population.

Not only the deformed creatures but also other prodigious events (which, as prodigious events, were signs of God's will or divine warnings) elaborated and first circulated in the domain of folklore would be used for precise political purposes by the court of Leo X in the years immediately following. This is what we shall examine next.

---

mum Principem Divum Herculem Estensem Francisci Rococioli Mutinensis Libellus de Monstro in Tyberi reperto anno D.ni MCCCCLXXXXVI (n.p., n.d. [Modena: Domenico Rocociolo]), 4 fols. I refer to the copy in the Biblioteca Estense, Modena.

3

APPARITIONS AS SIGNS: THE KINGS OF THE DEAD ON THE BATTLEGROUND OF AGNADELLO

Ghostly Combatants in the Bergamo Countryside

A PRINTED pamphlet circulated in Cesena in January 1518, the chronicler Giuliano Fantaguzzi tells us, that told "about the visions and combats of spirits taking place in the Bergamasco."[1] About the same time, word that near Bergamo "were seen visions and prodigies of great quantities of armed men on foot and on horseback [fighting] against one another" was reported in the journal of an anonymous French cleric who had long lived in Rome,[2] Marin Sanudo gathered a number of letters concerning the incident, and it was even noted in the *Journal d'un Bourgeois de Paris*. The printed pamphlets mentioned by the Cesena chronicler circulated in Italy in at least two different versions, and they were also translated into French and German. One version from Rome reached Valladolid, where a copy came into the hands of Pietro Martire d'Anghiera, who mentions it in a letter dated 23 February 1518.[3]

Obviously, the incident had repercussions far and wide. On 12 January, Gian Giacomo Caroldo, secretary to the doge of Venice attached to Viscount de Lautrec, governor of Milan, gave a disparaging explanation of it, however. Caroldo wrote to his brother: "There is no truth to what has appeared in the Bergamasco. Some simple people saw the fumes above

[1] *Occhurrentie et nove notate per me Juliano Fantaguzzo Cesenate*, in Claudio Riva, "La vita in Cesena agli inizi del '500. Dal 'Caos' di Giuliano Fantaguzzi," tesi di laurea discussa presso l'università di Bologna, a.a. 1969/70, relatore Paolo Prodi, which transcribes parts of Fantaguzzi's chronicle not included in the earlier edition edited by Dino Bazzocchi: *Caos. Cronache cesanati del sec. XV* (Cesena: Tip. Arturo Bettini, 1915), pp. 158–59.

[2] Biblioteca Apostolica Vaticana, MS Barb. Lat. 3552, fol. 32*v*. See Louis Madelin, "Le Journal d'un habitant français de Rome au XVIe siècle (1509–1540). (Etude sur le Manuscrit XLIII–98 de la Bibliothèque Barberini)," *Mélanges d'archéologie et d'histoire. Ecole française de Rome* 22 (1902): 251–300.

[3] *Opus epistolarum Petri Martyris Anglerii* (Amsterdam: typis Elzevirianis, 1670), p. 337. Anghiera connected the apparitions at Verdello with the Ravenna monster: "De ravennate monstro ex Urbe ad nos misso, priusquam Gallorum saevitiae Ravenna succumberet, vidistis suo tempore. Nunc accipite quae nuper prelis formata chalcographorum et sparsa per universum emerserunt. . . . Est in bergomensi agro in Insubria, quae vulgo Lombardia dicitur, nobile vicina sylva oppidulum, nomine Verdelum. . . ."

some manure piles, and in their great fearfulness they thought they were armed men. . . . So you should not lend credence to such things."[4] Nonetheless, this does not explain why some "simplice persone" should have seen hosts of specters fighting in the vapors released in the winter from dung heaps. We also need to place this incident within the broader question of how traditions circulated through nonhomogeneous cultural strata, how they were transformed by such shifts, and by what means (means that often were related to their function within a specific social context) they were transmitted. In this instance, we shall see that an item of ascertainable folk origin was connected, on a second level, to a prophetic system of signs, only to be picked up again on a different and higher cultural and social level and ultimately used for political purposes by Pope Leo X himself.

Supernatural Visions and Visions of Battles

Portentous visions were not unheard of in the early years of the modern era.[5] They were singular experiences, but not totally out of the ordinary scheme of things. We have already seen examples from the times of the War of Cambrai. In general, they represented one aspect of the complex set of manifestations and warnings of the divine presence discussed earlier. Supernatural apparitions—both religious and nonreligious—are an extremely interesting field of investigation, because visions (and, in many cases, dreams)[6] provide us with an external (hence definable) projection of an inherited set of mental images. By that token, they offer a valuable opportunity for learning about that heritage. Italian chronicles of the early

[4] Marino Sanuto, *Diarii*, 58 vols. (Venice: R. Deputazione Veneta di Storia Patria, 1879–1903), vol. 25, col. 209. On Caroldo, see Antonio Carile, "Caroldo, Gian Giacomo," in DBI, vol. 20, pp. 514–17.

[5] See William A. Christian, Jr., *Apparitions in Late Medieval and Renaissance Spain* (Princeton: Princeton University Press, 1981); Ottavia Niccoli, "Visioni e racconti di visioni nell'Italia del primo Cinquecento," *Società e storia* 28 (1985): 253–79. On apparitions in the Paleo-Christian age and the early Middle Ages, see Johannes Lindblom, *Geschichte und Offenbarungen. Vorstellungen von göttlichen Weisungen und übernatüralichen Erscheinungen in ältesten Christentum* (Lund: Gleerup, 1968); Michel Aubrun, "Caractères et portée religieuse et sociale des 'Visiones' en Occident du VIe au XIe siècle," *Cahiers de civilisation médiévale Xe–XIIe siècles* 23, no. 2 (1980): 109–30; Vito Fumagalli, "Il paesaggio dei morti. Luoghi d'incontro fra i morti e i vivi sulla terra nel medioevo," *Quaderni storici* 59 (1982): 411–25; Paolo Siniscalco, "Pagani e cristiani antichi di fronte all'esperienza di sogni e visioni," in Vittore Branca, Carlo Ossola, and Salomon Resnik, eds., *I linguaggi del sogno* (Florence: Sansoni, 1984), pp. 143–62.

[6] For a historical reading of dreams, see Peter Burke, "L'histoire sociale des rêves," *Annales E.S.C.* 28 (1973): 329–42, and Jacques Le Goff, "Dreams in the Culture and Collective Psychology in the Medieval West," in his *Time, Work and Culture in the Middle Ages*, tr. Arthur Goldhammer (Chicago: University of Chicago Press, 1980), pp. 201–4.

modern period include a wealth of materials of this sort. For instance, only a few months before the apparitions that concern us here, the shipwrecked sailors of the galley *Magna*, which went down off Cyprus, declared, when they arrived in Famagusta after many adventures that "they had seen a number of saints . . . in the sky with lighted candles."[7] The phenomenon did not cease with the spread of the Reformation, nor was it limited exclusively to Catholic confessional circles, as we might suspect from this tale, which calls to mind well-known passages in Erasmus and Rabelais on devotion to the saints on the part of mariners caught in storms. Apparitions and dreams appear often in the pages of Melanchthon,[8] and one need only pick up the *De spectris, lemuribus . . . variisque praesagitationibus* of the Protestant physician Ludwig Lavater, published in Zurich in 1570, to find an impressive and varied picture of supernatural visions. Among the variety of phenomena he discusses, Lavater devotes particular attention to spectral combats, which, he states, are to be understood as bad omens. Such were swords, lances, and a large number of other objects seen in the air; clashing armies or fleeing troops seen or heard in the air or on the ground; the horrible sound of shouting voices and the clangor of clashing arms.[9]

There are vast numbers of examples of the specific typology of visions of clashing armies outside Lavater's pages, beginning with a passage in Pausanias concerning the battlefield of Marathon.[10] A phantom army accompanied Attila to the battle of the Catalaunian Plains, in premonition of his defeat.[11] In the tenth century, when the Persian voyager Ibn Fadlans was making his way from Baghdad to the Volga, he saw on the night of 11 to 12 May 922 two fire-red armies clashing in the air with a muted roar.[12] Analogous examples are plentiful for the late Middle Ages,[13] and in the sixteenth century aerial battles had become so common that on several occasions they were predicted by preachers.[14] In France the topic appears to have been a favorite of the broadsheets on current occurrences known as

[7] Sanuto, *Diarii*, vol. 24, col. 25.

[8] In particular in Philipp Melanchthon, *Historiae quaedam recitatae inter publicas lectiones*, *Corpus Reformatorum* (Brunswick: Schwetschke et filium), vol. 20 (1854), cols. 519–608.

[9] Ludwig Lavater, *De spectris, lemuribus et magnis, atque insolitis fragoribus, variisque praesagitationibus* . . . , 4th ed. (Leiden: J. Luchtmans, 1687), pp. 112–13.

[10] Pausanias, *Descriptio Graeciae* 1.32.4.

[11] Leo Weber, "Die katalaunische Geisterschlact," *Archiv für Religionswissenschaft* 33 (1936): 162–66.

[12] Otto Weinreich, in a note added to Weber, "Die Katalaunische Geisterschlact," p. 166.

[13] There is an ample list in Knut Martin Stjerna, "Mossfunden och Walhallastrom," *Från filologiska föringen i. Lund, Språkliga uppsatser* (1906): 148ff., which I was unable to consult but which is cited in Otto Höfler, *Kultische Geheimbünde der Germanen* (Frankfurt am Main: M. Diesterweg, 1934–), p. 242.

[14] Sanuto, *Diarii*, vol. 10, cols. 48–49; Tommaso di Silvestro, *Diario*, ed. Luigi Fumi, in RIS 15, pt. 5 (Bologna: Nicola Zanichelli, 1923), vol. 2, p. 482. The two mentions refer, respectively, to the years 1510 and 1513.

canards.[15] On 28 January 1664, during an eclipse of the sun observed in the territory around Ljubljana, a Capuchin friar from Friuli, Cristoforo da Cividale, saw in succession in the sun, "with the interval of about one *Miserere*" between them:

1. Four men seen in the sun.
2. Two men on horseback.
3. Four men on horseback.
4. A company of cavalry.
5. An army of cavalry.
6. A church.
7. A giant on horseback.
8. A squadron of infantry.
9. A great body of cavalry.
10. A very large army of cavalry . . . and for a good length of time fierce and doleful combats were seen.[16]

These prodigies were signs of wars to come, and the pamphlet narrating them concludes with the hope of "weakening the pride of the haughty Ottoman and giving glorious victory to the Christian armies."

[15] Jean-Pierre Seguin, "Notes sur des feuilles d'information relatant des combats apparus dans le ciel (1575–1656)," *Arts et traditions populaires* 7 (1959): 51–62, 256–70. Aerial battles are included in all treatises on *mirabilia* of the age: Freidrich Nausea, *Libri mirabilium septem* (Cologne: P. Quentell, 1532), fols. 37*r*–38*r*; Conrad Lycosthenes (Conrad Wollfhart), *Prodigiorum ac ostentorum chronicon* (Basel, 1557), pp. 556, 608, and so forth; Ambroise Paré, *Des monstres et prodiges*, ed. Jean Céard (Geneva: Droz, 1971), pp. 146–47 [*On Monsters and Marvels*, tr. Janis L. Pallister (Chicago: University of Chicago Press, 1982), pp. 156–57]; Pietro Pomponazzi, *De naturalium effectuum admirandorum causis seu de incantationibus liber* . . . (Basel: ex officina Henricpetrina, 1567), p. 130; Ulisse Aldrovandi, *Monstrorum historia* (Bologna: Marco Antonio Bernia, 1642), pp. 143, 717. As late as 1650 a Spanish pamphlet appeared describing the passage of a "fantastic army . . . formed of many infantrymen and cavalry" (*Copia de una carta embiada a esta corte, en que se da cuenta de las notables visiones que en diversas vezes se ha visto entre Rosell y Traiguera, y otras partes, en el Reino de Valencia, de exercitos formados de infanteria y cavalleria y que se vieron pelear unos con otros* [Madrid: Alonso de Paredes, 1650]). Even the English almanac, *Nuncius coelistis or The Starry Messenger*, compiled in 1682 by Henry Coley, described an aerial battle between ships and armies in its 1682 edition, for which see Bernard Capp, *English Almanacs 1500–1800: Astrology and the Popular Press* (Ithaca, N.Y.: Cornell University Press, 1979), p. 24. Naturalistic interpretations have seen in the phenomenon a fantastic description of the aurora borealis or the effect of sunspots: Frantisek Link, "On the History of the Aurora Borealis," *Vistas in Astronomy* 9 (1967): 297–306; D. Justin Schove, *Sunspot Cycles* (Stroudsburg, Pa.: Hutchinson Ross Pub. Co., 1983).

[16] Cristoforo da Cividale, *Prodigii portentosi osservati in vari luoghi da molte persone degne di fede. E da PP. Cappuccini con ogni fedeltà osservati e posti in scritto* (Parma, Milan, and Genoa: per Gio. Ambrosio de Vincenti, n.d. [c.1665]), fols. 2*v*–4*r*. The same events were reported in a letter from Gorizia dated 2 February 1664, conserved in the Archivio di Stato di Bologna, Senato, Diari, 1656–1671, fols. 45*v*–46*r*. I owe the last item to the courtesy of Giovanna Ferrari.

It is of course difficult to give a single explanation for materials that, although repetitive, are culturally so heterogeneous. Still, the battles of spirits that were observed in the territory of Bergamo toward the end of 1517 seem to have a greater specificity, and it is perhaps possible to situate them within a more precise scheme in folklore and to show their specific but multiple political reverberations. What makes them even more relevant is that it is possible, given the various accounts of these events available to us, to suggest a historical reading of them and to grasp the gradual and ongoing construction of that scheme and its subsequent rapid disintegration.

"Littera de le maravigliose battaglie"

The fullest description of an apparition and the one with the most details comes from an octavo-sized pamphlet of four leaves with no imprint entitled *Littera de le maravigliose battaglie apparse novamente in Bergamasca.*[17] The pamphlet is in the form of a letter sent by "Bartholomeo de Villachiara al suo charissimo misser Onofrio Bonnuncio veronese" and is dated from the castle of Villachiara 23 December 1517. The text plunges right into its topic: Three or four times daily for eight days in Verdello, in the territory of Bergamo, formidable battalions of infantry, cavalry, and artillery were seen advancing in battle array "with the greatest organization and in perfect order." Before them rode three or four kingly figures, led by another sovereign who appeared to be the greatest among them. They advanced to parley with another king standing before his own troops and who awaited them, surrounded by his barons, halfway between the two armies.

> And there, after much negotiation, one sees one armed king, with most ferocious aspect and little patience, take the glove (which is of iron [mail]) from his hand and toss it in the air, and at once at once [*sic*] with a troubled expression he shakes his head, and immediately turns toward his men in battle array. And in that instant there are heard so many sounds of trumpets, drums, and rattles, and the most terrible racket of artillery (no less, I believe, is made by the infernal forge; in fact, truly one cannot believe that they come from anywhere but there). And then one sees no small array of banners and standards come into the fray, and with the greatest fierceness and force assault one another, and in most cruel battle all are cut to bits. . . . Half an hour later everything is still and nothing else is seen. And anyone who has the courage to draw

17 The *Index Aureliensis* hypothesizes the following publication data: Rome: Gabriele da Bologna, 1517. As we shall see, the place of printing seems to be confirmed by the documentation, but the date is more probably 14 or 15 January 1518.

> near to that place [sees] an infinite number of pigs, which stay a short while and then enter into the said wood.[18]

The writer adds that he wanted to verify these events in person, so he went there with other gentlemen. They confirmed that at the end of the apparitions, "nothing is found in that very place but marks of horses' hoofprints and men's footprints, cart tracks and burned spots, and many trees torn to bits." The letter concludes with expressions of marvel and terror ("truly the thing is so terrible that I cannot compare it to anything but one's own death"), and the writer states that he would have added other news, but refrains from doing so because "this is so great that the others would be naught."

The Furious Horde of the Dead of Agnadello

The components of this account seem to be: first, the place and date of the apparitions; next, four (or five?) kings, one of whom has command, at the head of an endless army on the march; a sole, terrible king leading another army; his terrifying aspect and fierceness as he throws his mail gauntlet into the air; the battle between the two forces; the tremendous noise that accompanies the battle; the tracks remaining on the ground; the pigs that at the end of the apparition are seen returning to the wood; finally, the author of the letter. We shall return to him later. For the moment, let it suffice to say that he was a historical person, Count Bartolomeo III Martinengo da Villachiara, who belonged to one branch of the Martinengo family, some of whom opted for the Reformation in later generations and had to emigrate to the Graubünden and to Geneva.

The apparitions took place in an open space before a wood, from which the armed specters emerged. In one account, this space is described as "spacious fields covered with snow, and in them two heaps of stable litter, and not far from there is a wood."[19] The village of Verdello is a few kilometers from the confluence of the Adda and the Brembo; Agnadello is not far away, and the battle left such a mark on the entire district that the first accounts Sanudo gathers of the apparitions in Verdello (29 December) speak, with characteristic imprecision, of "a certain thing that occurred around Treviglio or Cassan [now Cassano d'Adda], where the encounter with the French and the Swiss took place."

As for the date, the *Littera de le maravigliose battaglie* was dated 23 December, as we have seen, but it stated that the apparitions had begun eight

[18] *Littera de le maravigliose battaglie*, fols. A ii*v*–A iii*v*.

[19] Antonio Verdello to Paolo of the late Marco Morosini, Brescia, 4 January 1518, in Sanuto, *Diarii*, vol. 25, cols. 187–88.

days earlier, thus pushing the date back to 16 December, which in 1517 was the first of the winter Ember Days. As it happens, the four series of Ember Days, the winter ones above all, were the times of the year when phantom armies were most apt to appear. This was a myth of Germanic origin, tied to the origins of witchcraft,[20] which until now has been supposed to have had little influence in Italy, but which seems without doubt to apply in this instance.

The saga of the furious horde existed in a good part of Europe, branching off into Scandinavian and Slavic lands, but it seems certain that it originated in the Germanic world. As has rightly been remarked,[21] a fairly ancient trace of this myth can be seen in a passage from the *Germania* of Tacitus in which he records that the Harii were the most ferocious of the Germanic warriors, fighting at night with black shields and their bodies dyed black: "feralis exercitus . . . nullo hostium sustinente novum et infernum aspectum" (The sudden and funereal gloom of such a band of sable warriors are sure to strike a panic through the adverse army).[22] Thus they appeared as an army of the dead, like ghosts risen from the tomb, defeating all enemies by striking terror in their hearts. This tradition was doubtless based, on the one hand, on the custom, documented among the Germans, of using disguises to terrorize their adversaries;[23] on the other, on beliefs concerning the dead and their night wanderings that were widespread in the Germanic world. As early as the time of Tacitus, the army of the dead was thought to be led by Wotan, whom Tacitus equates with Mercury, thus emphasizing his role as a psychopomp god. Warriors who had died in battle followed this spectral guide, but with the Christianization of the myth, all those who had died before their time (suicides and unbaptized infants, for instance) were added to their number. The myth found a ready

[20] This is the hypothesis offered in Carlo Ginzburg, *I benandanti. Stregoneria e culti agrari fra Cinquecento e Seicento*, 2nd ed. (Turin, G. Einaudi, 1971), esp. pp. 61–103 [*The Night Battles*, tr. John and Anne Tedeschi (Baltimore: Johns Hopkins University Press, 1983), pp. 33–68]; Ginzburg, "Charivari, associazioni giovanili, caccia selvaggia," *Quaderni storici* 49 (1982): 164–77; Ginzburg, "Présomptions sur le Sabbat," *Annales E.S.C.* 39 (1984): 341–54; and now Ginzburg, *Storia notturna. Una decifrazione del Sabba* (Turin: G. Einaudi, 1989), esp. pp. 65–98. For further bibliographical information on the myth of the furious horde, see these studies and the comments of Vittore Branca in his edition of Giovanni Boccaccio, *Decameron*, 2nd ed.; 2 vols., (Florence: Le Monnier, 1960), vol. 2, p. 83.

[21] By Ludwig Weniger, "Feralis exercitus," *Archiv für Religionswissenschaft* 9 (1906): 201–47, and 10 (1907): 61–81, 229–56.

[22] Tacitus, *The History, Germania and Agricola*, tr. Arthur Murphy, Loeb's Classical Library (London and Toronto: J. M. Dent; New York, E. P. Dutton, 1926), p. 339.

[23] Gunter Müller, "Zum Namen *Wolfhetan* und seinen Verwandten," *Frühmittelalterliche studien* 1 (1967): 200–212; Müller, "Germanische Tiersymbolik und Namengebung," *Frümittelalterliche studien* 2 (1968): 202–217; Claude Lecouteux, "Les Cynocéphales. Etude d'une tradition tératologique de l'Antiquité au XIIe siècle," *Cahiers de civilisation médiévale Xe–XIIe* 24 (1981): 117–28, esp. p. 27. I owe these citations to the courtesy of Vito Fumagalli.

reception in learned circles as well, since it coincided at least partially with traditions in Roman religion according to which the souls of the dead periodically rose from the infernal regions to the earth's surface through certain crevasses in the earth, notably through the *mundus*, the pit dug at the center of every Latin city at its founding to establish yearly contact between the upper and the lower earth.[24] In Roman religion, what is more, the spirits of those who had suffered premature or violent death, warriors killed in battle in particular, were destined to wander in the air. Such spirits could be formidable and were often invoked by necromancers.

Parallels between the Germanic myth and the Roman myth probably favored the spread of this notion over ever larger and more varied cultural and territorial areas. It appears well-rooted in France in the thirteenth century, where a number of literary texts—the *Tournoiement Antechrist*, the *Roman de Fauvel*, *Le Jeu de la feuillée*, and others—contain rhetorical comparisons between some unusually noisy event and the racket made by the Mesnie Hellequin, as the furious horde appears to have been called in France (Hellequin or Herlechinus—from which the stock figure of Harlequin was derived—was the demon who took over from Wotan the task of leading the troops of the dead).[25] Soon after 1250, Etienne de Bourbon gave fixed form to the myth, by that time totally Christianized and demonic, in one of his sermons: "Aliquando [diaboli] ludificant transmutando se . . . in similitudinem militum venacium vel ludencium, qui dicunt de familia Allequini vel Arturi."[26]

A text dated 1278 explicitly and for the first time places the army of the dead on the battlefield of their last combat,[27] which was to remain an intrinsic part of the myth. It lends significance to the fact that the apparitions of 1517 took place not far from Agnadello, or at least that the battle was referred to in order to locate the site of the apparitions. In the sixteenth century the temporal placement of the phantom army during the Ember Days, particularly the winter Ember Days, seems definitive, as is clear from a passage in a sermon of Johannes Geiler von Kaisersberg, a Strasbourg

[24] Franz Cumont, *Lux perpetua* (1949; reprint ed., New York: Garland, 1987), pp. 58, 82–89, 105, 332; Ernesto De Martino, *La fine del mondo. Contributo all'analisi delle apocalissi culturali* (Turin: Einaudi, 1977), pp. 212–15.

[25] Otto Driesen, *Der Ursprung des Harlekin. Ein kulturgeshichtliches Problem* (Berlin: A. Duncker, 1904), pp. 34–35, 41, 106. See also John Colin Dunlop, *John Dunlop's Geschichte der Prosadictungen oder Geschichte der Romane, Novellen, Märchen, u. s. w.*, tr. and ed. Felix Liebrecht (Berlin: G.W.F. Müller, 1851), p. 474, n. 170 and p. 546, n. 541a [*The History of Prose Fiction*, ed. Henry Wilson, 2 vols. (London: George Bell and Sons, 1888), vol. 1, pp. 229–30, n. 2].

[26] Albert Lecoy de La Marche, *Anecdotes historiques, légendes et apologues tirés du receuil inédit d'Etienne de Bourbon, Dominicain du XIIIe siècle* (Paris: Librairie Renouard, H. Loones, successeur, 1877), pp. 321–22.

[27] Lavater, *De spectris*, pp. 116–17.

preacher, given in 1508 but printed in 1516 and again in 1517, the same year as the apparition at Verdello ("die lauffen aller meisten in der fronfasten, und vorausz in den fronfasten vor Weinnachten; das ist die heiligest Zeit").[28]

Nonetheless, the place and the date of the visions—the fact that they involved armies that clashed during the winter Ember Days on or near a former battleground—are not the only reasons to define them as manifestations of the furious horde. According to all the eyewitnesses, the appearances were always accompanied by a fearful racket.[29] We have even seen that in thirteenth-century France this noise had become such a cliché that it could be applied to any unusual amount of noise, even to a charivari, as in an interpolated incident in the *Roman de Fauvel*. We also know of an unusual manifestation of Herlechinus's troops in a somewhat earlier period (mid-thirteenth century) in which the horde appears to be composed of craftsmen who fill the skies with the clanging of the tools of their trades. The armies at Verdello clashed amid a "terribilissimo strepito" judged not inferior to the racket that "si faccia all'infernal fucina, che veramente altro non è da credere se non che de lì eschino." Even the terrible aspect and ferocity of the king who throws his mail gauntlet into the air, the traditional gesture to set off a battle,[30] has a parallel in the terrible countenance always attributed to the leader of the troops of the dead,[31] whether he was Herlechinus or the "man of the four Ember Days," as he was called (Kwaternik, Quatembermann) in the northern and eastern border areas of Italy (Trentino, Carniola, Carinthia, Slovenia, Switzerland).[32]

One last important element of the account remains to be clarified: the

[28] Johannes Geiler von Kaisersberg, *Zur Geschichte des Volks-Aberglaubens im Anfange des XVI. Jahrhunderts. Aus der Joh. Geilers von Kaisersberg Emeis*, ed. August Stöber (Basel: Schweighauser, 1856), p. 21.

[29] Felix Liebrecht, *Des Gervasius von Tilbury Otia Imperialia. In einer Auswahl neu herausgegeben* . . . (Hannover: C. Rümpler, 1856), app. 2, "La Mesnie furieuse ou la chasse sauvage," pp. 181–82; Driesen, *Der Ursprung des Harlekin*; Höfler, *Kultische Geheimbünde*, pp. 8–9, 108–10, 300; Lucia Lazzerini, "Preistoria degli zanni: mito e spettacolo nella coscienza populare," in *Scienze, credenze occulte, livelli di cultura. Convegno internazionale di studi (Firenze, 26–30 giugno 1980)* (Florence: L. S. Olschki, 1982), pp. 445–76; p. 459. On two examples given later, see Ginzburg, "Charivari."

[30] According to Luigi da Porto, before the battle of Agnadello the king of France, Louis XII, sent a herald to Venice who "in sign of challenge . . . threw at the feet of the doge the bloody glove"; before the battle of Ravenna in 1512 "monsignor Foix sent to Don Raimondo di Cardona the bloody glove of the battle." See *Lettere storiche di Luigi da Porto vicentino dall'anno 1509 al 1528*, ed. Bartolommeo Bressan (Florence: Felice Le Monnier, 1857), pp. 35, 302.

[31] Liebrecht, "La Mesnie furieuse," p. 177.

[32] Waldemar Liungman, *Traditionswanderungen, Euphrat-Rhein. Studien zur Geschichte des Volksbräuche*, 2 vols. (Helsinki: Suomalainen tiedeakamia, Academia scientiarum fennica, 1937–1938), vol. 2, pp. 640–41.

four kings (though this number can vary) who head the second army. The oft-cited passages from Guillaume d'Auvergne concerning the phantom army contain a few additional details. When Guillaume speaks of night armies at the end of the 1230s ("quos alii hellequin vocant, alii exercitum antiquum") and of the troops led by Abundia or Satia, he also speaks of four kings who, when the necromancers call on them (thus making them kings of the dead), "a quatuor mundi partibus cum exercitibus innumerabilibus suis convenire dicuntur."[33] In a later passage, still in connection with the phantom army, Guillaume returns to the topic: The four kings who spring out of the earth followed by their armies at the call of the necromancers receive their names from the parts of the world from which they come: "ita ut primus vocatus sit Oriens, secundus Occidens, tertius rex Austri, quartus rex Septentrionis."[34] Chief among them is the king of the East. Guillaume goes on to argue that the four kings can only be kings of the demons and are themselves demons, thus attempting to reduce to Christian coordinates a myth that appears to precede Christianity and to be extraneous to it. Other traces of this myth can be found in a well-known passage of the *Historia ecclesiastica* of Ordericus Vitalis, which relates the encounter of a priest, Gauchelin, with the nocturnal army on 1 January 1091 near Saint Aubain de Bonneval: Among the dead there stood out "quatuor horrendi equites . . . terribiliter vociferantes," who intervene when Gauchelin attempts to catch a riderless horse that belongs to the horde.[35]

This part of the myth of the furious horde—that the army of the dead was led by four kings and that it was possible to call them up by means of the necromantic arts—was not completely spent in the sixteenth century. In 1544 some students wandering about the countryside of Swabia boasted of being able to call up the furious horde on nights of the sabbath during the four Ember Days and the three Thursdays of Advent.[36] They experimented with necromantic techniques to discover hidden treasure and used a circle traced on the ground, salt and holy water, magic herbs,

[33] Guillaume d'Auvergne, *Opera omnia*, 2 vols. (Paris: Edmundus Couterot, 1674), vol. 2, p. 948. In medieval culture the number four was of course the number of the cosmos: "the *fabrica mundi* developed in a vast *ordo quadratus* that remained permanent within temporal flux" (Henri de Lubac, *Exégèse médiévale. Les quatre sens de l'Ecriture*, 4 vols. [Paris: Aubier, 1959–1964], vol. 2, p. 27).

[34] Guillaume d'Auvergne, *Opera omnia*, vol. 2, p. 1037.

[35] Ordericus Vitalis, *Historiae ecclesiasticae libri treaecim*, ed. Augustus Le Prevost, 5 vols. (Paris: apud J. Renouard et socios, 1838–1855), vol. 3, p. 372. The work is available in English as *The Ecclesiastical History*, ed. and tr. Marjorie Chibnall, 6 vols. (Oxford: Clarendon Press, 1969–), where the citation is in vol. 3, p. 245.

[36] Martin Crusius, *Annalium Svevicorum dodecas tertia* (Frankfurt: ex officina typographica Nicolai Bassai, 1596), pp. 653–54.

lighted candles, and glowing embers as part of a scheme to befuddle and cheat a peasant from Chomburg. The Swabian students thus emulated Wotan, the god who called up the dead and knew the places in which treasure was buried. Their science may have had other sources besides folk tradition, for example (and this is a hypothesis), the *De occulta philosophia* of Heinrich Cornelius Agrippa, published eleven years earlier in Cologne.[37] Agrippa discusses techniques for finding buried treasure and the necromantic arts most easily exercised on the "sepultura carentium vagabundas umbras, manesque Acheronte remissos et hospites inferum, quos immatura mors in Tartara astraxit." Both the classical tradition and the Germanic and folk tradition seem evident in these lines. Contaminations of this sort must have been frequent, as Agrippa's own work shows. Elsewhere he speaks of the four kings of the subterranean world, giving them names that derive from rabbinic wisdom:

> In malis spiritibus praesunt . . . quatuor reges potentissimi iuxta quatuor partes mundi, quorum nomina appellantur Urieus, rex Orientis, Amaymon, rex Meridiei, Paymon, rex Occidentis, Egyn, rex Septentrionis; quos Ebreorum doctores forte rectius vocant Samael, Azazel, Azael, Mahazael; sub quibus plures alii dominantur principes legionum et presides.

Thus the myth of the four kings of the world who led the army of the dead and whom the power of the necromantic arts could raise out of the earth was certainly alive in sixteenth-century Germany, even if it had classical and Oriental admixtures. Furthermore, fragments of the same mythology persisted in the Po valley as well. A formula for invoking the four kings of the world by the names Agrippa had attributed to them appears in an Inquisitional document from Modena that bears no date but is probably from approximately the same period as the apparitions in Verdello.[38] Fragments of these beliefs are also discernible in the *Littera de le maravigliose battaglie*, which seems to evoke a combat between several armed groups, some led by the king of the four seasonal Ember Days, the others by the four kings of the world under the leadership of the king of the East.

37 Heinrich Cornelius Agrippa von Nettesheim, *De occulta philosophia libri tres* (n.p. [Cologne: Johann Soter], 1533). The two quotations that follow are on pp. cccv and cclvi. The reference to Wotan's functions is taken from Georges Dumézil, *Gods of the Ancient Northmen*, ed. Einar Haugen (Berkeley: University of California Press, 1973), pp. 40–42.

38 This document is a loose page conserved in the Archivio di Stato di Modena in a file containing love spells and marked Inquisizione, envelope 1. It has been studied in Albano Biondi, "La signora delle erbe e la magia della vegetazione," in *Medicina, erbe e magia* (Bologna: Federazione delle Casse di Risparmio e delle Banche del Monte dell'Emilia Romagna, 1981), pp. 190, 192.

The Construction of a Myth

The *canard* described above seems to present a fairly fully developed version of the events. Although the myth of the spectral army is not mentioned explicitly, it is suggested with great exactitude and a wealth of detail. At the opposite extreme is the stripped-down version of the events in the skeptical letter written by the doge's secretary in Milan, Gian Giacomo Caroldo ("some simple people saw the fumes above some manure piles"). More relevant to our purposes, however, we can grasp the intermediate phases or, more accurately, the raw materials that were subsequently sifted, re-elaborated, and modified to create a mythical event. The first traces of this process go back even some years before the event, though they seem not to have had any direct result. In the anonymous minstrel's *frottola* (popular poem) published in 1511 under the title *Memoria delli novi segni*, already examined for the large number of signs it describes in connection with the War of Cambrai, we read the following lines:

Là dove fu il conflitto
delli Venitiani
de molti segni strani
son comparsi:

fochi per l'aere sparsi
de nocte visti sonno
da quei che guardar vonno
spesse volte;

rumor de squadre folte
e soni di trombette
di maggio a giorni sette
furno auditi.

(Where there was the conflict of the Venetians many strange signs have appeared: lights dispersed in the air have often been seen at night by those who care to look; the din of close-ranked squadrons and sounds of trumpets were heard on 7 May.)[39]

Thus as early as 7 May 1511 the nucleus of what later was to be seen as a clear manifestation of the furious horde was recorded in the sighting of will-o'-the-wisps (the souls of the fallen?) on the site of the battle of Agna-

[39] *Memoria delli novi segni et spaventevoli prodigii comparsi in piu loci de Italia et in varie parte del mondo lanno mille cinquecento undese* (n.p., n.d.), fol. 1*v* (unnumbered).

dello (by antonomasia, "il conflitto delli Venitiani").[40] Above all, the din of a large army was heard, accompanied by the shrill squeals of trumpets. No vision is recorded, however, and the date is not relevant, since in that year 7 May was the Wednesday following the second Sunday after Easter, known in Italy at the time as *Misericordia Domini* Sunday. What is more, the events of 1517 were by no means immediately placed within the winter Ember Days (which, as we have seen, lent them further significance). A letter dated 4 January 1518,[41] to which I shall return, declares that the visions began "about twenty days ago," thus around 10 December, whereas the *Littera de le maravigliose battaglie*, dated 23 December, refers to the week just past, thus placing the events within the feast days of the winter Ember Days.

The progressive construction of the myth, or rather the adaptation of materials that came from eyewitness reports to the myth is even clearer from a direct examination of the reports themselves. The most singular among these is the long letter just mentioned, sent by Antonio Verdello of Brescia on 4 January 1518 to Paolo Morosini. Verdello tells his correspondent that he had interrogated a number of people about the visions and, in particular, that he had discussed them at length with three trustworthy eyewitnesses. He gives an extremely precise description of the place and offers no fewer than six different accounts of the apparitions, all introduced by formulas such as "some say," "others say," and "another man says," which allow us an extraordinarily immediate grasp of both the subjectivity of the interpretations and the innate fluidity of this sort of phenomena (a quality that facilitates accommodation to the schemata of a preexistent mental image). The inherent interest of this multiple testimony is intensified by the fact that there is no indication that any of the informants had access to printed texts that may already have been in circulation or that they had based their reports on such texts, as is the case with other accounts. Here we see a culture still in an exclusively oral phase.

The first version reported seems already quite complex, however. As with the later printed text, it includes foot soldiers, horsemen, artillery, and supply wagons all racing full tilt across the snow-covered fields between a wood and a small church dedicated to St. George. The images are unclear, however, as if shrouded in clouds of dust ("per tal corere levarsi gran polvere a l'aiere"), and they soon dissolve into nothing ("poco andati inanti,

[40] Phosphorescent lights appearing on battlefields were a recurrent commonplace, to the point that in the mid-eighteenth century Lenglet Dufresnoy felt it necessary to state that they "are only gross exhalations that rise naturally from cadavers and that easily take fire." See Nicolas Lenglet Dufresnoy, *Recueil des dissertations anciennes et nouvelles sur les apparitions, les visions, et les songes*, 2 vols. (Avignon and Paris: J. N. Leloup, 1751), vol. 2, pt. 1, p. 247.

[41] Antonio Verdello to Paolo of the late Marco Morosini, Brescia, 4 January 1518, in Sanuto, *Diarii*, vol. 25, cols. 187–88.

disparere et perdersi totalmente"). Furthermore, here the furious horde leaves no trace of its presence on the snow ("non si vedeva ne la neve un minimo vestigio"), whereas the *Littera de le maravigliose battaglie* devoted a good deal of space to describing the footprints of the infantry and the hoofprints of the cavalry left to bear witness to the prodigy.

The next account is more subdued, speaking only of "shades like men with no heads" ("umbre a modo de homeni senza capo") that seemed to move about and group together in ever shifting number ("pareano se movessero et hora se unissero insieme, hora fusseno pur assai et hora pochissimi"). Still, those unstable shades, now many, now few, advancing and retreating, are perhaps a first sketch of the meeting and colloquy between the four kings of the dead and the king of the four seasonal Ember Days. The detail of decapitated shades has a certain relevance in that the soldiers risen from battle who made up the furious horde often appeared as death had overtaken them: "One carried his viscera before him, another bore his head in his hand," Geiler von Kaisersberg wrote only a few years earlier.[42]

The third report describes pigs running onto the field, just as the vision of the phantom combatants in the *Littera de le maravigliose battaglie* ends with "an innumerable quantity of pigs who grunted and rose up into the air, running wildly here and there." In the folk tradition of the furious horde, souls could take the form of animals or be accompanied by animals—horses and dogs above all, but also pigs, particularly in some cantons in Switzerland.[43] A large number of animals appear in the account of the fourth eyewitness as well. He reports that he saw first "several thousand black and white sheep walking on the snow"; next, "a great many red and white oxen"; then, "just as many friars [dressed in] black and white"; finally, as if he had been subjected to pressure from the collective imagination of the crowd around him (he was "led to look where there were many other people as well"), he "thought he saw an infinite number of armed men on foot and on horseback, and many with readied lances, all of them helmeted and all moving and running over those fields with a multitude of hay carts." In a notable qualitative jump that tells us much about the process involved in the creation of visions, this eyewitness reaches the more complex level of elaboration of the first account given in the letter.

The last two reports, relegated to a postscript, are almost completely negative. One "homo da bene" (the term indicates that he was a trustworthy witness, though it is not clear whether it is a judgment of his integrity or his social status) looks for a long time without seeing anything before he finally believes he can distinguish two decapitated shades that advance

[42] Geiler von Kaisersberg, *Zur Geschichte des Volks-Aberglaubens*, p. 22.

[43] See Hans Plischke, *Die Sage vom wilden Heere im deutschen Volke* (Eilenburg: C. W. Offenhauer, 1914), pp. 30–31.

over the snow and then disappear. Some in the crowd gather enough courage to approach the church. They see nothing unusual, but others watching them (from a safe distance) see them surrounded by shades. In conclusion, the writer of the letter adds that "some . . . took such a fright that they became sick, and . . . still others died of it."

Obviously the visions, as reported in this singular text, were extraordinarily fluid, flexible, and susceptible to being adapted to a specific model. This process of adjustment must have been enormously swift, as we can see from the dates of the various reports, which overlap to such an extent that it is nearly impossible to establish a clear, logical, and chronological order among them. Antonio Verdello's letter bears the date of 4 January; Bartolomeo da Villachiara's letter is dated 23 December; on 29 December, Marin Sanudo notes the events in his journal in terms that lead us to suppose that he had at hand a source of information that was already fairly well formalized.[44] Finally, there is a letter dated 28 December from one Marin Saracho or Saracco in Bergamo to Antonio Orefici in Vicenza that seems to represent a last phase in the construction of the myth before it reached its definitive form.[45] The letter speaks of the daily apparition of two friars ("appareno ogni zorno due frati sie miglia lontano di Bergamo"), then of two armed men bearing halberds who come out of a wood to climb a hill ("se levava fuora de quel boscheto dui armati con le labarde et vengono in zima de la colina"), who are finally transformed into two crowned kings conferring together until one of them throws his gauntlet into the air, setting off the battle. Thus we have arrived fairly close to our point of departure—to the *Littera de le maravigliose battaglie* and its presentation of the visions as a manifestation of the furious horde.

At this point we need to consider the cultural environment in which this parallel was drawn. Admittedly, the apparitions must have been seen and believed by people of very different social and cultural levels. We should not forget Caroldo's scornful opinion concerning the "simple people" who thought they had seen men in arms in the fumes rising from a mound of fertilizer; nor should we ignore the social distance separating Caroldo, secretary of the Venetian Republic in the service of the French commander in Italy, the "homo da bene" who saw only "due umbre . . . senza capo, forte obscure," and the "simplice persone" who saw infantry, cavalry, and baggage trains. Still, there seems to have been an inverse relationship between the elaborateness and complexity of the visions and the social level of the viewer. The *Littera de le maravigliose battaglie* (hence the interpretation of the apparitions as a manifestation of the furious horde) had an author whose name is given explicitly and to whom it would thus seem that we

[44] Sanuto, *Diarii*, vol. 25, col. 167.

[45] Ibid., cols. 189–90.

should attribute the elaboration of the visions in their definitive form. He was, as we have seen, a historical personage about whom we have precise information: Bartolomeo Martinengo, the son of Count Vettore, the late Giovan Francesco Martinengo.[46] The Martinengo family had split into a number of branches, the one that interests us here being the Villachiara branch, so called from the castle of that name (parts of which are still standing) east of the Oglio River not far from Crema. Bartolomeo was a military man and had participated in the battles of the Holy League, in particular in the autumn of 1514, when he had fought beside Lorenzo Orsini da Cere, the captain of the Venetian infantry, in the zone between Crema, Bergamo, and Brescia. In recognition of his services, the doge of Venice, with all due solemnity, raised Bartolomeo to count of Villachiara on 16 November 1516, and he held command of Cremona for the Venetian Republic. The letter was sent from the castle of Villachiara, where Bartolomeo probably was at the time. It is also probable that the visions that gave rise to the text printed in letter form under his name were related by one of his men, whether Bartolomeo actually wrote the letter or not. In fact, Marin Sanudo informs us in a journal entry for 29 December that "Count Vetor da Martinengo, or rather, the Contin [literally, the little count] his son, sent one of his serving men who, coming too near these phantasms or spirits or whatever they were, was severely beaten by them."[47] Perhaps it was this unknown "fameglio," to whom Bartolomeo himself probably alludes in his letter when he says that "one or two of our own [men] are sick from fear," who, besieged by his terror of the "phantasms," tipped his own personal experience definitively into the realm of myth.

Letters and Pamphlets in Italy and in Europe

The event had vast notoriety, thanks to the publication of the piece whose genesis I have attempted to reconstruct. It gave rise to another text printed in Italy that gives a somewhat different version of the events at Verdello and thrusts them into an eschatological framework ("I sorely suspect that

[46] On the Martinengo family in general, see Paolo Guerrini, *I conti di Martinengo* (Brescia, 1930), a work that contains inaccuracies, however. On Bartolomeo in particular, see pp. 484–89 of Guerrini, and Carlo Pasero, *Francia, Spagna, Impero a Brescia, 1509–1516*, Supplemento ai Commentari dell'Ateneo di Brescia per il 1957 (Brescia, 1958), pp. 339–40 and 356, to which should be added the many pertinent entries in Sanuto, *Diarii*, vols. 19, 20, 21, 23, *ad indicem*. On the castle of Villachiara, for which Bartolomeo ordered frescoes painted by the Campi brothers, see Adriano Peroni, "L'architettura e la scultura nei secoli XV e XVI," in *Storia di Brescia*, 5 vols. (Brescia: Morcelliana, 1963–1964), vol. 2, pp. 717–19.

[47] Sanuto, *Diarii*, vol. 25, col. 167.

in our times we can rightly say *consummatum est*").[48] This publication must have had a much more restricted circulation than the *Littera de le maravigliose battaglie*, which was certainly used as the basis for a French translation (in at least two different editions) and a German translation.[49] The German translation, destined for a market that might grasp the affair, set the visions explicitly within the myth of the furious horde. Along with the name of the sender and the recipient, as in the Italian original, the letter also bore the indication, "von Dieterichs Bern" (in Italian tradition, the name Dietrich von Bern was one name for King Theodoric of Verona, but in Germanic folklore he had become one of the leaders of the phantom army).[50] The translator thus recognized a formulation of that myth in the text, probably seeing the Ostrogothic king in the king of "ferocissimo aspetto e di poca paciencia armato" who sets off the infernal battle by throwing his mail gauntlet into the air.

Thanks especially to the print piece we have examined, the battle of the spirits of Verdello was thus famous far and wide, its renown reaching into France and Germany. This means that it is possible to reconstruct the progress of its notoriety, the channels that news of it followed, and the time this required, which gives us an opportunity to go beyond strictly oral transmission and to trace one example of the itineraries open to cultural images in Europe of the early modern age. The itineraries for information that circulated by epistolary means and those followed by printed publications should be kept distinct, however. Letters moved more rapidly, but over shorter distances. The visions began toward the middle of December; Marin Saracco could write about them from Bergamo to Vicenza on the 28th, and Marin Sanudo noted them in his journal on 29 December. News must have reached Venice several days before, however, if Antonio Verdello had time to gather information and then answer Paolo Morosini's request for particulars on 4 January. Milan also heard of the

[48] *Copia delle stupende et horribile cose che ne boschi di Bergamo sono a questi giorni apparse* (n.p., n.d.).

[49] *La terrible et merveilleuse bataille que a este veue novellement en la duche de Millan VIII jours durant au pres de la cite de Bergamo: translate de italien en françoys* (n.p., n.d. [Paris, 1518]); *La translacion de italien en francoys de la lettre des merveilleuses et horribles batailles nouvellement apparues au pays de Bergame, translate par maistre Michel du Pont, banquier a Troyes. Lan mil cinq cent et dix sept* [Troyes: Nicolas le Rouge]; *Ein wunderbarlich, grausam und erschrockenlich Geschichte von Streyt woelche ist geschehen und neuwlich gesehen worden In dem land Bargamasca* . . . (n.p., n.d.).

[50] Plischke, *Die Sage vom wilden Heere*, p. 39; Renato Serra, "Su la pena de i dissipatori (*Inferno*, C. XII, vv. 109–129)," *Giornale storico della letteratura italiana* 43 (1904): 278–98; p. 294; Claude Luttrell, "Folk Legend as Source for Arthurian Romance: The Wild Hunt," in Kenneth Varty, ed., *An Arthurian Tapestry* (Glasgow: Published on behalf of the British Branch of the International Arthurian Society at the French Dept. of the University of Scotland, 1981), pp. 94, 99.

apparitions fairly soon because Gian Giacomo Caroldo wrote on the subject to his brother on 12 January but was apparently aware of the events several days earlier.

Thus news moved rapidly within a fairly restricted geographical area, for the most part within the confines of the Venetian Republic. Word reached Rome a bit later, probably in the form of a manuscript copy of Bartolomeo da Villachiara's letter and of other letters. On 21 January 1518, in fact, Leo X read "some letters on the apparitions of Bergamo" to the cardinals assembled in consistory.[51] It was also in Rome that the *Littera de le maravigliose battaglie* was most probably printed (by Gabriele da Bologna), since the anonymous French cleric cited earlier states in his journal that "the aforesaid books were printed in Rome and sold publicly . . . to persons of note and in great favor."[52] It was from Rome, then, that the most complete working out of the news of the battles of the dead made its way, in the form best adapted to wide circulation and over a longer distance, arriving in France and Germany, as we have seen, and Valladolid, as we know from a letter of Pietro Martire d'Anghiera dated 23 February. In the meantime, the pamphlet lost no time circulating within the confines of the Pontifical States. In Cesena, as we have seen, the chronicler Giuliano Fantaguzzi noted in his *Caos* that "books printed about the visions and combats of spirits taking place in the Bergamasco" began to circulate in his city by 20 January (a date that indicates, taking the entire chronology into consideration, that the *Littera* came off Gabriele da Bologna's presses around 14 or 15 January).

From Rome news of the spectral battles rapidly rebounded to northern Italy. Bartolomeo da Villachiara's letter—certainly in the Roman edition, the only one to mention him by name—was put into verse by a Po valley tale singer, and his poem was used to pad out a reprinting of the minstrel's *frottola*, *Memoria delli novi segni*, already mentioned several times. The additions—sixteen quatrains of limping verse—were even clumsier than the doggerel into which they were inserted, but they did give a faithful description of "the signs that have appeared / again in Geradada / where every road was full / of armed men." Ghiaradadda (now Gera d'Adda) confirms the reference to the battle at nearby Agnadello, also referred to in the work's title, now modified to read: *Segni e prodigi spaventosi apparsi in Lombardia nel confino de Trevi e Rivolta seccha: quali appareno doi o tre volte al zorno a combattere in ordenanza e con ferissime artelarie viste visibilmente per el magnifico Bartolomeo da Villa Chiara: et molti altri uomini degni di fede.*[53] Trevi and Rivoltasecca (now Treviglio and Rivolta d'Adda) were in fact

[51] Sanuto, *Diarii*, vol. 25, col. 219.

[52] Biblioteca Apostolica Vaticana, MS Barb. Lat. 3552, fol. 32*v*.

[53] (n.p., n.d.).

fairly pertinent topographical references for the battle called "of Agnadello" or "of la Ghiaradadda." There is no longer any mention of Verdello, and the permanent alteration of the circumstances of the place and the time in which the spectral battles took place is a persuasive confirmation of their definitive assimilation into a mythic model.

From Myth to Propaganda

Rome functioned well as a sounding board of international scale for the prodigious—for the apparitions at Verdello as earlier for the monster of Ravenna. The impression is inescapable that the success of these two events in Rome was due to the circumstances that favored their use for propaganda purposes. In the case of the Verdello apparitions, the political context was furnished by the crusade against the Turks. When Leo X read the letters describing the visions at Verdello to the assembled cardinals, he commented that these prodigious apparitions were "signals that the Turk will soon be attacking Christianity . . . thus we need to make proper provisions and not shilly-shally."[54] As is known, the notion of a crusade against the Turks frequently arose in sixteenth-century Italy, often in quite concrete terms, involving the collection of alms and the establishment of diplomatic contacts. This was precisely the situation during the months in question. As early as the beginning of November 1517, Leo X was considering the organization of a league of Christian princes against the Turk, and after a successful Egyptian campaign the previous spring, Selim I was then at the peak of his dangerous power.

Among the many missives offering advice received by the pope was a Latin epistle from a humanist in Imola, Giovanni Antonio Flaminio, which merits a brief word. Flaminio had spent long periods of his life in Serravalle (now Vittorio Veneto), not far from the eastern borders of Italy. He was there in 1499 when the Turks reached the Tagliamento River, which is probably why he approached the problem of Turkish pressure with particularly intense feeling. From 1514 until 1536, the date of his death, he sent letters to every pope who was elected to urge him to declare a crusade. Aside from the letter of 1517 (in prose), he had already sent Leo X an epistle on the same subject in hexameters in 1514.[55] The 1517 letter dif-

[54] Sanuto, *Diarii*, vol. 25, col. 219.

[55] Biographical and bibliographical information on Giovanni Antonio Flaminio can be found in Alessandro Pastore, *Marcantonio Flaminio. Fortune e sfortune di un chierico nell'Italia del Cinquecento* (Milan: Franco Angeli, 1981), pp. 15–17; the epistles to the popes are in Ioannis Antonii Flaminii, *Silvarum libri II. Eiusdem epigrammatum libri III* (Bologna: per Hieronymum de Benedictis, 1515); Flaminii, *Epistolae familiares*, ed. Fr. Dominico Josepho Capponi (Bologna: ex typographia Sancti Thomae Aquinatis, 1744).

fered from its rather repetitive predecessor in that it gave fuller treatment to the "ingentia prodigia, quae futurae calamitates praenunciant . . . et ad consulendum in commune monere, hortari, impellere non cessant."[56] Flaminio urged the pope to use his authority to mitigate the discord among Christians and to unite their forces under the sign of the cross in order to march against their common Ottoman enemy. Leaving aside its rhetorical scheme, Flaminio's letter is truly singular for its sources, a major portion of which, surprisingly enough, turns out to be a somewhat pedestrian translation into Latin of the *Memoria delli novi segni*,[57] quite evidently in the 1511 version that bore this title (as Flaminio's letter precedes the apparitions at Verdello, it thus also precedes the edition with the title *Segni e prodigi spaventosi* quoting Bartolomeo's *Littera*). In short, Giovanni Antonio Flaminio, a humanist and teacher of Latin, used a text from the culture of the city streets to invite the reigning pontiff to declare a crusade. Not only did he borrow its description; he took over its general thrust, which was, precisely, an invitation to Christian princes to unite for the purpose of liberating the Holy Sepulchre, thus diverting from mankind the divine wrath that was revealed by the prodigies it described—a fine example indeed of the complex relations between humanists and the vernacular.

Given the situation that faced the pope, Flaminio's letter found Leo X well disposed to listen to its arguments. On 7 November a commission of cardinals was formed, which prepared a fairly broad-ranging questionnaire to be sent to Christian rulers so as to know their thoughts on the most opportune strategy to follow and on how to organize the crusade and raise the necessary military forces.[58] Early in January 1518 the pope received word from Constantinople, via Ragusa and Ancona, that the Turks were on the move, which set off a new flurry of preparations. In particular, Leo X sent briefs to all the sovereigns of Europe, and it was precisely to discuss the responses he had already received that the cardinals had been called together on 21 January.[59] Thus the apparitions of combating armies could have been considered premonitory, a warning of the imminent and expected struggle between the Cross and the Crescent (according to the interpretive scheme proposed by both Flaminio and the anonymous tale singer who preceded him) and could prove useful in preparing the way for a request for new taxes. The projected expedition against the Turks never

[56] Flaminii, *Epistolae familiares*, p. 59.

[57] Ibid., p. 60 for the passage in Flaminio closely translating quatrains 6–31 of the *Memoria delli novi segni*.

[58] Sanuto, *Diarii*, vol. 25, cols. 76 and 95–106. On preparations for the crusade of 1517–1518, see Charles Göllner, *Turcica*, 3 vols. (Bucharest: Editura Academiei R.P.R., 1961–1978), vol. 3, *Die Türkenfrage in der öffentlichen Meinung Europas im 16. Jahrhundert*, pp. 73–74.

[59] Sanuto, *Diarii*, vol. 25, cols. 204 and 219.

took place, but in the early months of 1518 the pope worked diligently to raise financial aid, sent out a number of briefs, and urged that ceremonies and penitential processions be organized.[60] The pope was not alone in raising money: Franciscan friars moving about the Venetian *terraferma* also collected funds, at times abusively. To increase the appeal of their requests for alms for St. Peter's they included propaganda for the crusade in their sermons, thus incurring protests from the Venetian Council of Ten.[61]

The propagandistic context into which the visions at Verdello were placed, particularly in Rome, was evident from various facts. The pamphlet about the "the visions and combats of spirits" reached Cesena on 20 January, as we have seen, together with another work entitled *Signuri stupende del grando aparato face il Turco per pasare in cristianità*. In all probability, this print piece, whose title already announces the Turks' large-scale mobilization, contained a letter that both Sanudo and Tommasino Lancellotti report.[62] It gave a highly colored description of the terrifying aspect of the fleet of the Great Turk in the Levant: The ships bore banners with a black cross on a red field; the galley of the Great Turk himself was all black—sails, rigging, oars, and all—with only the banners in gold bearing a red cross placed upside down. All the ships were laden with large wood crosses (clearly, for the eventual martyrdom of captured Christians). That the two pamphlets circulated at exactly the same time might simply reflect the widespread presence of these topics in Roman circles, but it may also have been a deliberate move to prepare people's minds for the collection of funds. Even Francesco Guicciardini, who was at the time serving as pontifical governor of Reggio Emilia, received the two news items together and appears to have made a connection between them. On 19 January he wrote to Goro Gheri in Florence:

> The prodigy has disappeared, but it is confirmed from so many places that, as for me, I cannot laugh at it, above all hearing so much about the Turk's

[60] Scipione Vegio, *Historia rerum Insubribus gestarum sub Gallorum dominio* in *Bibliotheca Historica Italica* (Milan: Brigola, 1876–1901), vol. 1, p. 31; *Bando delle processioni per la unione dei principi Christiani contra Turchi* (Rome, 1518); Giovanni Cambi, "Istorie," in Fr. Ildefonso di San Luigi, ed., *Delizie degli eruditi toscani*, 24 vols. (Florence: Gaetano Cambiagi, 1770–1789), vol. 23 (1786), pp. 138–41; Leonello Beliardi, *Cronaca della città di Modena (1512–1518)*, ed. Albano Biondi and Michele Oppi (Modena: Panini, 1981), p. 142.

[61] Sanuto, *Diarii*, vol. 25, cols. 390–91.

[62] Ibid., cols. 335–36; Tommasino Lancellotti, *Cronaca modenese*, ed. Carlo Borghi, 12 vols. (Parma: P. Fiaccadori, 1863), vol. 1, pp. 438–39. Analogous and dramatic news of the Turkish fleet was also contained in a letter dated Milan, 18 February 1518, from one Fra Giovanni Antonio to the minorite Zaccaria da Ravenna in Cremona, which also gives a description of a number of prodigies interpreted as omens of the imminent arrival of the Turk in Italy, for which see Francesco Novati, ed., "La vita e le opere di Domenico Bordigallo," *Archivio Veneto* 19 (1880): 327–56; pp. 334–35.

preparations, and believing that now is like the past [and] that great things have been signified ahead of time by great prodigies.[63]

The connection that Guicciardini establishes between the "apparati del Turco" (mentioned in a letter dated two days earlier) and "the prodigy" of Verdello does not figure in the news that he received from the place where the apparitions were seen, so we can suppose that he linked the two on the basis of what he heard from Rome. As early as 8 January, Guicciardini sent Gheri a copy of a letter on the visions that he had received from near Brescia, in which (thus differing somewhat from all those examined up to this point) there is no suggestion of any relationship between the prodigy and preparations for war against the Turks.[64] We know of this letter thanks to Giovanni Cambi's summary of it in his *Istorie*, where he states explicitly that Guicciardini was the source of his information:

> On a plain, in the daytime, near certain woods and pastures, [people] saw a great King coming to parley from one side, and from the other another King with six and eight lords, and when they had been there awhile they disappeared; and then two great armies came to parley and to do battle together and stayed an hour fighting together. And this thing happened several times, but there were more than three days from one time to the other: on which the common voice [*la brighata*] judged it a combat of great lords. In that [part of] Lombardy there were some curious [people] who wanted to get close to the said armies to see what they were and who, as they drew near, out of fear and terror immediately fell sick and lay at death's door.[65]

This version of the events—which, obviously, was written independently of Bartolomeo da Villachiara's letter—was sent directly from Lombardy and contains no anti-Turkish sentiments. All that "la brighata" drew from the visions is a generic prognostication of a "combattimento di gran signori." We learn somewhat more about the matter through another source that, although late in date, offers a wealth of particulars. Toward the end of the seventeenth century, Father Gregorio di Valcamonica published a work on the history of the Camuni, the prehistoric inhabitants of the valley and their descendants. In it he relates that in 1518 the rectors of Brescia had manned the castle overlooking Breno, contrary to previous custom, because of "fears conceived because of some prodigious signs [that] appeared in those days in the territory of Bergamo, in the general system of which people saw presented the affairs of Italy." Thus concern for the political situation in Italy was mixed, in the minds of the rectors of

[63] Francesco Guicciardini, *Carteggi*, ed. Roberto Palmarocchi, 17 vols. (Bologna: Nicola Zanichelli, 1938–), vol. 2, p. 240.

[64] Ibid., p. 236.

[65] Cambi, "Istorie," p. 131.

Brescia and of the local population, with a holy terror aroused by "prodigious signs." But just what did the population of the area really think about those signs? "Everyone interpreted them in his own way, but the most sensible ones took them as a prediction that King Francis of France and King Charles of Spain, who was later Emperor Charles V, were to tussle between them in Italy for the Duchy of Milan."[66] Father Gregorio was doubtless using hindsight when he stressed this interpretation over others that he may have had available, but it communicates the sense of alarm (whether or not it was shared) that suggested to the rectors of Brescia that it would be prudent to keep the commander of the castle in Breno on duty. It also contributes to an understanding of what a Lombard meant when he stated that "si faceva giuditio di combattimento di gran signori." These "great lords" were the kings of France and Spain, and what was feared was yet another foreign invasion to seize possession of the Duchy of Milan. Another report, of a different origin, offers an interesting comparison. We know of it from a summary given in the *Journal d'un Bourgeois de Paris*:

> In the said year 1517 [1518] in January, in Rome and like parts, both in the air and on the ground in a wood were heard a great number of armed men fighting (they seemed to be around six or eight thousand men); and [people] heard [something] like cannon, bombards, and arms clashing against one another; which battle lasted a good hour at the most, without [their] seeing anything, however. Afterwards, [they] heard a great many pigs, in equal number, fighting, from which the terrified populace judged that those pigs signified the Mahometan infidels.[67]

The version of events that the Parisian burgher had in hand was substantially different from those we have available (the phantasms are only heard fighting, and nothing is seen), and certainly came from Rome (the visions, in fact, are placed "à Rome et par de là"). In all probability, the Bourgeois had seen the French translation of a Roman print piece other than the *Littera de le maravigliose battaglie* (Leo X, after all, had "some letters" on the apparitions in Bergamo read to the assembled cardinals). In this second piece, the pigs of the vision were interpreted as Muslims. We know well, however, that it would be difficult to impute this interpretation to the "populaire espouvanté"—the equivalent of the *brighata* of the letter forwarded by Guicciardini—to judge from the spontaneous reactions of which we have evidence. From the beginning, all the reports speak of the presence of pigs, but as animals without particular significance who, together with oxen and sheep, painted a picture familiar to Bergamo country dwellers in

[66] Padre Gregorio di Valcamonica, *Curiosj trattenimenti continenti raguagli sacri e profani de' Popoli Camuni* (Venice, 1698; reprint ed., Bologna: Forni, 1965), pp. 561–62.

[67] *Journal d'un Bourgeois de Paris sous le règne de François Premier (1515–1536)*, ed. Ludovic Lalanne (Paris: J. Renouard et c., 1854), p. 62.

those days. The oxen and the sheep disappeared in the mythic tradition of the visions because, unlike the pigs, they had no function in the furious horde. In the final stages, the lost Roman pamphlet definitively removed the visions from their peasant roots by placing the pigs in an ecclesiastical tradition that, as early as the twelfth century, saw pigs as an incarnation of sin and vice.[68] This last shift reworked the visions to serve anti-Turkish ends with the aim of encouraging a broader consensus for the projected crusade.

Twenty years later, in 1538, the Venetian printer Giovanni Andrea Valvassori published a pamphlet entitled *Avisi da Constantinopoli di cose stupende et maravigliose*. The work had two parts, the second of which was a wholly fictional account of the victory of the armada under Andrea Doria over the Turks. The first part, which served as a sort of preamble to the second, was little more than a nearly literal repetition of the *Littera de le maravigliose battaglie*, followed by explanations that the astrologers of the Great Turk were supposed to have given of these prodigies. The last of these to speak, the sage Odobassi, admonishes the sultan in these terms:

> The highly honored king who is seen coming to parley on the field will be that Caesar, emperor of the Christians, so much our enemy, who before he enters into combat will come to meet you in mid-course, and he will ask you whether you want to become a Christian, and you will answer him, no. And then, in a meadow, he will turn around to his men, and will throw the gauntlet in the air as a sign that they should enter into battle, with a face so full of fury that it will strike terror in your men, and in an instant you will see so many arquebuses and so much artillery discharged that it will be impossible to resist them, and at the end they will set your men to flight like pigs, without resistance and in greatest disorder.[69]

The king of the four Ember Days had thus become Charles V. The propagandistic purpose and the aim of supporting anti-Turkish and pro-imperial sentiment that are explicit here reflect elements that were simply latent in the pamphlet's predecessors.[70] One detail should be stressed: The *Avisi* specifically mentions the myth of the furious horde, but only to deny it. One of the wise men whom the Great Turk invites to give his interpretation in fact states that "in ancient days some armed combat must have taken

[68] Lecouteux, "Les Cynocéphales," p. 124.

[69] *Avisi da Constantinopoli di cose stupende, et maravigliose novamente apparse in quelle parti . . . Et unaltro aviso dell'armata del Principe Andrea d'Oria* . . . (Venice: Giovanni Andrea Valvassori, n.d. [1538]), fol. 3*v*.

[70] Although Marcel Bataillon appears unaware of the underlying sources of this and other similar texts, he interprets them correctly; see his "Mythe et connaissance de la Turquie en Occident," in Agostino Pertusi, ed., *Venezia e l'Oriente fra tardo Medioevo e Rinascimento* (Florence: Sansoni, 1966), pp. 451–70.

place in that locality, for which reason those generations still appear in that place with their damned spirits."[71] The ranks of the dead are no longer made up of souls undergoing purification (as in the preceding phase of the Christianization of the myth) but of the damned. Their demonization, in parallel to that of witchcraft, was by then fully achieved.

From Folk Culture to Leo X

One of the many interesting aspects of this entire affair seems to me to be that it confirms connections (postulated before) linking mythology and Germanic folklore with aspects of the cultural and religious life of sixteenth-century Italy, particularly among the subalternate classes.[72] As we have seen, the myth of the furious horde (well defined and widely known in the German world, where, among other things, it was connected with the origins of witchcraft) was sufficiently well known on the plains of Lombardy to be called to mind accurately as a way of dealing with prodigious events in a highly confusing early phase. That we are exceptionally fortunate in being able to follow this development from an unstable visionary creation to a later clear formulation as a specific myth is probably due to an unusually precise and rich documentation.

That is not all, however. This affair also provides an excellent example of the communication of cultural information through social levels that were not only different but notably complex culturally.[73] If we look at the chan-

[71] *Avisi da Constantinopoli*, fol. 2*v*.

[72] More than a century ago, Aleksandr Veselovskii, in an introduction to the *Novella della figlia del re di Dacia* (Pisa: Nistri, 1866), p. xlv (now reprinted in Alexandre Veselovskij, François de Sade, and Giovanni Boccaccio, *La fanciulla perseguitata*, ed. D'Arco Silvio Avalle [Milan: Bompiani, 1977], p. 65), launched the hypothesis that a complex of Nordic traditions, among them the myth of the phantom army, had persisted in Italy at least until the fifteenth century in the territories formerly occupied by the Longobards and, in some parts, also by the Goths. This hypothesis seems confirmed beyond doubt by studies such as Carlo Ginzburg, *The Night Battles*, and Maurizio Bertolotti, "Le ossa e la pelle dei buoi. Un mito popolare tra agiografia e stregoneria," *Quaderni storici* 41 (1947): 470–99. It has even been claimed that Nastagio degli Onesti's novella in the style of Boccaccio is symptomatic of the persistence of the myth, at least until the battle of Ravenna (Boccaccio, *Il Decamerone*, vol. 2, p. 83; Serra, "Su la pena de i dissipatori"; Veselovskij, Sade, and Boccaccio, *La fanciulla perseguitata*, pp. 64–67). This hypothesis finds indirect confirmation, moreover, in the suggestion that the Ravennese dialect word *biatricol* (devil) derives from the name Dietrich von Bern, for which see Manlio Cortelazzo, "Concordanze linguistiche fra Venezia e Ravenna," in Dante Bolognesi, ed., *Ravenna in età veneziana* (Ravenna: Longo, 1986), pp. 188–89.

[73] The importance of investigating both the exchanges between different cultural levels and the various functions of the traditions analyzed is well expressed in Jean-Claude Schmitt, "Les traditions folkloriques dans la culture médiévale. Quelques réflexions de mode," *Archives de Sciences sociales des religions* 52, no. 1 (1981): 5–20.

nels of transmission through which word of this affair traveled between 10 to 15 December 1517 (the hypothetical date of the beginning of the visions) and 23 February 1518 (the date of Pietro Martire d'Anghiera's letter from Valladolid), we see that the time limits are singularly narrow—about two months. Still, we find evidence of a goodly number of means used during those two months: private conversation (oral transmission), private correspondence (written), performance by *cantastorie* (oral again), and printed pamphlets (written). Furthermore, accounts now lost and known only through diaries or chronicles (Giovanni Cambi's *Istorie* and the *Journal d'un Bourgeois de Paris*) allow us to deduce the existence of letters that were manuscript before they appeared in print, but in some fashion no longer fit the category of private correspondence because they were detached from both their sender and their addressee to become "copies of letters" and, in that guise, achieved a wide autonomous, manuscript circulation that often ended up in print publication. This is in all probability what happened with the *Littera de le maravigliose battaglie*. At first a private letter (which was already a written version of an oral account by the "fameglio" who was stricken by the phantasms, according to the reconstruction outlined above), it was then a copy of a letter, and finally a print piece used for propagandistic purposes. Then, however, it was taken up again by a tale singer, and thus was returned to oral transmission.

There are other unknowns superimposed on this already complex picture. As our investigation has progressed, we have found three distinct strata or levels—those of the visions, of the myth, and of propaganda. These three levels stand out clearly in the reconstruction I have attempted and, in my opinion, they are confirmed by the minor but telling detail of the different presentation of the pigs. On the level of the visions, the pigs appear as a reality within the vision, yet they are in some fashion concrete and free of symbolism. The pig, as we know, was a highly important domestic animal between the Middle Ages and the early modern age.[74] For a long time, pigs were allowed to forage in the woods (where the pigs of the vision take refuge), but in early sixteenth-century Lombardy they were more probably kept under a roof. One clear allusion to the presence of pigs or other domestic animals in the area is provided by the heaps of manure, the fumes of which Gian Giacomo Caroldo took as an explanation of the origin of the entire affair. On the mythic level, the pig became an integral part of the myth. We can see this from the fact that the oxen and sheep that accompanied the pigs in the visions of the Bergamo country people no longer have a role in the myth. Finally, at the third level, the pigs acquire a

[74] See *Porci e porcari nel Medioevo. Paesaggio, economia, alimentazione*, ed. Marina Baruzzi and Massimo Montanari (Bologna: IBC: Cooperativa Libraria Universitaria Editrice Bologna, 1981), esp. pp. 29–30 and 72 concerning the raising of pigs in the woods and in pig barns.

symbolic and propagandistic value. They are the Muslim infidels, an emblem of vice, inchoate hordes destined to be routed. In short, the image of the pig remains constant in all versions, but the animal's function varies substantially.

We might well ask, finally, how all these variants fit into the different pigeonholes of social hierarchy. Is there any correspondence between a particular means of communication (oral transmission, letter, print, etc.) and a given social category? What seems to emerge is the interclass character of people whose accounts are on the purely visionary level and, in part, on the mythic level (folklore, as we know, is not exclusively rural or tied to a specific social class).[75] Nonetheless, as the preceding pages have shown, the lower classes (the "simplice persone" and the "fameglio") pay greater attention to the visions and display a greater capacity for elaborating them in complex forms. Those who furnish or who accept a propagandistic interpretation of the apparitions seem to form a much more compact group, not in the channels of communication they use but in their social and cultural status. They are "gens notables et de grant favoir"; they are Francesco Guicciardini or Pope Leo X.

Let me go one step further and add one last variant to the picture outlined thus far, a distinction between two vast territorial and political spheres—Italy of the Po valley, on the one hand, and the Pontifical States, on the other (leaving to one side, for the moment, reverberations of the affair outside Italy). The unknowns in the system I have attempted to construct seem to fall into place. Word of the affair first circulated on the plains of the Po valley within a social context of lay people of middle to lower social status who were receptive to folk influences. The affair received a first political interpretation—that had no sequel, however—in Lombardy, pointing to foreign powers struggling on Italian soil for control of the Milanese state. When Roman circles took over the affair it underwent a radical qualitative shift from the lay realm to the ecclesiastical, from the underclasses to the governing classes, from folk culture to "high" culture (when Guicciardini refers to "cose grande" signified "ora come per el passato" by "prodigi grandi," he is alluding, by implication, to classical divination), from the Italian wars to the crusade against the Turks, and from the visionary and mythic level to that of propaganda. The recasting of folkloric materials as they passed through Rome is, of course, not an isolated fact, as we have seen in connection with the monsters of Ravenna and Bologna. In the early years of the sixteenth century the papal court and circles in Rome tied to it did not refuse "popular" culture, but they did remove

[75] Schmitt, "Les traditions folkloriques," p. 7. See also analogous remarks by D. S. Likhachev cited in Aron Ja. Gurevich, *Categories of Medieval Culture*, tr. G. L. Campbell (London and Boston: Routledge and Kegan Paul, 1985), pp. 59–60.

its constituent parts from their original context and use them in a different sense and for a specific purpose. Certainly in this period exchanges between high and low culture seem extraordinarily rich and frequent: the *Memoria delli novi segni*, translated into Latin by a humanist who offered it, without mention of its origin, to the pope, acquired a second life and more ample telling thanks to the insertion in it of a text—the *Littera de le maravigliose battaglie*—that was given notoriety and further circulation by no less a personage than Pope Leo X. Thanks to the pope, a divinatory interpretation of a folk tradition achieved international fame. Twenty years later it led to an identification of the king of the four Ember Days as Charles V and to a prediction of the rout of the Turks based on the disorderly flight of a herd of pigs.

4

THE APOCALYPTICAL PREACHING OF ANDREA BAURA AND ZACCHERIA DA FIVIZZANO

Was Andrea Baura a Lutheran?

ON CHRISTMAS DAY 1520, Maestro Andrea Baura of Ferrara, a hermit of Saint Augustine, preached in Venice from the balcony of Palazzo Loredan, overlooking Campo Santo Stefano. Marin Sanudo, whose ear was, as always, attuned to every religious event that had social implications, recorded his homily in these terms:

> On Campo San Stephano there was a sermon by Master Andrea of Ferrara that drew a large crowd. The square was full, and he was up on the balcony of the Pontremolis' house . . . and he spoke ill of the pope and of the Roman curia. This man follows the doctrine of Fra Martin Luther, [who] in Germany is a most learned man who follows St. Paul and is much opposed to the pope, for which he is excommunicated by the pope.[1]

Baura's sermon must have been truly extraordinary if it held the attention, out of doors and in the middle of winter, of a larger audience than could fit into the nearby church of Santo Stefano, where he had preached before, as we shall see. It is hardly surprising, then, that echoes of his homily, accompanied by the redoubtable name of Martin Luther, from whom he seemed to take his inspiration, soon reached the ears of Leo X (sharply attacked by Maestro Andrea). The pope was swift to react. Looking upon Baura more as a new Luther than as a Lutheran, he summoned the Venetian ambassador, Alvise Gradenigo, to ask him to see to it that a work Baura had written that was still in manuscript not be printed. Pietro Bembo, who was present as pontifical secretary, later suggested to Gradenigo, privately and on his own initiative, that he have Baura imprisoned,[2] and other requests in the same vein reached the Venetian Signoria from the papacy in the next two weeks. An answer arrived from Venice, through an interlocutor, "that Brother Andrea of Ferrara being no longer in Venice, neither his conclusion nor other things against the Holy See have been or

[1] Marino Sanuto, *Diarii*, 58 vols. (Venice: R. Deputazione Veneta di storia patria, 1879–1903), vol. 29, col. 495.

[2] Ibid., col. 552.

will be printed."[3] In reality, Baura had remained "in secret" in the city, and he later went to Ferrara under the protection of Alfonso d'Este,[4] where, toward the end of the year, he dedicated the work to Cardinal Corner. The piece was, somewhat disconcertingly, entitled *Apostolicae potestatis contra Martinum Lutherum defensio*,[5] and thus was a defense of papal power against Luther. Was this a politic change of mind or a cover-up? In either case, the situation seems to have been resolved, and as early as 23 March 1521 a pontifical brief arrived in Venice authorizing Baura to return to preaching.

These events are well known.[6] If I return to them here it is because these events had another meaning than the one usually suggested for them. Baura, as is known, had already preached in Venice in the churches of Santo Stefano and San Marco in April 1517 and January 1519. Sanudo was certainly present when he gave the homily on Easter Day, 12 April 1517, as he reports:

> After dining, I was urged to go to San Marco for the preacher of San Stefano, Master Andrea da Ferrara of the order of the hermits, who has a great following. He preached a poor sermon, in my judgment, who was there to hear it, reproving vices well, but without adducing any doctor, philosopher, or poet.[7]

Two years later Sanudo offers further information on this and other sermons of Baura:

> [17 January 1519] This morning in San Stefano there preached one of the first of his order, named Master Andrea da Ferrara, who preached two years ago about prophecies, etc. And thus he preached today, saying that her enemies have now begun to group together against Italy (that is, the Turks). He will preach Saturday and Sunday and will say great things about what is going to

[3] Ibid., cols. 561, 609–10, 614, 615.

[4] Fedele Lampertico, "Ricordi storici del palazzo Loredan," *Nuovo archivio veneto* 5 (1893): 250–54.

[5] The work was later published in Milan in 1523. See below.

[6] On Baura, see Lampertico, "Ricordi storici," pp. 249–55; Franco Gaeta, "Baura, Andrea," in DBI, vol. 7, pp. 296–97; David Gutiérrez, "I primi agostiniani italiani che scrissero contro Lutero," *Analecta augustiniana* 39 (1976): 19–38; Silvana Seidel Menchi, "Le traduzioni italiane di Lutero nella prima metà del Cinquecento," *Rinascimento* 17 (1977): 33–108; pp. 34–36; Antonio Samaritani, "Contributo documentario per un profilo spirituale-religioso di Lucrezia Borgia nella Ferrara degli anni 1502–1519," *Analecta Tertii Ordinis Regularis Sancti Francisci* 14 (1981): 975–90, later included in Samaritani, "La 'Defensio' di Pietro Scazano in favore di Andrea Baura contro Lorenzo Castrofranco (*a.* 1520). Ai prodromi della polemica antiluterana in Italia," *Analecta augustiniana* 47 (1984): 7–42.

[7] The transcription of this passage is based on the original manuscript of the *Diarii* (Biblioteca Marciana di Venezia, MS it. VII 252 [= 9239], fol. 90*r*) because the printed edition (vol. 24, col. 158) erroneously reads "maestro Andrea da Franza" rather than "maestro Andrea da Ferrara."

happen, then he will leave to go preach elsewhere. . . . [20 January 1519] That master from Ferrara preached in San Stefano. He had a large crowd. He made some prophecies: This year Italy will be badly smitten; two cities will be preserved, one of them Venice, if [people] resolve to do good.[8]

Thus Bauer had preached *di profetie* in both 1517 and 1519, perhaps also in 1520, foretelling in detail God's punishment for men's vices, with the Turks serving as the instrument of divine wrath. There was a possible way out, however: "volendo far bene"—that is, by amending one's ways. It is quite understandable that this type of apocalyptical preaching based on divine inspiration would scornfully reject learned citations and any "alegation di alcun dotor, philosopho né poeta."

Itinerant Hermits from the Fifteenth to the Sixteenth Centuries

Apocalyptical preaching was an extraordinarily widespread homiletic genre in Italy in those years, and, added to other channels for the diffusion of prophecy, it assured a broad hearing for the prophetic message among a great variety of social strata. The Neapolitan chronicler Angelo Tummulilli noted as early as 1450 that "ceperunt undique insurgere predicatores fratres de ordine minorum et predicare populo penitentiam." Such men threatened terrible chastisement, "nisi fuerimus conversi . . . et non cessabant profetare nisi malum et ve."[9] Nearly fifty years later, in 1496, Giuliano Dati admonished Italy in his *Diluvio di Roma* in the following terms:

> Tu hai tanti profeti già veduti
> e scribi e sapienti predicare
> . . .
> O quanti n'è venuti anchor da poi
> che gli ha possuti tutti quanti udire!
> ma tu se' obstinato come suoi
> e non ti vuo' per niente pentire.
> . . .
> E la voce di molti ancor rimbomba
> che portano una croce sempre in mano.

> (You have already seen so many prophets and scribes and wise men preaching . . . O! how many have come in recent days

[8] Sanuto, *Diarii*, vol. 26, cols. 363, 378, 386.

[9] Angelo de Tummulillis, *Notabilia temporum*, ed. Costantino Corvisieri (Livorno: Tip. F. Vigo, 1890), pp. 57–58.

> whom you have had to hear! But you are as obstinate as ever and will not repent for anything. . . . And the voice still echoes of many who forever carry a cross in their hand.)[10]

Thus Italy in 1496 had seen "tanti profeti."[11] Indeed, contemporary chronicles give frequent testimony to itinerant hermits who went "preaching and wailing," often in an apocalyptical key, through the same town squares in which the *cantambanchi* declaimed their tales of catastrophes and prodigious happenings. In the prophecies in verse, hermits and prophets often appeared as signs and messengers of the divine will. The *Diluvio di Roma* gives an excellent picture of apocalyptical preaching, and of prophetic tension in general, in Italy during those years. Dati says:

> Non ti ricorda Guglielmo barbato
> che predicò per Roma con la croce
> el prim'anno de Sisto, in ogni lato
> predicendo tutto 'l male ad alta voce?
> Fulli tolta la croce e bastonato,
> ma tristo chi fa 'l male e poi li nuoce:
> el beato Gulielmo da Morano
> ogi lo chiama al mondo alchun christiano.
>
> Un altro che un san Paulo pareva
> che in Campo di Fior pur predicava,
> e tanta longa barba al pecto haveva,
> e vestito d'azuro sempre andava,

[10] Giuliano Dati, *Del diluvio di Roma del MCCCCLXXXXV adi iiii di dicembre et daltre cose di gran meraviglia* (n.p., n.d.), fol. a iii*r*–*v*.

[11] Melchior de Pobladura, "La 'Severa riprensione' di fra Matteo da Bascio (1495?–1552)," *Archivio italiano per la storia della pietà* 3 (1962): 281–302; Cesare Vasoli, "L'attesa della nuova era in ambienti e gruppi fiorentini del Quattrocento," in *L'attesa dell'età nuova nella spiritualità della fine del Medioevo* (Todi: Accademia tudertina, 1962), pp. 370–432; Giampaolo Tognetti, "Sul romito e profeta Brandano da Petroio," *Rivista storica italiana* 72 (1960): 20–44; Marjorie Reeves, *The Influence of Prophecy in the Late Middle Ages: A Study in Joachimism* (Oxford: Clarendon Press, 1969), pp. 367 and 447–48; Antonio Volpato, "La predicazione penitenziale–apocalittica nell'attività di due predicatori del 1473," *Bullettino dell'Istituto storico italiano per il Medioevo* 82 (1970) [1974]: 113–28; Giovanni Miccoli, "La Storia religiosa," *Storia d'Italia*, 6 vols. (Turin: G. Einaudi, 1972–1977), vol. 2, *Dalla caduta dell'Impero romano al secolo XVIII*, pt. 1, pp. 968–75; Adriano Prosperi, "Il monaco Teodoro. Note su un processo fiorentino del 1515," *Critica storica* 11 (1975): 71–101; Prosperi, "Gian Battista da Bascio e la predicazione dei romiti alla metà del '500," *Bollettino della società di studi valdesi* 138 (1975): 69–79; Giampaolo Tognetti, "Profezie, profeti itineranti e cultura orale," *La cultura* 18 (1980): 427–34; and, in particular, Bernardo Nobile, " 'Romiti' e vita religiosa nella cronachistica italiana fra '400 e '500," *Cristianesimo nella storia* 5 (1984): 303–40. I have taken into account, whenever it seemed to me opportune, the observations in the latter two articles concerning my own previous works, and I now want to thank the two authors, in particular Bernardo Nobile, who has kindly allowed me to read his essay in typescript. Given his ample treatment of the subject, I will not go into hermits in depth here.

el mal che t'è seguito ti dicieva
. . .
Vedi quel che ti dice suor Palomba,
e Margerita, virgo da Magliano,
. . .
e quel da Ginazano, e 'l ferrarese,
e quel che t'ha già detto Caterina,
seconda verginella fu sanese,
che chi l'udì paria proprio divina.

(Do you not remember bearded Guglielmo, who preached through Rome with the cross the first year of Sixtus, in every place predicting all evil at the top of his lungs? The cross was taken away from him and he was beaten, but woe befell those who do evil and did him harm: the blessed Gulielmo da Morano many Christians in the world call him today. Another who seemed a St. Paul, who preached in the Campo dei Fiori and had a long beard down to his chest and always went about dressed in blue, told you of the evil you have done. . . . See what sister Palomba tells you, and Margarita, the virgin from Magliano, . . . and the one from Ginazano and the Ferrarese, and what Caterina told you, [the] second virgin from Siena, who to those who heard her seemed truly divine.)[12]

We can recognize Colomba da Rieti,[13] Mariano da Genazzano, and Girolamo Savonarola on this list, and other lesser-known persons to whom Dati gives equal importance, such as Guglielmo da Morano and Antonio da Padova, who preached throughout Italy and even in Sicily in the winter of 1472–1473.[14] A long list of prophets, beginning with the illustrious name of Joachim of Fiore and extending to other, more recent "messengers of the Almighty" (St. Vincent Ferrer, blessed Anselmus, St. Bridget, blessed Tommasuccio da Foligno, Osanna da Mantova), figure in the appropriately titled *Imminente flagello de Italia*, which presumably appeared about 1510.[15] There was also the anonymous *cantastorie* of the *Memoria delli novi segni*, which gives an admirable picture of the hermit:

un antico romitto
cum barba longa e chioma
va gridando per Roma

12 Dati, *Del diluvio di Roma*, fol. a. iii*v*.

13 Dati mentions Colomba of Rieti twice, once giving her name as "suor Palomba," and the second time using the term "second Catherine of Siena," by which she was known.

14 On these, see Volpato, "La predicazione penitenziale-apocalittica," and Nobile, " 'Romiti' e vita religiosa," pp. 317–21.

15 *Imminente flagello de Italia* (n.p., n.d.), fol. 2*r*.

"pace, pace"
poi quando che li piace
invisibil va via
e multi ch'el sia Elia
credon fermo.

(an old hermit with long beard and hair goes crying "peace, peace" through Rome, then when he pleases, invisible, he goes away, and many firmly believe that he is Elijah.)[16]

The suggestion in these lines that the "antico romitto" is the prophet Elijah is important for its eschatological tone. There was in fact a well-established pseudo-Joachimite tradition (probably spread through preaching) that Elijah would return to the earth, together with Enoch, in the last days. For example, the expression "fin a che Henoch apparerà et Helya" had the sense of "until the end of the world" in a Venetian sonnet published anonymously in 1509, and in the *Libellus* of Telesphorus of Cosenza, published in Venice in 1516 but well known before that date, Elijah and Enoch are given as the "two witnesses" mentioned in the Apocalypse ("And I will give unto my two witnesses, and they shall prophesy a thousand two hundred sixty days, clothed in sackcloth": Apoc. 11:3).[17] Sackcloth (or even wild animal skins—*pelle salvatica*)[18] was a constant in the dress of itinerant prophets. Added to the cross, the long beard, and the bare head, such clothing produced a faithful imitation of the current iconography of St. John the Baptist and the prophet Elijah.[19] Matthew says

[16] *Memoria delli novi segni et spaventevoli prodigii comparsi in piu loci de Italia et in varie parte del mondo lanno mille cinquecento undese* (n.p., n.d.), fol. 1*v*.

[17] The 1509 sonnet appears in *Laus Venetorum* (Venice, 1509), fol. 4*r*. On Telesphorus, see Emil Donckel, "Studien über die Prophezeiungen des Fr. Telesphorus von Cosenza O.F.M., 1365–1386," *Archivum franciscanum historicum* 26 (1933): 29–104, 282–314; Herbert Grundmann, *Studien über Joachim von Floris* (Leipzig and Berlin: B. G. Teubner, 1927), p. 193, which contains a careful analysis of the publication. See also Dennis E. Rhodes, *Gli annali tipografici di Lazzaro de' Soardi* (Florence: L. S. Olschki, 1978), pp. 76–77, 80; Roberto Rusconi, *L'attesa della fine. Crisi della società, profezia ed Apocalisse in Italia al tempo del grande scisma d'Occidente (1378–1417)* (Rome: Istituto storico italiano per il Medio Evo, 1979), pp. 171–84; Bernard McGinn, *Visions of the End: Apocalyptical Traditions in the Middle Ages* (New York: Columbia University Press, 1979), pp. 246–47. The return at the end of time of Enoch and Elijah, united in the one person of "er Nocchilia," was familiar to the Roman populace of Belli's day: See Giuseppe Gioacchino Belli, *I sonetti*, ed. Maria Teresa Lanza, 4 vols. (Milan: Feltrinelli, 1965), vol. 1, p. 300, no. 274, "La fin der monno."

[18] Niccola della Tuccia, *Cronache di Viterbo e di altre città*, ed. Ignazio Ciampi, in *Cronache e statuti della città di Viterbo* (Florence: Tipi di M. Cellini e c., 1872), p. 106; Bernardino Zambotti, *Diario ferrarese dall'anno 1476 sino al 1504*, ed. Giuseppe Pardi, RIS vol. 24, pt. 7, no. 2 (Bologna: Nicola Zanichelli, 1937), pp. 3–359; p. 191.

[19] See, for example, Antonio de Vascho, *Il diario della città di Roma dall'anno 1480 all'anno 1492*, ed. Giuseppe Chiesa, RIS vol. 23, pt. 3 (Città di Castello: S. Lapi, 1910–1911), pp. 449–546; p. 523; *Continuazione della cronaca di Bologna detta Varignana (Cronaca B) dal*

of John (Matt. 11:14) that "he is Elias that is to come," a parallel that was frequently drawn.[20] In short, they (John the Baptist in particular) were the models and the archetypes for hermits, lent the hermits epithets such as *Missus a Deo*, for example, which derives from John 1:6 ("There was a man sent from God, whose name was John"), or provided them with names, as was the case with Giovanni Novello, which was not, as has been thought, that preacher's given name and family name, but more probably an epithet qualifying Giovanni as a second John the Baptist.[21]

Although these prophets resembled one another in their fidelity to this stereotype and in their itinerancy, they differed widely in their levels of culture and their social status. They could be friars, priests, or laymen, illiterates or *docti*, physicians, doctors, or ex-peasants. Nonetheless, very few sources show traces of any great degree of complexity in the prophetic preaching of the hermits.[22] For the most part, city chronicles repeat monotonously that the prophets foretold "widespread death, famine, and war," "many future ills," "famine, war, and food shortages"—in short, that "they all say, 'Repent, for God intends to punish Italy.' "[23]

1471 al 1500 in *Corpus Chronicarum bononiensium*, ed. Albano Sorbelli, RIS vol. 18, pt. 1, no. 26 (vol. 4 of the text) (Bologna: Nicola Zanichelli, 1924), p. 435; Dati, *Del diluvio di Roma*, fol. a. iii*v* ("e la voce di molti anchor rimbomba / che portano una croce sempre in mano"); Zambotti, *Diario ferrarese*, p. 191; Tommasino Lancellotti, *Cronaca modenese*, ed. Carlo Borghi, 12 vols. (Parma: P. Fiaccadori, 1863), vol. 6, p. 150.

[20] Louis Réau, *Iconographie de l'art chrétienne*, 3 vols. (Paris: Presses Universitaires Françaises, 1955–1959), vol. 2, pt. 1, p. 349; Réau, "L'iconographie du prophète Elie," in *Elie le prophète*, 2 vols. (Tournai and Paris: Desclée de Brouwer, 1956), vol. 1, pp. 236–37. On John the Baptist, see also Marilyn Aronberg Lavin, "Giovannino Battista: A Study in Renaissance Religious Symbolism," *Art Bulletin* 37 (1955): 85–113, and "Giovannino Battista: A Supplement," *Art Bulletin* 43 (1961): 319–26. For the parallel between John the Baptist and Elijah, see Antonio Pinelli, "La 'philosophie des images.' Emblemi e imprese fra Manierismo e Barocco," *Ricerche di storia dell'arte* 1–2 (1976): 12–13, 21. On the Renaissance tradition of the prophet Elijah, see Katharine R. Firth, *The Apocalyptic Tradition in Reformation Britain, 1530–1645* (Oxford and New York: Oxford University Press, 1979), pp. 5–6, and, for a later period, Guy Demerson, "Un mythe des libertins spirituels: le prophète Elie," in *Aspects du libertinisme au XVIe siècle* (Paris: J. Vrin, 1974), pp. 105–120. Bibliography for the medieval period is given in Rusconi, *L'attesa della fine*, p. 40, n. 5 bis. I might also note that John and Elijah are placed facing one another on the double door of the cathedral of Ravello sculpted by Barisano di Trani in 1179.

[21] Prosperi, "Gian Battista da Bascio," p. 69, changes the name Giovanni Novello to Giovanni Novelli, thus turning his nickname into a family name. On Giovanni Novello, see Nobile, " 'Romiti' e vita religiosa," pp. 322–27.

[22] One exception to this rule was Guglielmo da Morano, who preached in a number of Italian cities and demonstrated wide knowledge of the Bible (see Niccola della Tuccia, *Cronache di Viterbo*, p. 106); another was the "homo quidam natione incognitus," who, preaching in Rome some twenty years later, "reducebat ad concordiam testamentum vetus usque ad novum," hence followed Joachimite models (Stefano Infessura, *Diario della città di Roma*, ed. Oreste Tommasini [Rome: Forzani e c., 1890], pp. 264–65).

[23] Tommaso di Silvestro, *Diario*, ed. Luigi Fumi, RIS vol. 15, pt. 5, no. 2 (Bologna: Nicola Zanichelli, 1923), p. 50; Zambotti, *Diario Ferrarese*, p. 191; *Diario ferrarese dall'anno 1409*

Naturally, these reports do not necessarily tell us what the actual contents of the sermons were but only what the hearers could grasp and make their own. In this sense, the problem of context is related to how the prophets were received. The chroniclers do not always offer explicit comment on the question, but in general it would seem that the prediction of calamities had a wide audience. The anonymous chronicler who describes the preaching of one hermit in Bologna (perhaps Guglielmo da Morano) during the winter of 1472 states that he "had a great following of women and of men . . . and most of the citizens revered him and he was held to be almost a saint."[24] A hermit who rode about Rome on a steer in 1485 "aroused great admiration," although, the chronicler adds, "the better people (*gli huomini da bene*) esteemed these things, but not with as much enthusiasm as the common people (*il volgo*)."[25] Thus these preachers had greater success among the lower classes in the cities. The chronicler says of Giovanni Novello of Siena, who preached in Ferrara during the winter of 1487–1488, that he "showed himself to be a man of good life and merciful."[26] To end the series, "a mass of persons thronged" to hear the unnamed prophet who preached in Rome in 1491.[27]

A reverent hearing did not prevent isolated episodes of intolerance, but on the whole respectful attitudes must have been the rule. Giuliano Dati says of Guglielmo of Morano that "the cross was taken away from him and he was beaten," but he adds that at the time he was writing—1495–1496—many Christians called him blessed.[28] Guglielmo's twenty-five years of popular veneration entitle us to suppose that he had a large following and that his hearers believed his words. Such men must still have found it easy to gather a crowd in 1516, when the fathers assembled for the Fifth Lateran Council felt it necessary to place strict controls on prophetic preaching, as seen in the histories, both contemporary and later, of Brandano, Bonaventura, and Theodore (not by chance, the latter two came to a poor end). The situation was radically different after 1530, however. The preacher dressed in sackcloth who spoke in Modena in June 1532 "in the square where there is the market, in front of the bishop's palace, and spoke about great things that are to come" aroused the alarmed attention of the

---

sino al 1502 di autori incerti, ed. Giuseppe Pardi, RIS vol. 24, pt. 7, no. 1 (Bologna: Nicola Zanichelli, 1928–1933), p. 167; Lancellotti, *Cronaca modenese*, vol. 4, pp. 11–12.

[24] *Continuazione della cronaca di Bologna*, p. 435. On the problem of the identity of this personage (which is not relevant here), see Nobile, " 'Romiti' e vita religiosa," pp. 317–19.

[25] De Vascho, *Il diario della città di Roma*, p. 523. On this same personage, see, aside from Nobile, " 'Romiti' e vita religiosa," p. 322, the *Notationes* of the Roman grammarian Paolo Pompilio in Giovanni Mercati, "Paolo Pompilio e la scoperta del cadavere intatto sull'Appia nel 1485," *Opere minori*, 6 vols. (Vatican City: Biblioteca Apostolica Vaticana, 1937–84), vol. 4, p. 276.

[26] Zambotti, *Diario ferrarese*, p. 191.

[27] "Cum accurrisset ibi copia hominum" (Infessura, *Diario*, p. 264.

[28] Dati, *Del diluvio di Roma*, fol. a. iii*v*.

vicar of Bishop Giovanni Morone, who was away at the time, who ordered him to cease preaching. Not only did the preacher prompt ecclesiastical repression; it is even more interesting that he provoked laughter among the citizenry: "Most people mock them because they are not well dressed and are not even literate."[29] What fifty years earlier had elicited admiration and an attentive hearing—the inspired man's lack of worldly culture and clothing that reflected his qualifications as a precursor and a prophet—were now the objects of ridicule and laughter.

This was certainly not an isolated case. The hermit who passed through Modena in May of 1539 (probably Brandano) had no greater success. Lancellotti tells us:

> A poor man dressed in sackcloth, barefoot, his hair full of ashes, with a cross of Christ in [his] hand, went about the main square of Modena today, crying, "Repent, repent, for God is going to punish you," and every man laughed and he went on his way.[30]

In his appearance, this personage respected all the elements of the traditional stereotype. Dressed in sackcloth, bareheaded, barefoot, and carrying a cross in his hand, he urged the populace to repentance, predicting future afflictions exactly as had the prophets of fifty years before. The people had said of the earlier prophets that they were dressed "like an apostle"; now they said that this man was "a poor man." The earlier men aroused admiration; this man prompted hilarity. The equating of a certain way of dressing and a particular physical appearance with the image of the prophet now seems lost. The religious value of the poor man as the image of Christ also seems to have nearly disappeared during these decades. Here the poor man is no longer either Christ or a prophet, but only a deviant, an outsider to both civil and ecclesiastical society. The hypothesis that repression of the poor paralleled that of hermits finds apparent confirmation in the behavior of Agostino Zanetti, vicar to the bishop of Bologna. That same year, 1539, Monsignor Zanetti meted out exactly the same treatment to two beggars, caught pretending to have been slaves of the Turks and to have had their tongues cut off, who "went around the churches begging" and, several months later, to a hermit who was predicting earthquakes, storms, war, and pestilence in the city's main square. With perfect equity, Monsignor Zanetti had them all given a good flogging and sentenced them to a

[29] Lancellotti, *Cronaca modenese*, vol. 4, pp. 11–12.

[30] Ibid., p. 150. On preaching in Modena in those years, see Susanna Peyronel, "I conventi maschili e il problema della predicazione nella Modena di Giovanni Morone," in *Il rinascimento e le corti padane. Società e cultura* (Bari: De Donato, 1977), pp. 239–56 (Peyronel does not mention the passage cited, however).

few days in prison.[31] From the 1530s on, tighter and more careful control was gradually established over poverty, sanctity, and the presumption of divine inspiration.

Apocalyptical Preaching in the Churches: Francesco da Montepulciano and His Companions

For the most part, the itinerant hermits preached not in churches but in the public squares, rubbing elbows with "the charlatans, the quack dentists, the butcher surgeons" and with "crowd pleasers who, with the lyre and lascivious novellas hoodwinked the common people."[32] Hermits were an integral part of that scene, and they shared not only the audience but the repertory of gestures of the other actors on that stage. Eyewitness accounts agree that this was the general rule, the most illustrious isolated exception certainly being the *Missus a Deo*, who normally preached in the principal church of the city he visited, however "without ringing of the bells"—that is, with no official announcement.[33] Still, there is no lack of evidence of apocalyptical sermons given in church by friars and monks and even by official preachers; indeed, the sources are singularly abundant and are often quite specific. Perhaps because such sources are in better condition, mentions are particularly frequent after the turn of the sixteenth century, while evidence of the hermits' activities is largely (though not exclusively) earlier. It may be that the case of Savonarola encouraged the proliferation of preachers, which does not mean, of course, that prophetic preachers should necessarily be considered Savonarolans.

In this fashion, an Observant Franciscan of Corsican origin arrived in Orvieto in June 1496. We are told that he

[31] Jacopo Rainieri, *Diario bolognese*, ed. Olindo Guerrini and Corrado Ricci (Bologna: R. Deputazione di storia patria per le provincie di Romagna, 1888), pp. 42–48.

[32] The two quotations come, first, from a preacher who prophesied the sack of Rome in the Campo dei Fiori and, second, from Matteo da Bascio, for which see Francisco Delicado, *Portrait of Lozana: The Lusty Andalusian Woman*, tr. Bruno M. Damiani (Potomac, Md.: Scripta Humanistica, 1987), p. 63; and Paulo da Foligno, *Origo et progressus ordinis Fratrum Minorum Capucchinorum*, ed. P. Melchior a Pobladura (Rome: Institutum Historicum Ord. P. Min. Cap., 1955), p. 124. The tradition of gesture in preaching went back to Francis of Assisi: See Raoul Manselli, "Il gesto come predicazione per san Francesco d'Assisi," *Collectanea franciscana* 51 (1981): 5–16. "Merciless competition among jesters and Franciscan orators" is well illustrated in Vittorio Dornetti, "Sulla predicazione popolare francescana: la parodia di Zaffarino da Firenze," *Cristianesimo nella storia* 3 (1982): 83–102, citation on p. 102.

[33] Giovan Francesco Negri, *Annali della patria*, BUB, MS 1107, vol. 7, pt. 1, fol. 163*r*. On this figure, see Nobile, " 'Romiti' e vita religiosa," pp. 328–29. In spite of several discrepancies, I believe that this was the same person who had already appeared in Venice in May and June 1516 (Sanuto, *Diarii*, vol. 22, cols. 195–96, 206–7, 292–93).

always predicted woes—that is, widespread death, famine, and war—such that all, or rather few, would escape. He had [his listeners] cry out "Jesus, Jesus" at all his sermons and go in procession around the streets with the cross before them and the little children behind them, all continually crying, "Jesus, Jesus, God help us!"[34]

This was a penitential sermon, then, in which prediction presumably drew upon acknowledgment of real problems: the end of peace in Italy and the explosive rise of epidemic syphilis. The chronicler does not speak in very precise terms, however. We know somewhat more about several instances of prophetic preaching in Venice, thanks in particular to Marin Sanudo, who was unfailingly sensitive to the possible political implications in religious life and to the need to keep them in hand. Thus on 7 April 1501 he notes:

> at San Salvador there preached a friar of San Stephano, of Veronese nationality, who said in his sermon on Palm Sunday that until 1505 Italy will be torn to shreds, and that the French will be broken in Tuscany, and that he could not tell about Venice. He spoke of the pope and the kings of Spain. Then it was told to the heads of the [Council of] Ten, who ordered him to preach no more. And this was done at the request of the ambassador of France.[35]

If this Veronese friar came from the monastery of Santo Stefano, he was presumably an Augustinian. This is far from certain, in spite of the ambiguous title of *heremita* given to another preacher who "said he was a hermit" when he preached on 31 March 1507 in the church of the Servi and who threatened his hearers with "many things of a prophetical sort from the pulpit . . . about plagues and war with the Turks, saying he was a prophet."[36] Three years later, during Lent, another Veronese reeled off a long list of short- and long-term predictions involving bloody wars in Tuscany and Lombardy.[37] Still another Veronese preacher, Fra Girolamo da Verona, *heremito* (in this case, as we shall see, an Augustinian hermit), who had preached at an earlier date in the church of San Salvatore and had been silenced because he predicted "that the king of France will break the faith," preached *per profetia* in Santo Stefano on 20 March 1513, Palm Sunday:

> He said that in the Old Testament up to Christ there were sixty-four generations, and after Christ, fifty-one generations, and that [the two periods] corresponded . . . and thus in the seventeen years to come there will be very great things in Italy, and in this land there will be an upheaval *in Ecclesia Dei*, etc., concluding "blessed are those who will not be alive," and [saying] that tomor-

[34] Tommaso di Silvestro, *Diario*, p. 50.
[35] Sanuto, *Diarii*, vol. 4, col. 11.
[36] Ibid., vol. 7, col. 40.
[37] Ibid., vol. 10, cols. 48–49.

row and the day after he will preach on this matter, which sermon, in my opinion, should not be given. The church was completely full.[38]

Several aspects of this report are interesting. First, there is the clear political context of at least the first of the Veronese preacher's sermons. At the time, Venice was concluding the alliance with France from which, as we have seen, Pope Leo X was to seek to dissuade it in the months to come. It is also interesting to note Sanudo's disapproval—the same disapproval that we see nearly every time he records prophetic preaching, here apparently directed in equal measure toward the more strictly political aspects of Fra Girolamo's homily and its apocalyptical aspects and the warm reception they received ("era tuta la chiesia piena"). But the most relevant detail is perhaps the computation of the generations of the New and the Old Testament, counted not according to the indications given in the Bible but according to the calculations that Joachim of Fiore proposed in his *Concordie Novi ac Veteris Testamenti* (still unpublished at that date but quite evidently known to the preacher).[39] The seventeen years of schism and suffering predicted by the friar from Verona exactly matched the number of years remaining until the end of the fifty-first generation ($51 \times 30 = 1530$; $1530 - 1513 = 17$), and, by implication, they refer to the eschatological passage in Matt. 24:23: "This generation shall not pass, till all these things be done."

The anti-French tone of Fra Girolamo's homiletics and the evocation of Matthew the Evangelist recall another and much better-known preacher whose voice had already been heard during the same months, Francesco da Montepulciano. His famous sermon of 18 December 1513 was shot through with reminiscences of the eschatological theme in Matthew, and it predicted (among other things) the collapse of French aspirations in Italy.[40] It is clear from contemporary reports that Francesco's sermon was

[38] Ibid., vol. 16, col. 53.

[39] Joachim of Fiore, *Divini vatis Abbatis Joachim liber Concordie Novi ac Veteris Testamenti* (Venice: Simone da Lovere, 1519), fol. 134*r*: "ab Adam usque ad Jacob fuere generationes viginti una, a Jacob vero usque ad Christum generationes quadraginta duarum." The count of generations is less in Matt. 1: 1–16 (thirty-eight from Jacob to Christ) and greater in Luke 3: 23–38 (seventy-seven from Adam to Christ). For the calculation of thirty years for one generation, "recte spatium generationis in Novo Testamento triginta annorum numero terminatur," see *Liber Concordie*, fol. 12*v*.

[40] On Francesco da Montepulciano, see Cesare Vasoli, "Temi mistici e profetici alla fine del Quattrocento," in his *Studi sulla cultura del Rinascimento* (Manduria: Lacaita, 1968), pp. 217–19; Roberto Ridolfi, *Vita di Niccolò Machiavelli*, 7th ed., rev. (Florence: Sansoni, 1978), p. 516, available in English as *The Life of Niccolò Machiavelli*, tr. Cecil Grayson (Chicago: University of Chicago Press, 1963), p. 259, n. 32; Giampaolo Tognetti, "Note sul profetismo nel Rinascimento e la letteratura relativa," *Bullettino dell'Istituto storico italiano per il Medioevo* 82 (1970) [1974]: 129–57, esp. pp. 143–46; Donald Weinstein, *Savonarola and Florence: Prophecy and Patriotism in the Renaissance* (Princeton: Princeton University Press, 1970), pp.

not an isolated incident but the most significant and most talked-about of a composite series of sermons. Not only do we know that several friars followed his example, among them two non-Florentines who "exclaimed much against Rome and against the present government of the city," but that he inspired others, even women and illiterate common people ("monks, tertiary nuns, young girls, peasants"), to do so as well. Machiavelli wrote to Vettori near the beginning of February 1514 that about Florence "there is nothing to say, except prophecies and announcements of misfortune."[41] Even outside Florence the weeks during December 1513 and January 1514 were filled with prophetic tension in part connected, as we have seen, with the shifting policies of the Holy See. Furthermore, Francesco da Montepulciano himself seems to have had a less specifically Florentine and Tuscan background than has been thought. The Perugian chronicler Teseo Alfani commented, as he noted the sermons that Francesco gave in Perugia between 20 April and 3 May 1513, that "seventeen years ago he was in Perugia studying, then in Padua, and recently [spent] many years in the Kingdom [of Naples] in a hermitage."[42] The *Storia fiorentina* of Jacopo Pitti also records that Francesco was not alone, but was

---

348–49. There is another edition of the sermon of 18 December 1513 not mentioned in these works: *Predica di frate Francesco da Montepulciano de' frati minori conventuali di san Francesco. Fatta in Santa Croce di Fiorenza a di XVIII di dicembre 1513. Raccolta dalla viva voce del predicatore per Ser Lorenzo Vivoli notaio fiorentino, mentre che predicava* (Florence: Stampa ducale, 1569).

[41] Piero Parenti, *Storia fiorentina*, ed. Joseph Schnitzer, in Schnitzer, *Quellen und Forschungen zur Geschichte Savonarolas*, 4 vols. (Munich: J. J. Lentner [E. Stahl, jun.], 1902–1910), vol. 4, *Savonarola nach den Aufzeichnungen des Florentiners Piero Parenti* (Leipzig: Dunker and Humblot, 1910), p. 308; Jacopo Pitti, *Dell'Istoria fiorentina*, *Archivio storico italiano* 1 (1842): 1–208; p. 112. Machiavelli's letter of 4 February 1514 can be found in Niccolò Machiavelli, *Lettere*, ed. Franco Gaeta (Milan: Feltrinelli, 1961), p. 323, and in *The Letters of Machiavelli*, tr. and ed. Allan Gilbert (New York: Capricorn Books, 1961), p. 153 (Gilbert translation used here). Another well-known letter of Machiavelli, dated 19 December 1513, gives an ironic report of the sermon of the previous day, which he himself did not hear, however ("The preaching I did not hear, because I am not given to such doings": Gaeta ed., pp. 308–9; Gilbert trans., p. 148). Vettori answers from Rome on 24 December with prudence: "I shall not respond concerning the hermit because, as you say, Florence is founded under a planet [that makes] such men abound, and they are heard willingly there" (Gaeta ed., p. 313).

[42] Teseo Alfani, *Frammenti inediti delle memorie di Perugia di Teseo Alfani dall'anno 1506 al 1527*, in *Cronache della città di Perugia*, ed. Ariodante Fabretti, 4 vols. (Turin: coi tipi privati dell'editore / dell'autore, 1887–1892), vol. 3, p. 50. Alfani also offers the information that Francesco had preached earlier in the territories of Siena and Florence, and that when he left Perugia "he went to Assisi and then on his trip" (pp. 50–51). The friar's widespread fame is confirmed by Leonello Beliardi, who records that an earthquake occurred in Florence in January 1514, adding that "it had been predicted by a preacher of the Conventual Order of St. Francis, together with many other woes that were supposed to occur in Florence. And that friar nearly died in Florence because of his aversion to the Florentines, and he was held to be a saint. Thousands of people followed after him": Leonello Beliardi, *Cronaca della città di Modena (1512–1518)*, ed. Albano Biondi and Michele Oppi (Modena: Panini, 1981), p. 90.

part of a group of twelve friars—an obviously symbolical number—who "went about Italy, each one in the province assigned to him, preaching and pronouncing on things to come."[43] To judge by the dates of Francesco's itinerant preaching, the group must have formed (perhaps in the hermitage in the south to which Alfani refers) as early as the spring of 1513, and we can suppose that Girolamo da Verona was part of the same group. There are others, however, whom we can place in the same circle, at least hypothetically. There was a Florentine hermit named Giovanni Battista who sent a letter in early May 1513 to the Treasurer of the Patrimony of St. Peter in Orvieto in which he made complex meteorological and political prophesies. We also know that on Christmas Day 1513 a Franciscan preached a sermon in Padua containing predictions that the Venetians would find reassuring, and that he was received "as a saintly man who said many truths about these wars." During the same period, another Franciscan in Naples, "who has a great following among the people, but is held as mad by the principal [citizens]," was forecasting that within two years the Turks would be on Italian soil and the Church would be profoundly shaken and in deep turmoil. He was eventually chased out of the city, but his place was taken by a Carmelite who confirmed this catastrophic picture and added his own prediction that on 2 February 1514 an earthquake would raze Naples. The population spent the night in the streets, quaking with terror and marching in procession, while the Carmelite prudently fled to Sicily.[44]

Even in the context of the intensive preaching activity that was taking place, and even though it is impossible to prove the hypothesis that these preachers were among the companions of Francesco da Montepulciano, it is nonetheless singular that so many instances of prophetic preaching should occur within such a limited time period. The series does not end there, however. In January 1515, the hermit and prophet Bernardino da Parenzo arrived in Venice, accompanied by the Augustinian Anselmo Botturnio.[45] During the same period a friar, Elia da Brescia, who "professed

[43] Pitti, *Dell' Istoria Fiorentina*, p. 112.

[44] Tommaso di Silvestro, *Diario*, pp. 482–83; Sanuto, *Diarii*, vol. 17, cols. 417 and 496; *Cronica anonima dall'anno 1495 all'anno 1519* in *Raccolta di varie croniche, diarj, ed altri opuscoli così italiani come latini appartenenti alla storia del regno di Napoli*, ed. Alessio Aurelio Pelliccia, 5 vols. (Naples: B. Perger, 1780–1782), vol. 1, p. 284.

[45] Sanuto, *Diarii*, vol. 19, cols. 348–49, 383. On Bernardino da Parenzo, see Maria Pia Billanovich, "Una miniera di epigrafi e di antichità. Il Chiostro Maggiore di S. Giustina a Padova," *Italia medioevale e umanistica* 12 (1969): 197–293; Maria Pia Billanovich and Giovanna Mizzon, "Capodistria in età romana e il pittore Bernardino Parenzano," *Italia medioevale e umanistica* 14 (1971): 249–89; Billanovich, "Bernardino da Parenzo pittore e Bernardino (Lorenzo) da Parenzo eremita," *Italia medioevale e umanistica* 24 (1981): 383–404. On Anselmo Botturnio, see Adriano Prosperi, "Botturnio, Anselmo," in DBI, vol. 13, pp. 505–

to be a hermit," preached in the church of the Servites. Fra Elia (whose name alone is indicative) wore the gray mantle of a hermit and preached repentance and fasting to placate the divine wrath directed at Venice. Above all, he organized penitential processions for children that closely recalled other processions through the streets of Orvieto twenty years earlier. In them there were

> little girls and little boys dressed in white with a candle in [their] hands, and there came so many of them that they made more than four hundred, [it was] a terrifying thing to see their agitation, and [there were] many women, and others of the people. . . . And thus with the torches leading them and the cross these boys and girls came out of the church, [followed by] the friars and the preacher, and they went in procession to San Marzilian [San Marziale], Santa Fosca, [and] Rio Terao [Rio Terrà], and went to the bridge of the Axeo [Aseo], returning to the church, singing the litanies, which was terrifying to see and a fearful thing.[46]

Sanudo probably found the procession not to his liking because it offered no chance for political control and because it failed to express the cohesiveness of city life, as was usual in Venetian civic ritual. He spoke of the matter to "someone who can take care of it." In reality, Elia da Brescia had already been called before the Council of Ten two days earlier, along with other preachers, "and they were admonished that in their preaching they not speak of things of state, but only about sins."[47] Prophetic preaching could indeed have political implications and arouse concern among those in charge of public institutions. Sanudo's reservations and those of the Council of Ten did not put a stop to apocalyptical preaching, however. In April 1517 and January 1519, Andrea Baura preached, also prompting Sanudo's disapproval, as we have seen.

One last case that should be mentioned here is that of an unnamed friar who preached in the church of the Friars Minor on Easter Day (4 April) 1518. Sanudo calls him an "homo sanza lettere" and reports his sermon with his usual expressions of disapproval ("he said a thousand crazy things today"). The friar's discourse covered the usual topics, picturing vices and describing divine wrath and consequent castigation ("God is angry with us, soon ruin will be seen . . . God has loosed three million devils and then three thousand"). According to him, the sign of the end would be an earthquake, which could be averted only by the prayers of two saintly men and the good works of the Venetian government.[48]

7; Gutiérrez, "I primi agostiniani italiani," pp. 8–19. In general, see Bernard McGinn, "Circoli gioachimiti veneziani (1450–1530)," *Cristianesimo nella storia* 7 (1986): 19–39.

[46] Sanuto, *Diarii*, vol. 19, col. 462. See also vol. 20, col. 20.

[47] Ibid., vol. 19, col. 460.

[48] Ibid., vol. 25, cols. 338–39.

Condemnation by the Fifth Lateran Council

A clearly defined literary genre emerges from this complex picture. It met with increasing success until 1516, particularly among the *popolari*, and although it faded somewhat with the decrees of the Fifth Lateran Council, it did not cease completely. The Council's decisions, as is known, laid down guidelines for the persecution of preachers who,

> perverting the multiple sense of Holy Scripture . . . preach terrors, threats, imminent catastrophes . . . daring to affirm that they speak through the inspiration and impulse of the Holy Ghost . . . so that simple people, who are the most disposed to be tricked, easily turn to many errors.

Moreover, these preachers inveighed against prelates and even the pope himself, thus giving a scandalous example to the lay population; finally, they pinpointed with undue precision the moment of the advent of the Antichrist and the Day of Judgment.[49]

This picture obviously coincides with what has been outlined in the preceding pages. Significantly, it expresses concern over the success that these preachers encountered among the *semplici*, the *volgo*, and the laity in general. Sanudo repeatedly expresses similar preoccupations, but for somewhat different reasons. For him, prophetic preaching had actual or potential political implications that were difficult to control and could be serious enough to interfere with "le cosse di Stado." Such implications were all the more dangerous because preaching could provide them with a sounding board among a large public of low social status. Sanudo also had little sympathy for the limited literary quality of a homiletics that had no connection with "high" culture.

To judge from the evidence, after 1516 the prophetic preachers toned down their references to the Antichrist and the Day of Judgment and eliminated allusions to precise dates, but they continued to predict approaching calamities (the Turks, earthquakes) and to draw connections between these disasters and the sins of humankind. We have already met Anselmo Botturnio as the companion of the hermit and prophet Bernardino da Parenzo. Botturnio was also credited with the first print edition of Joachimite writings in Venice. During the same period (in 1521) he wrote:

> Est autem duplex prophetia: altera de adventu Salvatoris, et de his quae pertinent ad divinum mysterium; altera vero de futuris comminationibus. Secundam concedunt doctores vigere; priorem vero perfectam esse et completam nullus dubitat.

[49] *Conciliorum Oecumenicorum Decreta*, ed. Giuseppe Alberigo et al. (Bologna: Istituto per le scienze religiose, 1973), pp. 635–37.

He adds:

> Non desunt etiam in Italia, qui divino afflati munere haec et maiora dictitent, et quae futura sint etiam in hoc saeculo in genus christianum maxime ab infidelibus, nisi reges et principes benevolentia et charitate uniti cum Pontifice Max. attentent obviare Dei flagello, et bonis moribus.[50]

A salutary repentance could thus remove the Turkish threat, considered to be the imminent fruit, now ripe ("perfectam . . . et completam"), of divine wrath. There was, of course, no lack of people around Botturnio and within his own order who, "divino afflati munere," had prophesied from the pulpit "de futuris comminationibus." Even Egidio da Viterbo had begun the homily before the Fifth Lateran Council that we have already seen by recalling that for the past twenty years—thus approximately from the start of the Italian wars (once again interpreted as a powerful, though not the only, impetus for the spread of prophecy)—he had worked to explain to the faithful the meaning of prophecies that announced great turmoil for the Church and its ultimate reform. Canisius used similar themes in his preaching as well, even after the decrees of December 1516. In Rome in January 1517 and in Zaragoza in July 1518 he was still preaching "about the things of the Turk and about prophecies."[51]

Andrea Baura's Vocation: A Clarification

Among Botturnio's fellow religious who shared his views and made them their own there was also Andrea Baura. As early as 1513 Baura wrote and published (with a dedication to Lucrezia Borgia) an *Exposition ingeniosa et accomodata a nostri tempi* (the accommodation to "our times" is interesting) of Psalms 14, 15, and 17. This short work noted the *malitia* and the *scandali* present in the Church, even in "ecclesiastical prelates and leaders," and quarreled bitterly, in barely veiled prophetic terms, with Julius II, then at the end of his life and who in fact died ten days after the work was published.[52] Baura states, speaking in the voice of the renewed Church that was to come addressing Christ:

> Other times, when I did not love you, I trusted in terrestrial fortresses, in arms, in soldiers, and in strong walls and ramparts, which I thought invincible; but I was deluding myself, because there is no fortress where you are not.

50 Anselmo Botturnio, *Christiana de indulcentiis assertio* (Venice: Bernardino Vitali, 1521), fol. O 1*v*.

51 Sanuto, *Diarii*, vol. 23, cols. 486–88; 25, col. 600.

52 *Exposition ingeniosa et accomodata a nostri tempi del xiiii. xv. et xvii. Psalmo. Facta per il Sacro Theologo Frate Andrea Ferrarese de lordine de S. Augustino* (Ferrara: Giovanni Mazzocchi, 11 February 1513), fols. A. iii*r*, C. ii*v*, E. ii*v*.

The future pope "chosen according to human will and not according to God" would be no better than his predecessor, and would bring down the severest punishment on the Church. God would of course send preachers throughout the world who, "will speak, preaching and pronouncing on future things" and thus on "the ruin that God has prepared for the Church," but none of them would be believed. Finally, however, Baura continues, the Church would be purged in the most terrible afflictions, the Muslims would be defeated under the sign of the cross, and finally "the peoples who never knew God will be converted just by hearing the divine word pronounced" (an evident echo of reports that had filtered through from the works of Columbus and Vespucci on how easy it was to convert the indigenous populations of the New World). As a final tribulation, the Church would undergo the advent of the Antichrist, but through divine mercy it would be liberated from his seductions and would rule over him and his minions.[53]

Thus by early 1513 Baura had already developed what seem to have been the fundamental motifs of his preaching in 1517 and 1519—the corruption of the Church, especially the vices of the prelates, and prophetic announcement of tremendous divine castigations. Later, and in particular in a sermon given in Ferrara on 21 October 1520, he made a number of affirmations that seemed to his hearers to smack of Lutheranism and he was obliged to retract them.[54] It is improbable, however, that he returned to those statements in the sermon given in Venice on Christmas Day 1520 that aroused the angry reactions of Leo X recorded at the beginning of this chapter: Baura's preaching in Ferrara in 1520 was strictly theological, concerning the nonmeritorious nature of good works and the sinfulness of all mankind, even of the saints, and it contained no criticism of or even any reference whatever to the ecclesiastical hierarchy. Thus it is likely that the sermon preached in Campo Santo Stefano on Christmas Day 1520 was more like the ones Baura had preached in 1517 and 1519, and that the connection with Martin Luther's doctrines was made by his hearers on the basis of information received from Ferrara.

These hypotheses seem confirmed by a work that Baura apparently wrote during the winter of 1520–1521 but that includes a dedication to Cardinal Marco Corner dated Ferrara, 8 November 1521, and was published only in 1523, probably in Milan. It was seen through the press by Anselmo Botturnio, who dedicated it to the general of the Augustinian order, Gabriele della Volta, in a letter dated from San Marco in Milan, 10 April 1523.[55] Baura's work was to be a defense of the apostolic power, as

[53] Ibid., fols. D. ii*r*–*v*; C. ii*v*; E. iiii*r*; G. ii*r*–*v* and iiii*r*; H. i*r*.

[54] Gutiérrez, "I primi agostiniani italiani," pp. 27–29.

[55] Andrea Baura, *Apostolice potestatis defensio. Reverendi patris fratris Andree Baurie ordinis Eremitarum Sancti Augustini sacre Theologie Doctoris eximii ac verbi divini predicatoris celeber-*

its title, *Apostolice potestatis defensio*, indicates. It concluded with the affirmation that the pope was the head of the Church, not in an absolute sense, because the only true head of the Church was Christ, but in the sense that the pope was the vicar of the head, Christ the Lord. The hypothesis that the work represented some sort of abjuration of positions that Baura had held or that it attempted to cover them up is invalidated by the dedicatory letter to Corner:

> Since the renewal of this world is imminent, O most reverend sir, the Lord has called upon me, an ignorant and inexpert and unknowing sinner, to speak. He sent me to scourge the multitude of their vices, to announce his wrath at the sunset with word of his power, and at dawn of his mercy; he sent me to sustain the weak, to comfort the afflicted, and to guide the minds of the reprobate. The impetus of the Spirit constrained me to this purpose, and yet I resisted. Jesus Christ, whose servant I am, is my witness to how many times I fled his presence; still, my mind, in his light, gave presage of future things. I went where the Lord called me; I wearied myself with crying until my throat was hoarse, until I saw the word of God transformed into a serpent, and good interpreted as evil. According to the imperious force of my calling, I reproached the vices of this world and detested them, and the world said, "Whoever disdains and detests the power of Rome scorns and condemns the authority of the Roman pontiff!" Yet I have always praised [that authority] and I have always upheld it to the best of my ability, since I knew that it derives from Christ—even if I have always put Christ before it.[56]

This passage offers an excellent grasp both of the ideology that underlay Baura's thought and of the general orientation of prophetic preaching in his time. We should note first that from the start Baura places his text against a background of apocalyptical expectation ("instante iam saeculi mutatione") and that it is a tissue of biblical echoes that add further meaning. What Baura does here is to put himself in the place of the psalmist surrounded by his enemies (Ps. 69:4, "laboravi clamans, raucae factae sunt fauces meae"; "I have labored with crying; my jaws are become hoarse") who says, a few lines later, "For the zeal of thy house hath eaten me up: and the reproaches of them that reproached thee are fallen on me." Even more, he identifies with the image of the Old Testament prophets, Jeremiah in particular, who "does not know how to speak" and on whom Yahweh prevails with force, constraining him to cry out ceaselessly against the iniquities of Jerusalem despite his attempts to contain the fire that burns in

---

rimi. In Lutherum (n.p., n.d.). Botturnio's dedication to Gabriele della Volta is on fols. 1*v*–2*r*, unnumbered; Baura's dedication to Cardinal Marco Corner is on fols. 2*v*–3*r*, also unnumbered.

[56] Ibid., fol. 2*v*, unnumbered. It can be found in Latin in Gutiérrez, "I primi agostiniani italiani," pp. 31–32.

his bones (Jer. 1:5–6 and 20:7–9). In this context, the phrase "Reprehendebam ego secundum imperium vocationis meae vitia orbis" (here translated "according to the imperious force of my calling, I reproached the vices of this world") leaves little room for doubt: It was the prophet's vocation that Baura feels has been imposed on him. Whether he wills it or no, his mind, enlightened by the light of Christ, foresees future things; he feels himself propelled by the force of the Spirit to cry out against reprobates. It is understandable, at this point, why this Ferrarese Augustinian might have spoken "ill of the pope and of the Roman court," but this does not mean that he adhered to Luther's positions. His work, then, was intended to clear up a misunderstanding. Because the pope had prohibited the publication of the work, the dedication continues, Baura was dedicating it to Cardinal Corner in the hope that Corner would transmit his sentiments to the pope, along with his desire to be a defender of power and of the Church of Rome forever, but it would also send word that he was an implacable adversary ("usque ad mortem oppugnator pro viribus infestissimus") of abuses among Christians.[57]

This dedicatory letter must not have been sufficiently reassuring, for the *Apostolice potestatis defensio* remained unpublished for yet another year and a half, until it was published in April 1523 through the good graces of an indefatigable protector of prophets, Anselmo Botturnio.

Friar Girolamo Piumazzo of Verona

In the meantime, during approximately the same weeks, a case was unfolding that involved Baura, albeit indirectly. On 26 March 1523 he wrote to his friend Gaspare Sardi that his teacher, Girolamo "the Bearded" of Verona, had been imprisoned in Piacenza on the accusation of having spread the heresy of Luther.[58] Maestro Girolamo was still in jail on 14 September of that year. In fact, Gabriele della Volta gave orders not to release him "so as not to confirm the calumnies relayed to the pope that the Order was hypocritical in suppressing heretics."[59] This was a rumor that certainly had also been spread at the time of the equivocal affair concerning Baura, whose work Della Volta, the general of the order, had only a few months before agreed to allow Botturnio to dedicate to him, thus in some measure becoming its sponsor. But who could this personage have been? Memory first suggests another Augustinian, Girolamo of Verona, who in 1513 had preached *per profetia* in Venice in the wake of the *Concordie Novi ac Veteris*

[57] Baura, *Apostolice potestatis defensio*, fol. 3*r*, unnumbered.

[58] Biblioteca Estense di Modena, cod. it. 833 (= α.G. I.15 [23]).

[59] Hubert Jedin, *Papal Legate at the Council of Trent, Cardinal Seripando*, tr. Frederic C. Eckhoff (St. Louis: B. Herder, 1947), p. 132, note.

Testamenti of Joachim of Fiore. This is an interesting hypothesis for several reasons. For one, if it were verified it would confirm, as was already apparent in the case of Baura, the complex, multifaceted relations between prophetic preaching and Lutheran preaching (or presumed Lutheran preaching). On the one hand, the emergence of new patterns of analysis and judgment, based on widespread knowledge of Luther and his work, might lead the public (or a part of the public) to judge as "Lutheran" preachers who were not and had no intention of being so. (This misunderstanding of course might also arise as an oblique effect of the diffusion of certain aspects of Lutheran propaganda, such as its antiecclesiastical tone.) On the other hand, familiarity with Lutheran themes could truly lead (as seems likely in the case of Girolamo of Verona) from prophecy to heresy, and all the more easily within an order in which the study of the works of Joachim traditionally accompanied that of the theology of St. Augustine and which identified the hermits of St. Augustine as the *eremiti* of the third age announced by the abbot of Fiore.[60]

A letter sent a few years later by Girolamo Aleandro, at that time papal nuncio in Venice, provides information on other aspects of the personality of Fra Girolamo of Verona. Aleandro says:

> One Friar Girolamo, Veronese, also called Piumazzo . . . was once retained [imprisoned] in Piacenza on the orders of the bishop of Fano [Goro Gheri], then governor of that city, and [was] sentenced to perpetual imprisonment as a Lutheran. He was sent to Bologna, where he remained in jail for six or seven years and then, at the bidding of I know not what important person [*prencipale*] he was pardoned, [and] was no sooner out of prison than he went to Verona, and in spite of the prohibition of the bishop he insisted on preaching, whereupon [he], returning to his vomit, was by the diligence of that bishop [and] the arm of the Signoria sent out of that city and diocese. It appears that now he boasts of planning to come to Rome and, through great people, of obtaining restitution of his citizenship and his preaching, which, if it were to happen, would much displease that good prelate.[61]

60 Marjorie Reeves, "Joachimist Expectations in the Order of Augustinian Hermits," *Recherches de théologie ancienne et médiévale* 25 (1958): 111–41.

61 Girolamo Aleandro to the apostolic protonotary Ambrogio Recalcati, Venice, 16 June 1535, in *Nunziature di Venezia*, ed. Franco Gaeta, Fonti per la storia d'Italia (Rome: Istituto storico italiano per l'età moderna e contemporanea, 1958–), vol. 1, pp. 316–17. Goro Gheri moved from Piacenza to Bologna as deputy of the papal legate, Innocenzo Cibo, in the autumn of 1524, and remained in that city until his death in 1528 (Maria Ferretti, "Legati, vicelegati e governatori di Bologna nel sec. XVI," tesi di laurea discussa presso l'Università di Bologna a.a. 1967–1968, relatore Paolo Prodi, p. 108). Consequently we can suppose that Piumazzo's transfer to the prison in Bologna occurred when Gheri moved from Piacenza to Bologna. In this case the dates would be, approximately: Lent 1523, arrest and imprisonment in Piacenza; 1524–1531, imprisonment in Bologna; 1532–1533, preaching in Verona and expulsion by Giberti.

Girolamo of Verona had thus been sentenced to life imprisonment. He must have enjoyed good protection, however, if he was subsequently liberated and if he was sentenced to no worse than exile when he relapsed in Verona. The letter (which is dated 16 June 1535) also tells us his last name, Piumazzo (thus *barbato* must have been an epithet), which enables us to identify him better. We know of the Augustinian Girolamo Piumazzo of Verona that he was a celebrated preacher much in demand, in particular thanks to his promotion of various state funds such as the Monti di Pietà and the matrimonial *monti*.[62] He preached in Venice during Lent in 1513, as we have seen; in 1514 he preached in Salerno;[63] in 1516 he was in Palermo, where in fact he incited the population against the city's Jews (preaching in favor of the Monti di Pietà was often violently anti-Semitic).[64] In 1517 he was invited to Ravenna by the Augustinian community there, and he received permission to accept from Egidio da Viterbo.[65]

A remarkable figure emerges from the picture we have gradually pieced together: a famous preacher requested throughout Italy, a man who until the Fifth Lateran Council adhered to the models of apocalyptical prophecy but who also propagandized for the Monti di Pietà, yet who ended up a Lutheran. Girolamo Piumazzo thus offers another example—with its own specific characteristics, and occurring at a precociously early date—to add to those of other famous preachers of the Augustinian order imprisoned for doctrinal reasons and then liberated, either under the guarantee of influential persons or because of their own ability to plead their own defense.[66] As we read in Aleandro, the affair had a sequel, since Piumazzo returned to Verona to preach, "non ostante la prohibitione del vescovo." We know how jealously Gian Matteo Giberti watched over the preaching in his diocese. The affair of Father Ludovico Mantovano, three and a half years after Aleandro's letter, clearly shows the great care the bishop of Ve-

[62] Onofrio Panvinio, *De urbis Veronae viris doctrina et bellica virtute illustribus* (Verona, 1621). The same information (taken from Panvinio's work in manuscript, however) can be found in Giuseppe Panfilo, *Chronica Ordinis Fratrum Eremitarum Sancti Augustini* (Rome: Georgii Ferrarrii, 1581), pp. 112–13, which gives Piumazzo's place and date of death (incorrectly, as we shall see) as Venice in 1534.

[63] As can be deduced from a letter dated 4 May 1514 from Gabriele della Volta to Ambrogio Flandino, named a commissioner of the order, along with Girolamo da Genazzano, "in decernenda controversia quae est inter magistrum Hieronymym Veronensem et conventum salernitanum super eleemosyna praedicationis," for which see Gutiérrez, "I primi agostiniani italiani," p. 39.

[64] Tommaso Fazello, *Le due deche dell'historia di Sicilia* (Venice: Domenico e Gio. Battist. Guerra, 1574), p. 894.

[65] Luigi Torelli, *Secoli agostiniani, overo Historia generale del Sacro Ordine Eremetano del gran dottore . . . S. Aurelio Agostino*, 8 vols. (Bologna: Giacomo Monti, 1659–1686), vol. 8, pp. 25, 191.

[66] *Nunziature di Venezia*, vol. 1, p. 316; Pio Paschini, "Episodi di lotta contro l'eresia nell'Italia del primo Cinquecento," *Euntes docete* 9 (1956): 497–513.

rona took to avoid any shadow of suspicion among his clergy. He preferred to nip any ambiguous affair in the bud, "considering," as he wrote to Contarini on 25 February 1539, "the place in which I live and the account that I have to give of myself both here and elsewhere."[67]

Giberti's anxieties are less interesting for our purposes than the precedents for the Augustinian's preaching and his ties with Baura. If we accept the hypothesis that Girolamo Piumazzo of Verona, Andrea Baura's teacher, was the same person as the Girolamo da Verona who preached in Venice *per profetia* on 20 March 1513 and who perhaps belonged to the group of twelve prophets connected with Francesco da Montepulciano who preached throughout the Italian peninsula during the course of 1513, several aspects of the work of the Ferrarese Augustinian would clearly take on a more specific meaning. The *Exposition ingeniosa* was in fact written and published at the beginning of 1513, and Baura did indeed speak of the imminent tribulations brought on by the Antichrist and warn that many preachers would "speak throughout the world, preaching, and predicting things to come." Was this a reference to Francesco da Montepulciano and his companions, who were at that very moment beginning their prophetic pilgrimage through Italy? Certainly, those final months of the papacy of Julius II and the first year of that of Leo X, a time of overlapping but changing pontifical policies, were also a time of high prophetic tension, still apocalyptic in tone.[68] In those months there were still some who awaited the end of time; when Baura returned to the same topic at the end of 1520—if indeed he did—people found it disconcerting because the situation had changed too much. Too many alarm bells (still uncoordinated at this point) were all set to ring, even at the touch of the wrong hands. Then in 1523, control over extremist preaching tightened further, and Girolamo Piumazzo spent many long years in prison.

Other Augustinian Prophets

The case of Baura, with all its aftereffects, did not close the era of prophetic preaching, however. In Milan, in the monastery of San Marco (where Botturnio was living at the time) there was between 1521 and 1523 a friar, "a man of very high repute, old, and he had a great beard, and he was of the order of St. Augustine, a hermit."[69] According to Giovan Marco Burigozzo, the chronicler to whom we owe this description, this friar was one

[67] Adriano Prosperi, "Un processo per eresia a Verona verso la metà del Cinquecento," *Quaderni storici* 15 (1970): 773–94; quotation on p. 792.

[68] See chap. 2, and Weinstein, *Savonarola and Florence*, pp. 350, 353–55.

[69] *Cronache milanesi scritte da Giovan Pietro Cagnola, Giovanni Andrea Prato e Giovan Marco Burigozzo, Archivio storico italiano* 3 (1842): 1–598; p. 436.

of the moving forces behind the resistance against the French. (There were a good number of anti-French Augustinian hermits during those years.) He preached during Lent in 1521 and again that year during Advent. On Candlemas in 1522 he led a great procession from the Duomo to the church of Sant'Ambrogio in a snowstorm ("it was snowing terribly that Sunday"). There were children dressed in white, singing; the clergy of Milan followed, first the regular and then the secular clergy. More important, all the able-bodied men from every parish in the city walked in the procession, each delegation with its captain, its banner, its corporals, its militia, and its drums, and all ready, according to Burigozzo, "to offer their lives and their possessions for the defense of the homeland and against the French." This same militia provided the city troops that did in fact fight against the French, along with imperial troops, in the victory over the French at the battle of the Bicocca the following April.

In the months that followed, the Augustinian seems to have played an increasingly important role: "In this time of war he comforted the souls of the Milanese against the French . . . and he had a banner made with a cross on it" that was kept in the Duomo "in order to carry it against the French" in an eventual conflict. Above all, Botturnio's fellow brother (and we cannot exclude the possibility that he was Botturnio himself) enlivened his preaching with prophetic inspiration: "he delighted in striving to seem a prophet and in divining things that were to come." He had a large following, particularly, as Burigozzo says with scorn, among "homenazzi, donazole e poltronaglia" (no-account men, idle women, and riffraff). Some in the ecclesiastical hierarchy were less enthusiastic, as can be seen from an episode that took place one Sunday in Advent in 1523. The bearded friar ("questo frate de Santo Marco della barbassa") was preaching in the Duomo and the sermon "was going on and on." The priests who were to officiate lost patience and while he was still preaching they began to chant the Introit at the high altar, thus provoking wrath and insults from "hangers-on and little women." The chronicler comments that "anyone among them who managed to say ought against these revered priests was lucky."[70]

This episode provides more than an evident case of prophetic preaching in support of political propaganda in the bosom of an order that seems to have been extremely open to such tendencies at the time. It also shows active disagreement within the Church in Milan, a disagreement that was not stilled by the preacher's embrace of the city's cause. Thus on one side we have the Augustinian friar's active supporters—"homenazzi, donazole e poltronaglia," the audience of choice of the prophets; on the other, the Ambrosian secular clergy, who took every opportunity to try to silence him. They got what they needed soon after in a letter dated 12 January 1524 from Clement VII, who enjoined the archbishop of Milan to enforce

[70] Ibid., pp. 443–44.

the Lateran decree of 1516 concerning preaching, a decree that gradually acquired a new urgency after 1520 and the first cases of Lutheran propaganda.[71]

An Umbrian Hermit and the Sack of Rome

Antiprophetic repression found it harder to move against the hermits. As we have seen, they continued to circulate for a decade after the decrees of the Fifth Lateran Council, flanked (after 1525) by the Capuchins, with whom they were for a time confused. Lancellotti says repeatedly that Giuseppe Piantanida went about "dressed as a hermit," and Matteo da Bascio followed the hermits' patterns of itinerant preaching for his entire lifetime.[72] The episode concerning Brandano is well known, so let us turn instead to a hermit who preached in Orvieto in March 1528. According to Giovan Maria della Porta, writing to Eleonora Gonzaga on 9 March, the hermit wore "the dress of St. John the Baptist," was twenty-four years of age, and "preaches in the public squares about other major disasters that are to come to Rome and to Italy, which will last for all XXIX [1529], and in XXX [1530] the Church is to be renewed." According to this man, the Turks would defeat the emperor, the pope, and the king of France in a great battle near Viterbo, but would later convert to Christianity.[73] He was perhaps the same person as the hermit who arrived in Camerino in July and "went through the city crying *misericordia* with the little children."[74] It

[71] Federico Chabod, *Lo stato e la vita religiosa a Milano nell'epoca di Carlo V* (Turin: G. Einaudi, 1971), p. 232. Contrary to Chabod's opinion, however, the provision was not directly correlated with the sermons of the prophet friar, as demonstrated by analogous letters sent at precisely the same time to the papal nuncios in Venice and Naples: See Bartolommeo Fontana, *Documenti vaticani contro l'eresia luterana in Italia* (Rome: R. Società di storia patria, 1892), pp. 12–13 and 16–17. See also below, p. 147.

[72] Lancellotti, *Cronaca modenese*, vol. 5, pp. 296–97, and vol. 6, pp. 237–38; Arsenio da Ascoli, *La predicazione dei cappuccini nel Cinquecento in Italia* (Loreto [Ancona]: Libreria S. Francesco d'Assisi, 1956), p. 244; Melchior de Pobladura, "La 'Severa riprensione' di fra Matteo da Bascio"; Costanzo Cargnoni, "Alcuni aspetti del successo della riforma cappuccina nei primi cinquant'anni (1525–1575)," in *Le origini della riforma cappuccina* (Ancona: Curia provinciale Frati Cappuccini, 1979), pp. 227–28 and 232–34.

[73] Archivio di Stato di Firenze, *Urbino*, cl. I, div. G 266, fol. 68*v*. Given the difference in their ages, it does not seem to me acceptable to identify this personage as Brandano, as in Ludwig von Pastor, *Geschichte der päpste seit dem ausgang des mittelalters*, 16 vols. (Freiburg im Breisgau; St Louis: Herder, 1886–1933). This reference can be found in the English version, *The History of the Popes from the Close of the Middle Ages*, 40 vols. (n.p.: Consortium Books, [1977?]), vol. 9, p. 379.

[74] Bernardino Lilio, *Diario* (at the date 10 July 1528), cited in Melchior de Pobladura, *Historia generalis Ordinis Fratrum Minorum Cappuccinorum*, 3 vols. (Rome: Institutum Historicum Ord. Fr. Min. Cap., 1947–1951), vol. 1, p. 53. To tell the truth, Lilio speaks of a "frate scappucino," but given the confusion between hermits and Capuchins, this may not invalidate the identification proposed.

is even more likely that he was the "hermit dressed in sackcloth" from near Perugia who came to Venice on 18 May 1529:

> This morning in several churches and later today when the Council had convened, a hermit dressed in sackcloth, barefoot and with nothing on his head, with a wooden staff with the cross at the top, also in wood, of Perosan [Perugian] nationality, from Torre, twenty miles from Perosa [Perugia], of [ ] years of age, named [ ], newly come to this land, climbed onto the banns stone and exhorted everyone to repentance and to doing good, saying, "the sentence has been passed, God intends to renew the world, Venice, mend your ways! The Turk has embarked, for the ruination of Christians, and will cross the Arete [Adese?]! Repent!" and other such words, and many wondered who he was. This man does not want money, only [food] to live on, he leads a rude life, and he beats his chest with a large marble stone as St. Jerome did. If someone gives him a *bezo* or two he takes it and gives it to the poor.[75]

What is striking about this account, beyond its most visibly spectacular aspects (the large stone with which the hermit beats his chest, in imitation of current iconography of St. Jerome), is its fidelity to a pattern we have seen several times before. Just like the learned Augustinian, Baura, fifteen years earlier, he promised destruction and castigation to Rome and to Italy, the coming of the Turks and their victory over Christian forces, their eventual conversion, and the renewal of the Church. These themes can also be found in prophetic works in vernacular verse such as the *Prophetia de santo Anselmo* or the *Prophetia trovata in Roma intagliata in marmoro*, which had begun to circulate some twenty years earlier.[76] One could certainly cite other texts that follow the same or an analogous pattern. We could also hypothesize direct knowledge of them on the part of the hermit (we know, for example, that Brandano read and used a Venetian vernacular edition of the *Pronosticatio* of Johannes Lichtenberger).[77] Furthermore, 1530 was the date that completed the fifty-first generation after the birth of Christ in the calculations that Girolamo of Verona presented in 1513 to the faithful of Venice, basing his predictions on Joachim of Fiore. The date had for some years circulated in other contexts as the moment at which the Church was to be totally renewed. In the last analysis, though, it seems more fruitful to place the preaching of this itinerant prophet (in Orvieto in particular)

[75] Sanuto, *Diarii*, vol. 50, cols. 341–42, 345.

[76] Also in circulation, but, from what I can gather, only in manuscript, was a *Profizia dell'anno 1180 nell'indizione nona per il Serenissimo e clarissimo Re di Jerusalem pacifico Signor del Regno di Cipri ad Urbano P.*, which was probably the direct source of the *Prophetia trovata in Roma*. The *Profizia* (which can be dated to the second half of the Quattrocento) is available under that title, edited by P. Fanfani, in *Il Borghini* 1 (1863): 755–57. There is a sixteenth-century copy with a few variants, untitled but bearing the notation "Reperta in antiquo codice scripta," inserted among other texts dated 1521–1522 in the MS Class. 287 of the Biblioteca Classense of Ravenna, Poesie italiane e latine, fols. 9*v*–11*r*.

[77] Tognetti, "Profezie," p. 327.

within the tense and confused atmosphere of Italy after the sack of Rome in 1527 and before the Congress of Bologna in 1529–1530. Both the hermit's words and the letter reporting them betray a greater sense of anxiety than preceding and apparently analogous texts do. They echo a sense of urgency for the immediate reform of the Church, which faced present *ruine* while *altre maggiori* lay in wait for it. In short, even if events in this viscous history are now so remote that they seem identical (or nearly so), we cannot lump them together or view them as equally important. Given that the conditions and circumstances of Italian political history were constantly changing in those early decades of the Cinquecento, such events acquire their full meaning only when we observe them as one would look at a transparent overlay placed on an ever-changing ground.

The Breakdown of Prophetic Preaching: The Story of Zaccheria da Fivizzano

As the imperial army made its way through Italy in 1529–1530, the pressure of events prompted a new rash of prophecy (less energetic than before, however) that even infected official preaching. Such was the case of the Spanish Dominican Tommaso Nieto, who preached in 1529 in the Duomo in Milan when Spanish troops and *Landsknechten* were bivouacked in the city ("whose fury anyone was indeed fortunate to rein in," Burigozzo commented, as he outlined a miserable but all too familiar picture of the violence and indignities to which the people were subjected by the Spanish and the *Lanzi*).[78] In April of that year Nieto organized a general procession to ask God to forsake his castigations, and as the months passed and tension mounted in the city, his sermons assumed a prophetic tone, remaining so vague, however ("for he was considered our prophet by the greater part of the people, and thus he prophesied and said, 'Stay, do not fear, it will not be, or it will be' "), that they give the impression—at least in Burigozzo's report of them—of aiming at little more than social control and quieting a nervous public opinion ("giving them to hear comforting rubbish"). Nieto's message was more pointed in a sermon that he gave on 5 September 1529, after an embassy had left Milan to confer with Charles V at Piacenza ("there they were to settle the affairs of Christendom"). Probably on the basis of that rumor, Nieto

> gave a most desperate sermon with great threats, not so much for Milan as for all Christendom; but he said that Milan would have the beginning of the renovation of the Church, and for this reason it must be the first afflicted and the last renewed; and he said much, particularly about the great carnage that will soon come to pass. And he said that it was not he who was speaking, no, but

[78] On Nieto, see *Cronache milanesi*, pp. 485–500.

by the mouth of the Holy Ghost . . . and [that] there was no cause to marvel at what he said, and furthermore, he said to me, "Write, when you are at home." And at the end of his sermon he had [everyone] cry *misericordia* two times.[79]

The interconnections between politics and prophecy are clear in this passage, particularly in the relationship between the emperor's approach as he traveled toward Bologna and the expectation of "la renovazion de la eclesia." In point of fact, as we shall see in a later chapter, the accent in the last burst of prophecy that occurred, precisely, in 1530 gradually shifted from the imminence of God's chastisement to proclamation of a peaceful reform of the Church by means of a long-awaited emperor who would inaugurate a new Golden Age.

The language of prophecy was wearing thin, however. Discouraged by the ecclesiastical hierarchy, less and less engrossing to the people, no longer able (after the accords of 1529–1530) to draw on the disasters that followed on the heels of military engagements or armies passing through, it lost its efficacy and its bite. One relevant example of how prophetic language lost significance is a sermon given by the Dominican Fra Zaccheria da Fivizzano in the church of Santa Reparata in Florence, on Sunday, 10 January, thus during the city's ten-month siege by the papal and imperial troops before it surrendered on 12 August 1530.[80] We know from Benedetto Varchi that it was the preaching of Fra Zaccheria, together with that of Benedetto da Foiano, that kept up the morale of the Florentines during those months by encouraging and praising the republican government of the city, bitterly criticizing Pope Clement VII and the Medici family, and promising certain victory to the besieged city in the name of God. Fra Zaccheria belonged to the monastery of San Marco and, in Varchi's words, he "followed the discipline of Savonarola."[81] Fra Zaccheria had in fact defended his reputation before the Synod of Florence in 1516 against the accusation of heresy, stating, in particular, that the concept of the renovation of the Church as Savonarola made use of it was not in itself heretical.

[79] Ibid., p. 498.

[80] The sermon, edited by Carlo Gargiolli, is published in *Il Propugnatore* 12, no. 1 (1879): 417–33. Gargiolli based his edition on a contemporary pamphlet in his possession, *Predica fatta la domenica fra loctava della Epiphania dal Reverendo P. fra Zacheria da Lunigiana frate di san Marcho in sancta Reparata Racholta da uno amico* (n.p., n.d.), in octavo, 12 fols.

[81] Benedetto Varchi, *Storia fiorentina*, ed. Lelio Arbib, 3 vols. (Florence: Società delle storie del Nardi e del Varchi, 1838–1841), vol. 1, p. 474, and vol. 2, pp. 258, 414. Benedetto da Foiano had preached in a prophetic vein in Venice, in the church of the Incurabili, in the weeks immediately following the sack of Rome: "He preached four hours; gave a prophecy of the Apocalypse which interpreted all this ruin of Rome; he said much ill of the pope, cardinals, etc. and much good of the emperor, and he talked much too much" (Sanuto, *Diarii*, vol. 45, cols. 321–22). Benedetto da Foiano had also preached in Venice during Lent 1526, but on that occasion he had asked only that "four things be taken care of: blasphemy, the Lutherans, having justice, and having pious places" (Sanuto, *Diarii*, vol. 41, col. 113).

Quite to the contrary, insofar as it signified moral renewal its urgency was even clear in the deliberations of the Council in course, "quia Iulius papa II non nisi pro reformatione Ecclesie concilium generale convocavit."[82] It is interesting that Fra Zaccheria thought it necessary to base this concept on a clearly prophetic passage in Joel ("ecclesiam . . . fore renovandam per abundantiam Spiritus sancti, quem Deus effundet super omnem carnem"). Joel 2:28 continues, "Your sons and your daughters shall prophesy: your old men shall dream dreams, and your young men shall see visions," going on to announce the "great and dreadful day of the Lord," probably the tacit basis for Zaccheria's proposed renewal of the Church.

If we examine the text of Fra Zaccheria's 1530 sermon in the vernacular, however, we realize that at that date not even this Savonarolan still accepted the models of prophetic preaching as they have been described above, and that if he speaks of the renewal of the Church, he does so on a very different basis than was the case in 1516. His homily, in fact, follows an outline that merits close analysis. Judicious men of the world and the timorous say that Florence has been sold out, he declares, but in reality

> when God sends a great scourge to a city that is full of sin, and when for all that reason it does not convert or repent, it is a manifest sign that it will go ill and that it has no remedy. As it happens . . . Florence . . . is filled with sins. . . . It has already been struck by God several times with great tribulations; it has had famine and great pestilence; now it has the war that wounds it to the bone, and nonetheless it will not convert. . . . What is there then to say, if not that it will be destroyed and that there is no remedy. There are still certain prophecies that strongly threaten the city and say that it is given over to fire and will be burned.

The *ragioni dei paurosi* are obviously those of the prophetic preachers of twenty years earlier. To oppose them, Fra Zaccheria continues, there are the reasons of the simple, who have faith in God. The simple know that the Lord can permit reason and justice to be oppressed, yes, but not extinguished; they know that there is sin in Florence, but there are also works of charity and mercy. As for the prophecies, "if we have to depend upon them, we have better, differently founded prophecies than those prudent men had, because we have heard them with our own ears and seen a great many of them come true thus far."

The living memory of Savonarola, whom Fra Zaccheria claims to have heard with his own ears, is thus opposed to a model of prophetic preaching that by that time had become rigid, a model that this Dominican rejected as good only for the timid. Even though he refers obsequiously to the

[82] Alceste Giorgetti, "Fra' Luca Bettini e la sua difesa del Savonarola," *Archivio storico italiano* 47, pt. 2 (1919): 164–231; p. 216. See also Weinstein, *Savonarola and Florence*, pp. 359–61.

prophecies of his master, somehow it was the prophecy practiced day by day in his own time that he denies.

> I am not a prophet, nor do I speak to you as a prophet, because I do not want to arrogate to myself what I do not possess; but I speak to you as a preacher according to Holy Scripture, according to the doctrine of the saints, according to the order of divine providence, insofar as we can know it, and according to reason and natural discourse.

It is precisely on the basis of natural reason that Fra Zaccheria moves on to his final and definitive argument:

> When the world is ruined and has grown old in vice, God is accustomed to renew it and take it back. . . . Now, we see the world more corrupt than ever, because the faith of Christ is nearly reduced to one corner of the world. . . . What shall we say, then? We shall say that God will do what he is accustomed to doing, that is, to renew it and yet another time purge it. Why do you think that he has begun to send so many scourges if not to reform and renew his Church? . . . Because it is nearly totally aged and corrupted by sins, he has begun to purge it with the scourge, and he will not rest until he has set it up again according to his way. . . . Thus believe me, God will take away the old rubbish that is in the Church today and will make a totally renewed house and vineyard.[83]

Taken as a whole, these arguments closely resemble those of Gasparo Contarini fifteen years earlier (in 1516, at a singularly early date), who used the image of the wheel of fortune to state (respectfully, to be sure) his disagreement with Savonarola:

> This renovation of the Church I know not by prophecy, but natural and divine reason dictate it to me. The natural because human things do not go according to an infinite straight line, but go according to a circular line; although all do not make a perfect circle and when they have come to a certain term in their augmentation they then move higher. You apply this. Divine reason also tells me that sometimes God must regulate his Church, the which should [be] highly desired by all Christians.[84]

The substance of the discrepancy between the figure of Savonarola as a symbol of prophecy and the demand for a reform of the Church dictated

[83] *Predica fatta la domenica*, pp. 428, 432, 434, 435–36.

[84] Felix Gilbert, "Contarini on Savonarola: An Unknown Document of 1516," *Archiv für Reformationsgeschichte* 59 (1968): 145–75; p. 149. See also Bartolomeo Cerretani, "Storie in dialogo della mutatione di Firenze," in Joseph Schnitzer, *Quellen und Forschungen zur Geschichte Savonarolas*, 3 vols. (Munich: J. J. Lentner [E. Stahl, jun.], 1902–1904), vol. 3, pp. 91–92, referring to the year 1520. On the image of the wheel of fortune, see Giorgio Stabile, "La ruota della fortuna: tempo ciclico e ricorso storico," in *Scienze, credenze occulte, livelli di cultura. Convegno internazionale di studi (Firenze, 26–30 giugno 1980)* (Florence: L. S. Olschki, 1982), pp. 477–503.

by natural and divine reason reemerges in the words of Fra Zaccheria. Moreover, speaking in the very name of Savonarola, Zaccheria rejects and refutes a model of preaching that for at least the two preceding decades had spread among extremely broad and socially differentiated segments of the population first an eschatological expectation of the end and then the expectation of catastrophes—the Turks, wars—that were human but immediate and terrible. From 1530 on, this channel for the diffusion of prophecy among a popular audience ran dry, as did the others. The hermits no longer found a hearing, *cantastorie* and printers turned to other materials, monsters acquired a different significance, and the pulpit no longer served to predict the future but rather to negate the present or to suggest a wide variety of changes in the Church. In this sense, it is singular and significant that it was precisely the preaching of a Savonarolan that gives us the most comprehensive sign of the end of a culture.

Fra Zaccheria was to preach again. We find him as an official reader (*lettore condotto*) of Sacred Scripture, paid by the Signoria of Venice "with a salary of fifty *ducati* a year for expenses and to buy books," first, in August 1532, in the church of the Trinità and, after June 1533, also in San Zanipolo.[85] He occasionally preached in other churches as well. Sanudo did not like his homilies ("he goes on and on . . . he did not give a good sermon . . . he said a lot of nonsense"),[86] and in fact the Dominican was much more appreciated by the *ignoranti* and the *idioti* than by the *dotti*, in particular in his readings of the epistles of St. Paul held in the church of the Trinità (in San Zanipolo he read Ecclesiastes). As the papal nuncio, Girolamo Aleandro, wrote to Iacopo Salviati, papal secretary, on 15 August 1533:

> [Fra Zaccheria] read . . . the epistles of St. Paul with the exposition always in the vernacular, for which he has an audience of many more ignorant and common people than of the learned, a thing that certainly pleased me little, because sacred doctrine is not subject to being put into the hands of common and simple people, particularly when we know that the Lutheran heresy has multiplied and grown in Germany by this way alone.[87]

Aleandro's fears were well founded. On 8 May a carpenter, Mastro Antonio da Rialto, was arrested as a Lutheran, and it came out in the interrogations that he had assiduously attended the readings from St. Paul at the church of the Trinità and, "after the readings . . . started to speak," denying free will, among other things.[88] The personal position of the reader aside, public readings of the Bible could thus in themselves give

[85] Sanuto, *Diarii*, vol. 56, cols. 777, 846–47, and vol. 58, col. 246.

[86] Ibid., vol. 57, col. 376; vol. 58, col. 22.

[87] *Nunziature di Venezia*, vol. 1, p. 104.

[88] Franco Gaeta, "Documenti da codici vaticani per la storia della riforma in Venezia. Appunti e documenti," *Annuario dell'Istituto storico italiano per l'età moderna e contemporanea* 7 (1955): 27. See also the other interrogations on pp. 25–26.

heretical opinions a chance to jell. Rome reacted with alarm, and on 1 October Tommaso Badia, master of the Sacred Palace, transmitted peremptory orders to Aleandro to prohibit this new custom of reading the Bible in the vernacular in public in the churches unless the preachers involved underwent preliminary examination.[89] Fra Zaccheria continued to preach in spite of everything. The last remaining trace of prophecy in his homiletics was a violent antiecclesiastical and antipapal tone. (Like Andrea Baura fifteen years earlier, he "spoke ill of the pope and of the Roman court," however, with a more specific political and anti-Medicean purpose.) Aleandro shrewdly noted that this was precisely why Zaccheria found favor with the Signoria and with the public, who were thus led to listen more trustingly to the refutation of Lutheran opinions that Aleandro encouraged.[90] Thus prophetic preaching could be taken as Lutheran, as in the case of Baura; it could become Lutheran, as with Girolamo Piumazzo; finally, a reformed Savonarolan could be manipulated and transformed into an anti-Lutheran preacher, as happened with Fra Zaccheria, thanks to Aleandro's political skill.

In the end, the last resistance was vanquished, and Fra Zaccheria was induced to throw himself at the feet of Clement VII and beg his pardon. On the return trip, however, he died unexpectedly, some said of poison.[91]

[89] Fontana, *Documenti vaticani*, pp. 73–74.

[90] Girolamo Aleandro to Pietro Carnesecchi, Venice, 13 March 1534, in *Nunziature di Venezia*, vol. 1, pp. 178–79.

[91] Benedetto Varchi asserts that the meeting with the pope occurred in Perugia, but this seems doubtful because Clement died on 26 September 1534 and had already been sick for many months (Varchi, *Storia fiorentina*, vol. 2, p. 498). The rumor of Zaccheria's death by poison is reported in Roberto Ridolfi, *Vita di Girolamo Savonarola*, 2 vols. (Rome: A. Belardetti, 1952), vol. 2, p. 46, which does not indicate the source of the item, however. In the English version, the reference is on p. 301 of *The Life of Girolamo Savonarola*, tr. Cecil Grayson (New York: Knopf, 1959).

5

ANTI-LUTHERAN PROPHECY: LUTHER AS MONSTER AND PSEUDOPROPHET

More on Monsters

THE PROBLEM of the relationship between prophecy and the spread of the Reformation has come up before in these pages. Thus far, the question has been what happened to prophetic preaching each time that it entered into contact with Lutheranism. There is another side to the problem, however. We might ask whether, and how, and in which of its aspects prophecy was used in Italy during these same years as a polemical weapon in the confessional dispute and, eventually, with what aims and with the use of what techniques.

To begin with, let us recall what has already been said on the combined divinatory and politico-religious meaning that was attributed to the monstrous births in Italy during that period. They were *segni*—generic signs of divine wrath and of God's will, thus warnings of a catastrophic future. But they were also indications that a merciful Providence offered to humankind so that if people were sufficiently inspired by piety they could disentangle themselves from events and read the true significance of history. The monsters display probably the clearest form of one of prophecy's most prominent characteristics during these years. As a global culture, prophecy provided the key to a unified interpretation of nature, of the supernatural, and of human history. This is why contemporary chronicles often ended by pointing to the monsters, which they took to be signs equal to the task of expressing their age. We have already seen this in Johannes Multivallis's continuation of the chronicle of Eusebius of Caesarea, which in fact ends with a description of the monster of Ravenna and its significance. It is also true, for example, of the *Chronica* of Joannes Nauclerus, which ends in the final years of the fifteenth century with a reference to the monsters that had captured the attention of the court of Maximilian I, and of Sebastian Brant in particular:

> Creator et stellas et cometas in caelo, et gladios igneos et dracones creat et apparere facit in sublimi; similiter et portenta in terra et in mari, monstra in hominibus etiam nasci, ut infantulos multorum capitum, propter quod et monstra dicuntur, non solum quod propter admirationem novitatis ea ho-

mines sibi monstrant, sed quoniam iram Dei monstrant imminere hominibus: quod Deus, supplex oro, bene vertat. Finis historiae Joannis Nauclerii tubingensis praepositi, quae a condito mundo in annum christianae salutis millesimum et quingentesimum deducta est feliciter.[1]

The most interesting aspect of this text is obviously not its theory of monsters, which is absolutely concordant with the current literature, but that it is presented, on the whole, as a historical and political comment on the present age. Nauclerus was writing at the very beginning of the sixteenth century; later, the gradual distinction between scientific fields that separated natural history from politics or theology contributed to the dismantling of this sort of prophetic analysis of monsters and, more generally, to the end of prophecy as a cohesive culture.

The two creatures born in Ravenna and Bologna had in fact already produced a great variety in the politico-ecclesiastical and prophetic meanings attributed to the monsters. Ten years later, that wealth of meaning persisted in the descriptions of the other monstrous creatures to which we now turn, and meaning acquired even greater complexity from the context of confessional polemics in which teratological interpretation was set. We need to examine how this context influenced prophetic techniques, first concerning the monsters, and in particular the so-called monk-calf, or the monster of Saxony.

The Monster of Saxony: Luther's Interpretation

The monster of Saxony was a deformed fetus found in the uterus of a cow in Waltersdorf near Freiberg in Saxony on 8 December 1522.[2] The monster, whose most salient characteristic was a large fold of flesh on its neck that might recall a monk's cowl, was dried and sent to Duke Frederick of Saxony ("apud quem nunc visitur," a contemporary witness noted).[3] At

[1] *Cronica d. Johannis Nauclerii praepositi tubingensis succinctim compraendentia res memorabiles saeculorum omnium ac gentium, ab initio mundi usque ad annum Christi nati MCCCCC* (Cologne, 1569), pp. 1121–22.

[2] On this question, see Martin Luther, *D. Martin Luthers Werke. Kritische Gesamtausgabe* (hereafter cited as *WKG*), 97 vols. (Weimar: H. Böhlau, 1883–1987), vol. 1 (1900), pt. 11, pp. 357–61; vol. 4 (1933), pt. 3, p. 10; Eugen Holländer, *Wunder, Wundergeburt und Wundergestalt in Einblattdrucken des fünfzehnten bis achtzehnten Jahrhunderts*, 2nd ed. (Stuttgart: F. Enke, 1922), pp. 322–25; Hartmann Grisar and Franz Heege, *Luthers Kampfbilder*, 4 vols. (Freiburg im Breisgau: Herder, 1921–1923), vol. 3, *Bilderkampf in den Schriften von 1523 bis 1545*, pp. 14–23; Robert W. Scribner, *For the Sake of Simple Folk: Popular Propaganda for the German Reformation* (Cambridge and New York: Cambridge University Press, 1981), pp. 127–32.

[3] Johann Georg Schenck, *Monstrorum historia memorabilis* (Frankfurt, 1609), p. 89. Apparently Schenck was citing a broadsheet similar to a colored drawing conserved in the Univer-

nearly the same time, other illustrated reports on the event appeared and had an immediate and wide distribution. As early as 26 December of the same year Johannes Magenbuch sent a print piece of the sort to Wolfgang Richard in Ulm. He comments:

> Monstrum tibi hic mitto, quod exceptum est e vacca, quam quidam volebat mactare Fribergae, quae civitas est ducis Henrici Misniae. Quid significet, difficile dictu est. Convocavit dux omnes monachos, ut dicerent quid prae se ferret hoc portentum; nihil volebant statuere. Tandem princeps ipse subridens conclusit et dixit vaccam esse matrem omnium monachorum.[4]

Beyond the gratuity of Duke Heinrich von Meissen's insulting remark on the parentage of monks, the final words give an accurate idea of how immediately the monster of Saxony was put into a context of religious polemics. Nor was this a one-way operation. On 5 January 1523, Margrave Georg of Brandenburg wrote to Luther from Prague to make his excuses for a regrettable incident. Several days before, he had received word of the monster of Freiberg, which he had passed on to an astronomer in Prague to get his explanation. Without the margrave's knowledge, the astronomer had printed an interpretation in verse that equated the monster with Luther. The work was sequestered and all the copies were burned.[5] Perhaps in reaction to this episode, Luther determined to furnish his own interpretation of the deformed calf. The piece must have been nearly completed on 16 January, when he wrote to Wenzeslaus Link:

> Gratiam et pacem. Unum monstrorum ego interpretor modo. Omissa generali interpretatione monstrorum quae significant certo rerum publicarum mutationem per bella potissimum, quo et mihi non est dubium Germaniae portendi vel summam belli calamitatem vel extremum diem, ego tantum versor in particulari interpretatione quae ad monachos pertinet.[6]

The monk-calf that Luther interpreted in these terms was only one of the many monsters to crop up in Europe at the time ("monstra cottidie crebrescunt," Luther wrote to Georg Spalatin four days earlier).[7] To balance the picture, Melanchthon commented during the same period on the so-called pope-ass, another monstrous creature known widely since its discovery on the banks of the Tiber in 1496. The two texts were published

sitätsbibliotek of Würzburg, cited in *WKG*, vol. 4, pt. 3, p. 10. A sheet containing the same text in French must have fallen into the hands of the Bourgeois of Paris, who describes it in the same terms: *Journal d'un Bourgeois de Paris sous le regne de François Premier (1515–1536)*, ed. Ludovic Lalanne (Paris: J. Renouard et c., 1854), p. 95.

[4] *WKG*, vol. 4, pt. 3, p. 17.

[5] Ibid., pp. 8–9.

[6] Ibid., p. 17.

[7] Ibid., p. 15.

together, splendidly illustrated with two engravings by Lucas Cranach, under the title *Deuttung der zwo grewlichen figuren, Bapstesels zu Rom und Munchkalbs zu Freyerberg in Meyssen funden*, a publication that had later printings, both together and apart, not germane to our concerns here.[8] What we should note is Luther's clear perception of the multiple layers of interpretation of monsters in general and of this one in particular (an interpretive variety that in all probability explains the vast and multifaceted success of this and other "monsters"). Luther makes a clear distinction between a global interpretation of the deformed creatures, used prophetically, and an interpretation in a political key and aimed at one specific topic, not intended to exclude or eliminate the more general meaning, but superimposed upon it. The text says of this type of reading:

> Die prophetische Deuttung dises Munchkalbs wil ich dem Geyst lassen, denn ich kein prophet binn. . . . Ein ander gebe die prophetische Deuttung. Ich will meyn Munchkalb meynem stand zu dienst deutten.[9]

Thus Luther intended to dedicate this work to the service of his *Stand* (in the medieval sense of *ordo monachorum*), or, to put it differently, to the service of the doctrinal and popularizing activities that he was pursuing during these very months regarding the uselessness and even the perniciousness of monastic vows. In the same month of January 1523, the *M. Lutheri ad Brismannum epistola de votis monasticis* appeared; a sermon on 25 January insisted at length on the hypocrisy of good works without faith that permeated monks like leprosy; between April and May he wrote and published the *Ursach und Antwort dass Jungfrauen Klöster göttlich verlassen mögen*, in which he justified his encouragement of twelve nuns who fled the convent of Nimpschen on 7 April and took refuge with him.[10] One of them, in fact, Katharina von Bora, was to become his wife.

The *monstra*, as we have seen, had been linked with divination since classical antiquity, and the connection between divination and Reformation and anti-Reformation propaganda was pointed out some time ago. We should note, though, that in the *Deuttung* Luther was not limiting himself to furnishing propaganda in the form of prophecy. Admittedly, he alludes

[8] On the various editions of the *Deuttung*, see *WKG*, vol. 1, pt. 11, pp. 361–68. On Cranach's engravings, see Fritz Saxl, "Illustrated Pamphlets of the Reformation," in his *Lectures*, 2 vols. (London: Warburg Institute, University of London, 1957), pp. 255–66; Werner Timm, "Notizen zur Graphik Lucas Cranachs," in Peter H. Feist et al., eds., *Lucas Cranach: Künstler und Gesellschaft: Referate des Colloquiums mit internationaler Beteiligung zum 500. Geburtstag Lucas Cranachs d. Ä.* (Wittenberg: Staatliche Lutherhalle, 1973), p. 93; Dieter Koepplin, Tilman Falk et al., *Lukas Cranach: Gemälde, Zeichnungnen, Druckgraphik: Austellung im Kunstmuseum Basel, 15. Juni–8 September 1974*), 2 vols. (Basel: Birkhäuser, 1974), vol. 1, p. 370, nn. 246–47.

[9] *WKG*, vol. 1, pt. 11, pp. 380–81.

[10] Ibid., pp. 284–91; 9–11; 394–400.

to the hidden divinatory meaning of the monster, but then, making good use of the same techniques of argumentation that he ascribes to the brand of prophecy practiced by others ("ein andere gebe die prophetische Deuttung"), he returns to the present, analyzing the meaning of the various parts of the calf (his closed eyes, his long tongue, his mangled thighs, and so forth), concluding that "all sistery and monkery is nothing but false and mendacious appearance." Thus the vague prophecy of catastrophe that was implied by the monster ("rerum publicarum mutationem . . . summam belli calamitatem . . . extremum diem") was a threatening confirmation of his interpretation.

The prophetic and the propagandistic approaches to analysis of the monster were not the only ones. When the Dominican theologian Johannes Cochlaeus, writing in April 1523, answered a piece that Luther had written against him (*Adversus armatum virum Cokleum*, composed early in February of the same year),[11] he did so by imitating the spirit of medieval marginalia and feigning an absurd and ridiculous combat between a snail and the Minotaur.[12] Luther had played on the sense of the word *cochlaea* ("snail," which, incidentally, he translates erroneously as *testudo*, "box turtle") to laugh at the *armatum virum Cokleum* and his useless shell of arguments, placing the Dominican among the "istae testudines, limacae, talpae, lacertae, erucae, locustae, bruci, vespae, imo viperae et stelliones, qui . . . pereunt in immundiciis suis sophisticis."[13] Cochlaeus responded in kind, not only identifying Luther with the monster of Saxony but going so far as to draw a parallel between the deformed calf and the Minotaur. This point of departure had a number of consequences for the composition and the structure of Cochlaeus's work (leaving aside for the moment its doctrinal content, which concerned grace through the sacraments and through faith). First, it forced Cochlaeus into a cultural framework of constant reference to classical mythology, so that along with the Minotaur we get Apis, the sacred bull, which had been known for several decades in connection with the *religio aegyptiaca*, thanks in particular to the popularizing activities of Annio of Viterbo (Giovanni Nanni). A second and perhaps more conspicuous result was that the work was in fact a series of elegant and superficial variations on the theme of the struggle between the

[11] Ibid., pp. 295–306.

[12] Johannes Cochlaeus, *Adversus cucullatum Minotaurum Wittenbergensem*, ed. Joseph Schweitzer, Corpus Catholicorum no. 3 (Münster, 1920). Cochlaeus returned to the topic in his *Historia Ioannis Cochlaei de actis et scriptis Martini Lutheri Saxonis* . . . (Cologne: apud Theodorum Baumium, 1568), fol. 99*r*. On Cochlaeus, see Remigius Bäumer, *Johannes Cochlaeus (1479–1552). Leben und Werk im Dienst der katholischen Reform* (Münster: Aschendorf, 1980); Gotthelf Wiedermann, "Cochlaeus as Polemicist," in *Seven-headed Luther. Essays in Commemoration of a Quincentenary, 1483–1983*, ed. Peter Newman Brooks (Oxford: Oxford University Press and New York: Clarendon Press, 1983), pp. 195–205.

[13] *WKG*, vol. 1, pt. 11, p. 305.

minax Minotaurus and the *parva cochlaea*, to the point that its rhetorical structure ended up getting the better of its theological content.

The text begins with a parody of the first lines of the *Aeneid*:

> Monstra bovemque cano, boreae qui primus ab oris
> Theutonicas terras profugus conspurcat. . . .[14]

The rest of the work continues in the same tone. Luther is called "saxonicus vitulus," "semicucullatus bos," "gloriosus Minotaurus," and finally "that great son of the Bohemian Pasiphae." The insult that Heinrich von Meissen had applied to Freiberg monks' parentage was thus turned against Luther and heightened by a mythological context. Rather than turning the image of the monster to prophetic or specifically propagandistic purposes, Cochlaeus consistently uses it for rhetorical and mythological ends. Only toward the end of his tract does he seem to abandon his pose as a humanist and return to a symbolic and religious interpretation of the monster of Saxony, identifying it, surprisingly enough, with Germany: "Deus optimus maximus resarciat has Germaniae scissuras, et conglutinet vulnera hiantia."[15] The *scissurae* in the body of the monk-calf had now become a physical laceration and a sign of the religious schism that divided Germany.

Luther as Monster

The monk-calf had a belated vogue in treatises on teratology of the latter sixteenth century from Paré to Rueff, Aldrovandi, and Fortunio Liceto,[16] but by that time its prophetic and symbolic connotations had been nearly totally lost and it belonged more in the ideal realm of the *Wunderkammern* than in the domain of doctrinal polemics. More interesting to our purposes is the stabilization and persistence of the image of Luther as the monster of Saxony. A year after the publication of the *Adversus cucullatum Minotaurum*, the Polish astrologer Johannes Ploniscus (Jan z Płonsk) blended the "monstrifica ac ridenda figura" of the monster of Saxony with a polemical position on the universal deluge predicted for 1524, accusing Luther, "hic

[14] Cochlaeus, *Adversus cucullatum Minotaurum*, p. 13.

[15] Ibid., p. 57.

[16] Jakob Rueff, *De conceptu et generatione hominis* . . . (Frankfurt am Main: [S. Feyerabendi], 1587, fol. 4*r*; Conrad Lycosthenes (Conrad Wollfhart), *Prodigiorum ac ostentorum chronicon* (Basel, 1557), p. 528; Ambroise Paré, *Des monstres et prodiges*, ed. Jean Céard (Geneva: Droz, 1971), pp. 36, 165 (available in English as *On Monsters and Marvels*, tr. Janis L. Pallister [Chicago: University of Chicago Press, 1982], pp. 46, 156–57); Pierre Boaistuau et al., *Histoires prodigieuses extraictes de plusieurs fameux autheurs, grecs & latins, sacrez & prophanes, divisées en cinq livres* (Antwerp: G. Ianssens, 1594), pp. 709–20; Fortunio Liceto, *De monstrorum caussis, natura, et differentiis libri duo . . . secunda editio correctior* (Padua: Apud Frambottum, 1634; colophon dated 1633), p. 100; Ulisse Aldrovandi, *Monstrorum historia* (Bologna: Marco Antonio Bernia, 1642), p. 371.

vitulus cucullatus et legislator saxonicus," of having spread fearful expectation of the flood in Germany.[17] Even many years later, Cochlaeus's work found an echo in the *Libri mirabilium septem* of Friedrich Nausea and the *Historia gentium septentrionalium* of Olaus Magnus.[18]

This image lost no time in penetrating Italy, even independently of Cochlaeus's work. As early as February 1523 an anonymous chronicler in Cremona wrote:

> There came a letter from Rome [about] how a peasant in Magna [Germany] had killed a cow, and when he had killed it, he left it that way three days, and after three days [when] the cow was opened he found a monster that had the face of a man and a friar's tonsure, but it was ugly to see and had a hood in front and in back like those of the friars, and had the body of a man, hairy arms and legs, and cleft hands and feet like a pig's, and the letter says that it lived three days.[19]

On 26 May Tommasino Lancellotti made an analogous entry in his chronicle:

> There was brought to Modena a picture of a monster born of a cow in Saxony that has a quasi-human head, and it has a tonsure and scapulary of skin like a friar's scapulary, and arms in front and legs and feet like a pig's and the tail of a pig. It is said that it is a friar who is called Martin Utero, who is dead and who several years ago preached heresy in Lamagna [Germany].[20]

These texts testify to the circulation in Italy of print pieces on "a monster born of a cow in Saxony." Internal evidence tells us several things. First, this is the earliest mention of Luther to be gleaned from Italian chronicles, the *Diarii* of Marin Sanudo excepted. Thus Luther was talked about in northern Italy early in 1523, but his name was distorted, he was reported as dead, and he was identified with an abnormal aborted calf. It is clear that we are in the realm of the most obvious anti-Reformation propaganda. We might also wonder what relationship there was between the *depintura* brought to Modena and the "littere da Roma" mentioned by the Cre-

[17] Johannes Ploniscus, *Judicium maius magnarum coniunctionum anno 1524 evenientium ad annos futuros quadraginta duraturum* (Cracow, n.d.), cited in Paola Zambelli, "Fine del mondo o inizio della propaganda? Astrologia, filosofia della storia e propaganda politico-religiosa nel dibattito sulla congiunzione del 1524," in *Scienze, credenze occulte, livelli di cultura. Convegno internazionale di studi (Firenze, 26–30 giugno 1980)* (Florence: L. S. Olschki, 1982), pp. 291–368, esp. pp. 331–34.

[18] Friedrich Nausea, *Libri mirabilium septum* (Cologne: apud P. Quentell, 1532), fols. xxiv *r–v*; Olaus Magnus, *Historia delle genti e della natura delle cose settentrionali d'Olao Magno goto* (Venice: D. Nicolini [for] gli heredi di Lucantonio Giunta, 1565), fol. 169*v*.

[19] *Cronache cremonesi dall'anno MCCCCIX al MDXXV*, ed. Francesco Robolotti, *Bibliotheca Historica Italica*, 4 vols. (Milan: Brigola, 1876–1901), vol. 1, p. 252.

[20] Tommasino Lancellotti, *Cronaca modenese*, ed. Carlo Borghi, 12 vols. (Parma: P. Fiaccadori, 1863), vol. 1, p. 440.

monese chronicler. It is not too improbable that the latter refers not to a private letter but to a print piece, since the term *littera*, as we have seen, was at the time often included in the titles of short works on prodigious events. It allowed the printer or the sponsor of the publication to claim credibility by referring to the direct testimony of the author, real or imaginary, of the supposed letter. That the terms *littera* and *depintura* might refer to the same publication (more likely a broadsheet than a pamphlet) seems possible from a close comparison of the two passages cited. Both, in fact, speak of a monster born of a cow but with an almost human face, who seemed to have a tonsure and a cowl like a friar's and who had feet and hooves like a pig's. Furthermore, the two chroniclers note these details in the same order. If the *littera* was illustrated, it could have been defined as a *depintura*; conversely, the *depintura* in Modena was most probably accompanied by an explicative text, perhaps even extremely short. We shall soon examine a true broadsheet on the same topic with these very characteristics. We might ask, finally (and this is not clear from the passages cited), whether identifying the monster as Luther and reporting him as dead (only in Lancellotti) were details in the text or texts that the two chroniclers had consulted.

One answer, on a hypothetical level, emerges from a comparison of these texts with a letter written by Pietro Martire d'Anghiera—as always, an indefatigable collector of print pieces on prodigies and monstrosities—several months later, on 25 August, from Valladolid. Anghiera states that two different pictures of monsters of "juvencae formam sub humana specie" had reached that city from Germany, and he comments: "Lutheri heretici et commilitorum eius referre specie populi summurmurant."[21] In this case, as perhaps with the Italian publication or publications, the monster was identified as Luther only by implication. The piece was to be understood and to serve as a warning to those who already knew the name of the German monk, but without furnishing inopportune information to anyone not yet aware of the heresy rife in Germany. As for a possible connection between the Italian print pieces and the German pamphlets from which they took their inspiration, it is clear that the Italian pieces were unrelated to either Luther's text or Cochlaeus's, but derived from one of the earlier, more anodyne accounts that had appeared in Germany as early as December 1522. Their early circulation in Italy (from February 1523) confirms this supposition. If we accept the various hypotheses that have been outlined thus far, we can conclude that the two Italian chroniclers were referring to an illustrated print piece of Roman origin (information traveled easily from Germany to Rome). Its text (presumably brief) was written in the form of a letter; it proposed—but only implicitly—that the monster be

[21] Pietro Martire d'Anghiera, *Opus epistolarum Petri Martyris Anglerii* (Amsterdam: typis Elzevirianis, 1670), p. 459.

equated with Luther; its aims were propagandistic and anti-Reformation. Furthermore, it is more than probable that the *depintura* mentioned in the Modenese chronicle also came from Rome: Modena belonged to the Holy See in this period, and for that reason there was a steady and privileged flow of information and propaganda between the two cities.[22]

The Monster of Castelbaldo

The image of Luther as a monster must have had a notable effect on the greater public in Italy, and even some years later interpretation of a monstrous creature still served anti-Lutheran propagandistic aims. Early in 1526 a broadsheet circulated in Venice (or at least in the territories of the Serenissima) that was printed on one side only, bore a small engraving and a short text printed in fine type, and was presented without title, author's name, or mention of the printer and the place of publication (Figure 9).[23] The incipit follows the conventions for this sort of literature:

> The lack of faith that reigns in the world today, my most illustrious lords, [is] the reason why the Eternal Father sends many monsters that are not believed [unless] we see them; and although they proceed from an ill-disposed, badly organized, or imperfect nature, or from superfluous sperm, nevertheless God the master of nature allows to happen what he could obviate for our most enormous sins, so that, as I said in the other exposition on the monster of Germany, seeing that we are of a perfect nature, we have cause to praise our father and Eternal God and fear him, considering that he could have made [others] similar and more monstrous.

The anonymous writer had thus already published an *Expositione del monstro d'Alemagna*, which, if it resembled this text in having an engraving and a brief text, might correspond to the descriptions of the *depintura* and the *littere* that circulated in Modena and Cremona. This is only a hypothesis, however, open to doubt, because the *littere* in Cremona came from Rome. We must admit the circulation of at least two or three print pieces on the topic in central and northern Italy, thus confirming that the image of Luther as a monster penetrated into this region.[24]

[22] See below, pp. 160–61.

[23] This piece was pasted into the original manuscript of Marin Sanudo's *Diarii* (Biblioteca Marciana di Venezia, ms. it. VII 268 [= 9255], fol. 435*r*). The text is reproduced in the printed edition of Marino Sanuto, *Diarii*, 58 vols. (Venice: R. Deputazione Veneta di storia patria, 1879–1903), vol. 40, cols. 652–53. Sanudo had occasion to see this creature while it was still alive (col. 650).

[24] Further confirmation comes from the recent discovery of an analogous sheet inside the manuscript of the *Historiae senenses* of Sigismondo Tizio: See Paola Zambelli, "Da Giulio II a Paolo III. Come l'astrologo provocatore Luca Gaurico divenne vescovo," in Fabio Tronca-

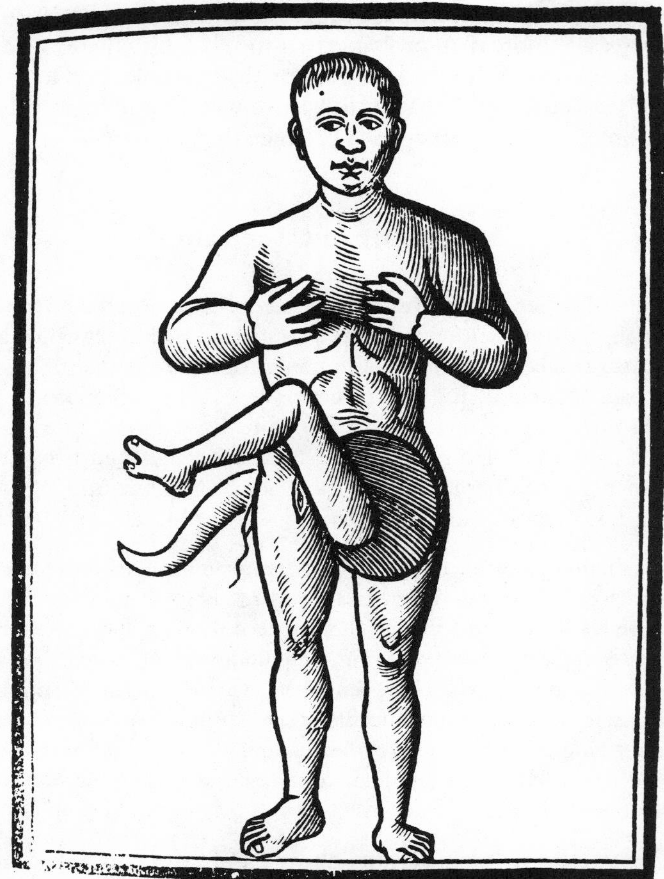

Fig. 9. The Monster of Castelbaldo. Illustration from an Italian broadsheet, Biblioteca Marciana, Venice.

Following the introductory paragraph in the Venetian broadsheet comes word of a creature born

> deformed and monstrous near Castelbaldo at Maxi [Masi, in the province of Padua, between Badia Polesine and Castelbaldo] in M.D.XXV, on the 28th day of December, with three legs, and the third leg between the [other] two, turned upward, and between the right leg and the middle one it had the nature [sexual parts] of a woman and behind it has the male member, and in the body it had [something] like a round ball or a head, and an imperfect arm behind.

---

relli, ed., *La città dei segreti, Magia, astrologia e cultura esoterica a Roma* (*XV–XVIII secolo*), Convegno Roma ermetica (1983: Rome, Italy) (Milan: Franco Angeli, 1985), pp. 311–12.

The anonymous writer then turns to an interpretation of the monster and of the symbolic and divinatory "significance" of every part of his body. The "bala tonda" signifies the vainglory of the world or perhaps the deceiving and hidden "cogitation" of princes; the upturned leg

> signifies a leader or a pseudoprophet who will predict falsely, and since a foot cannot walk turned against nature, so this one will not be able to make his way—that is, will not last long before he is annihilated. The imperfect arm signifies the imperfect works that he will make the holy faith of Jesus Christ display and he will ruin it, and since it is behind, counter to nature, so will he go against the holy faith. And by the woman's nature [we see] that he will promise that lust is no sin. And by the male member, which is turned backward, is meant the very great and putrid sin against nature that reigns in the world today, for which God will promise this false prophet that he will come to scourge Christianity.

Luther is quite obviously the false prophet turned against the body of which he is a member, whose works are imperfect, and who "will promise that lust is no sin." We know, in fact, and these pages offer further confirmation, that one of the most persistent rumors about Luther circulating in Italy was that he favored undue sexual freedom.[25] Thus although the great reformer was not explicitly equated with the monster of Castelbaldo, he was nonetheless tacitly associated with its deformity—a sign of moral deformity—and with lasciviousness, all the more so in that his preaching was taken as a divine punishment for sodomy, "il grandissimo e spuzolente peccato contra natura che ogidì regna al mondo." He is also presented as a false prophet, which makes this text interesting as a point of conjunction between the two different images of Luther as a monster and as a pseudoprophet. In any event, divine wrath would soon take care of him: "non durarà longo tempo che sarà anichilito." The prediction, like the false information of Luther's death given in Lancellotti, functioned as a prophecy, as an omen of things to come, and also as a warning.

An Anti-Lutheran Prophecy

Prophecy could thus be used for propagandistic, anti-Reformation ends when the bodies of deformed creatures were used for baneful predictions of the imminent coming of Luther (or his double) and coupled with pre-

25 When Gasparo Contarini went to the Diet of Worms in April 1520, he picked up, secondhand, the information that Luther "dicat . . . matrimonium . . . dissolvi posse, fornicationem simplicem peccatum non esse, ac innuit mulierum illam comunitatem de qua Plato in sua Republica": Sanuto, *Diarii*, vol. 30, cols. 211–12. See also, on a totally different level, the *Lamento de Italia contra Martin Lutherano. Opera nuova* (n.p., n.d., but written by a Florentine around 1530), fols. 4*v*–5*r*.

dictions of their ultimate annihilation and death (in some texts, such as the one Lancellotti saw, given as already achieved).[26] It is also interesting to note that, unlike the pieces that circulated at the time of Leo X, which were on a relatively higher cultural scale, the anti-Lutheran broadsides that we have examined or reconstructed were all in the vernacular and seem to have been of the "popular" sort. Thus they were addressed to a broad public who could be thought to be still interested, in the 1520s, in the literary genre of the *monstra* and who had the greatest need (in the eyes of those who put out such texts) to be protected against the lure of Luther's name.

The same propagandistic ends were pursued by means of other materials, again in a prophetic vein and again having a broad circulation. Thus the same popular typology is evident in an octavo-sized text of four leaves, with no indication of place or date of printing but apparently published around 1530, entitled *Vita de santo Angelo carmelitano martyre con la prophetia data a lui per el nostro signor Jesu Christo de tutto quello che e advenuto e advegnira alla christianitade per infedeli et della setta et leze falsa luterina*.[27] The pamphlet's title page bears an engraving taken from the *Pronosticatio* of Johannes Lichtenberger, a text whose extraordinary success in Italy can be traced through the wide distribution of its illustrations in other publications of a "popular" nature. The engraving used here shows Christ as he allots tasks to representatives of the three walks of life—priests, warriors, and peasants. We know, however, that the notion of the tripartite division of society was not common in Italy, where the image in question was interpreted as the Last Judgment, thereby giving it eschatological significance.[28] Thus both the title and the illustration place this short work in a prophetic context. It was, however, only a slightly revamped version of a *Vita sancti Angeli martyris* attributed to Enoch, patriarch of Jerusalem, and later known for the edition of it that Benoît Gonon produced from a fifteenth-century manuscript of the work for the *Vitae Patrum Occidentis* (Lyon, 1625), subsequently reprinted in the *Acta Sanctorum*.[29] The text was clearly biographical and recounted the life of St. Angelus, first on Mount Carmel and then in Rome (where he was supposed to have met St. Francis), his miracles, and his death, which took place in Licata on 5 May 1225 at the hand of one Berengario, a Cathar whom he had reprimanded

[26] The false news of Luther's death was also reported in 1529 in Leonardo and Gregorio Amaseo and Gio. Antonio Azio, *Diarii udinesi, dall'anno 1508 al 1541* (Venice: R. Deputazione di storia patria per le Venezie, 1884), p. 302, and in 1531 in Sanuto, *Diarii*, vol. 50, col. 308 and vol. 55, col. 279. In these cases as well, the news was quite evidently expedient for propagandistic purposes.

[27] See Victor Massena, prince d'Essling, *Etudes sur l'art de la gravure sur bois à Venise: Les livres à figures vénitiens de la fin du XVe siècle et du commencement du XVIe*, 4 vols. (Florence: L. S. Olschki and Paris: H. Leclerc, 1907–1914), vol. 2, pt. 2, p. 646.

[28] See Ottavia Niccoli, *I sacerdoti, i guerrieri, i contadini. Storia di un'immagine della società* (Turin: G. Einaudi, 1979), pp. 58–61.

[29] *Acta sanctorum*, 68 vols. (Paris: V. Palmé, 1863–1919), vol. 15, *Maius*, pp. 15*–47*.

for having an incestuous relationship with his own sister. This last note, which combines the themes of lust and heresy, provides us with a vantage point for understanding the sense of this publication. At the end of the 1520s, when Europe teemed with Reformation propaganda, this text, aimed at a wide audience, promoted the need to oppose, even at risk of one's life, a heresy that was spreading everywhere and was judged to lead to lasciviousness. Another, Latin version of the same *Life* was printed in 1526 under the auspices of Tommaso Bellorosi of Palermo, who added a prophetic note to it, in particular by reading into it a prediction of a Turkish victory in Italy ("de turcali victoria contra Italiam").[30] The *Life* published in the vernacular was addressed to a different public on a lower level (as is clear from the physical characteristics of the work); nonetheless, it too was presented as a prophetic text rooted in the present, especially through the use of one particular passage that deserves closer examination.

Angelus had lived in the Palestinian desert for five years when Christ himself appeared to him and predicted his martyrdom, to be followed by wars with the Turks and subsequent turmoil throughout a good part of Europe (which naturally was the first reason why sixteenth-century printers should have been interested in the *Life* and undoubtedly was what had attracted Bellorosi). At this point in the narrative a passage was inserted, which is given here first in the original Latin (subsequently published by Gonon) and then in the Italian paraphrase in order to show how small changes in the text adapted it to the contemporary scene. The passage runs thus:

Istud erit quando Ecclesia erit saepissime divisa et unusquisque alteri adversabitur, et quando duo vel tres summi Pontifices effici voluerint, et quando Ecclesia erit a multis tyrannis expoliata, et quando Ecclesia plena erit multarum Religionum hypocritarum, populos defraudantium sub colore sanctitatis: qui paucam caritatem erga proximum habebunt, et loco ejus superbiam, avaritiam, invidiam, luxuriam et sodomiam communiter habebunt. Et propter talia peccata permittam Italiam, et quasi omnes Christianos per manus inimicorum meorum castigari.

Et questo sarà come venirà scisma in la chiesa, simonia con altri mali, per li quali serà da diversi tyranni spogliata et malmenata. Et quando si levaranno male gente che sotto specie de sanctitade sedurà el popolo con nove et permixte lege, concorrendogli larga vita et bestial vivere. Onde questi lupi sotto tal manto levaranno ogni bon costume facendo licito lo illicito. Perhò surgerà la ira divina et permetterà che 'l gladi[o] deli inimici de Dio haverà vigore contra il christianesimo, aciò ch'el sequiti vendetta contra li soi inimici per li inimici.[31]

[30] Ibid., p. 13*.

[31] Ibid., p. 34* for the Latin text; *Vita de santo Angelo Carmelitano* (n.p., n.d. [c.1530]), fol. A iii*r*, for the vernacular version.

The reference to "two or three most high pontiffs" allows us, first of all, to date the Latin *Vita* (or at least its later interpolation) with some certainty, as this clearly refers to the years of the Great Schism in the West.[32] The same reference, by then no longer current, is left out of the Italian version, which speaks only of schism and introduces instead the concept of simony, indicated (unlike the Latin text) as the reason why the Church will be "despoiled and mistreated by various tyrants." The elaboration of this idea (the Latin text shows only the participle "expoliata") makes us think that the writer had in mind the sack of Rome. The most skillful and the most important modification, however, comes later, where the phrase "ecclesia plena erit multarum religionum hypocritarum, populos defraudantium sub colore sanctitatis," along with what follows, becomes "bad people will rise up, who under the guise of sanctity will seduce the people with new and mixed laws," and so forth.

In short, a commonplace of the late Middle Ages—deploring the proliferation and decadence of the religious orders—has been transformed into a denunciation of Lutheran preaching. Furthermore, the principal reason for the success of that preaching is seen as being the "broader life and bestial living" that it permitted when "the illicit" was made legitimate. The theme of the sexual license permitted by Reformed doctrine, which we have already encountered and will encounter again, is an extraordinarily tenacious *topos*. To sum up this print piece, however, we find in it signs of the same process that we have witnessed in connection with the verse prophecies published toward the end of the fifteenth century: When a traumatic event—first the arrival of Charles VIII, later the breakup of the unity of the *respublica christiana*—exerted pressure on society, people returned to the old texts, reread them, reworked them in the light of present events, and gave them titles that explained and justified their new currency. This phenomenon had been massive thirty years earlier, however; now it occurred only rarely.

God's Chastisement of Heretics

Another technique of the anti-Lutheran propaganda that also made use of popular print pieces of a prophetic nature was the use of celestial signs to predict horrible calamities as punishment for the rapid spread of heresy. The episode of the universal deluge expected in 1524 (to be discussed in the next chapter) provided an excellent opportunity to identify the feared catastrophic flood with God's castigation for the Lutheran heresy and to

[32] In another, probably earlier *Vita* given in the *Acta sanctorum: Maius*, Christ limits himself to foretelling Angelus's martyrdom when he speaks to him (p. 51*).

use it to try to destroy Lutheranism. It was not unique, however. As late as 1536 a rough and poorly printed octavo-sized leaflet of two leaves appeared, printed in Rome "per Albertin Zanelli" and entitled *El gran prodigio di tre soli apparsi in Franza adi nove de Setembrio a hore tredese. In di de sabbato cosa multo stupenda.* The text is epistolary in form (a technique frequently used for information on prodigious events, as we have seen), but it does not give the name either of the writer of the supposed letter or of its addressee.

The letter speaks of a phenomenon connected with the refraction of light that was often recorded during those years and to which we shall return, parhelia, or "parelia," as the text says: two "accidental suns that surround our natural sun." This phenomenon was, according to the writer, "most cruelly apart from nature," and the three suns were omens of the overturning of states and of bloody battles, earthquakes, pestilence, and famine. What had caused this disturbance? "The Lutheran sect and pagans, who with lasciviousness and their false laws have worked to subject the natural sun—that is, the Christian people, observant of the evangelical law."[33] The author later makes it clear that the natural sun represents the pope and the emperor and that this indivisible dual civil and ecclesiastical power, portrayed as the one true day star, will soon destroy (indeed, "burn up and annihilate") the other duality, the Turks and the Lutherans, "whereupon for one or both will follow the destruction of the leader and his sect . . . [they] and their followers will be punished, burned, and destroyed." Prophecy in the 1520s had stopped at foretelling the end of Luther and his followers by the action of God's wrath and providential catastrophes; now, in 1536, divine chastisement took a more human form, working through the Holy See, seconded by the secular arm, and leading directly to the flaming pyres. It was a significant change of direction in the struggle against heresy. The leaflet concludes with a warning to the "auditori" (can we then presume that the piece was read publicly?) that God would withhold the threatened scourges only if they could join their thoughts and turn their arms against those who sought to destroy the true law of Christ.[34]

One more time, and again in 1536, "lasciviousness" was the way the "Lutheran sect" entrapped the Christian multitudes. As we have seen, this was a truly recurrent theme in anti-Lutheran propaganda in Italy, at least (though not exclusively) in its more rudimentary, less refined forms. Although at first this certainly came of the application of a well-known stereotype connected with heresy, the insistence with which the theme recurs makes one wonder whether in some cases there was not some basis in

[33] *El gran prodigio di tre soli* (Rome: Albertin Zanelli, 1536), fol. 2*r*.

[34] Ibid., fol. 2*v*.

fact—whether, in other words, some defender of the Reformed word, in the fervor of preaching the Christian's newfound liberties, did not choose his examples from the realm of sexual morality as well.

A Case of Reformation Cryptopropaganda

Up to now we have seen that the language of prophecy was used, even after 1530, to combat the "pseudoprophet" of Saxony "who will predict falsities," who "will promise that lust is no sin," who "under the guise of sanctity will seduce the people with new and permissive laws," and with his "lasciviousness and false laws will work to subject . . . the Christian people."

In point of fact, a pseudoprophet had been expected for some time in Italy and in Europe in general, even several decades before Luther began to preach. The great conjunction of Jupiter and Saturn in 1484 (with its various interpretations) and the controversy concerning Antonio Arquato's *De Eversione Europae* are events too well known to merit further discussion here.[35] I might note, however, that when Arquato states (probably still in the Quattrocento), "veniet a septentrione heresiarcha magnus," he was without a doubt basing his prediction on the planetary conjunction, even if he did not say so explicitly. This was also the sense in which contemporary commentators understood him.[36] Andrea Bernardi, the barber chronicler from Forlì, gives living testimony to the circulation of these and other similar prognostications. In the waning days of 1484, Bernardi draws from a prognostication for the year 1485 written by the astrologer Marco Scribanario the disquieting conviction of the imminent rise of "new prophets who will make marvelous demonstrations of faith and of religion," adding that "in many places temples and oratories will be destroyed." Both Scribanario and Andrea Bernardi based their predictions on the conjunction of Jupiter and Saturn in the sign of the Scorpion.[37]

The text that perhaps contributed the most to expectations of a new prophet (still using the great planetary conjunction as a base) was the *Pro-*

[35] In connection with these events, see at least Eugenio Garin, "Il pronostico dell'Arquato sulla distruzione dell'Europa," in his *L'età nuova. Ricerche di storia della cultura dal XII al XVI secolo* (Naples: Morano, 1969), pp. 105–11. Zambelli, "Fine del mondo" reviews the bibliography on the topic (to which I might add Jean Deny, "Les Pseudo-prophéties concernant les Turcs au XVIe siècle," *Revue des études islamiques* 10 [1936]: 201–220, esp. "La Prédiction d'Antonio Torquato," 207–216) and treats the expectation of a pseudoprophet in the context of polemics concerning the flood (pp. 313–23).

[36] See Garin, "Il pronostico dell'Arquato," pp. 110–11.

[37] Andrea Bernardi, *Cronache forlivesi . . . dal 1476 al 1517*, ed. Giuseppe Mazzatinti, 2 vols. (Bologna: R. Deputazione di storia patria, 1895–1897), vol. 1, pt. 1, p. 156.

nosticatio of Johannes Lichtenberger in its fourteen Italian editions.[38] Lichtenberger's work can help us to a correct interpretation of the last text that interests us here, the *Pronosticho de Maestro Alberto Neapolitano sopra lanno 1523 Intitulato al Populo Christiano*, a work of four leaves with no indication of place or date of publication, as was usual for this type of publication. In its general lines the structure of this short work is not very different from that of others of the same sort. There is an astrological and theological introduction, then a few brief predictions relating to the seasons and the harvests, followed by a short note, "De le guerre et de la pace," a more general prediction, and, finally, a page devoted to conjunctions and oppositions of the moon and to the dates of movable feasts during the year.

A closer reading of the text shows, however, that the first part and the long concluding prediction are in reality literal borrowings of two long passages from Lichtenberger's *Pronosticatio*.[39] Worse, they are a plagiarism of a plagiarism in that they use the parts of Lichtenberger's work that he in turn had copied from the *Prognostica ad viginti annos duratura* of the Flemish mathematician (later bishop of Fossombrone) Paul of Middelburg (Paulus Middelburgensis).[40] It goes without saying that in this whirl of references reaching back to ever higher cultural levels, the figure of Maestro Alberto Napoletano dissolves into thin air. As no other notice of such a person can be found, the name obviously was a convenient shield for the unknown compiler of the publication. It would nonetheless be too restrictive to consider this unknown person (whom we shall continue to call Alberto Napoletano, out of convention) merely a plagiarist. The second of

38 To the thirteen editions cited in Domenico Fava, "La fortuna del pronostico di Giovanni Lichtenberger in Italia nel Quattrocento e nel Cinquecento," *Gutenbergjahrbuch* 5 (1930): 126–48, we should add at least one more, cited in Ugo Baroncelli, "Altri incunabuli bresciani sconosciuti o poco noti," in *Contributi alla storia del libro italiano. Miscellanea in onore di Lamberto Donati* (Florence: L. S. Olschki, 1969), pp. 53–65, esp. 58–60.

39 The first passage begins with the words "Benedecta sia la maestà del creatore" and ends "et è venuto da lo ascendente insino a duodeci gradi de Scorpione del quale Venere è divisore" (*Pronosticho de Maestro Alberto Neapolitano sopra lanno 1523 Intitulato al Populo Christiano*, fols. A *r*–A ii*r*); the second begins "Bisognera dare nova lege per la humana necessità" and ends "& instituirà epso profeta una nova religione" (ibid., fols. 3*r*–4*r*, unnumbered). The Italian version followed here seems identical (among all the Italian editions of Lichtenberger that I have been able to check) with the *Pronosticatione in vulgare rara et piu non udita* . . . , "Impressa in Venetia nel anno MCCCCCXXV. Adi XIII Septembrio. Cavada da unaltra stampada in Modena per maestro Pietro Francioso nel anno MCCCCLXXXXIj adi XIV de aprile." The passages indicated are on fols. a. iiii*r*–b. i*r*; f. i*r*–f. ii*r*.

40 Paul of Middelburg's work, in its turn, was a "servile" copy (Warburg's term is "sklavischer Benutzung") of passages from the *De magnis conjunctionibus* of Albumazar (Abū Ma'shar): Aby M. Warburg, *Ausgewälte Schriften und Würdigungen*, ed. Dieter Wuttke (Baden-Baden: Verlag Valentin Koerner, 1980), pp. 234–35; Italian translation of the first edition, *La rinascita del paganesimo antico*, tr. Emma Cantimori Mezzomonti (Florence: La Nuova Italia, 1966), p. 341.

the two passages that he picked up from Lichtenberger (and he from Paulus) predicts the coming of a new prophet from the north, one who would excel in the interpretation of Scripture, belong to a monastic order, found a new religion, and give humanity new laws for its changing needs. It is immediately apparent, then, that this brief work was more than a plagiarism or yet another proof (even another relevant proof) of the success of Lichtenberger's *Pronosticatio* in Italy. Once again, we see an earlier text reinterpreted and reappropriated because there was a profound sentiment that it was again current. It responded to a situation that it had prefigured when it was written, and now, when that situation had taken on concrete form, it cast new light on it to show its hidden potentialities. In short, Alberto Napoletano's text should not be read simply as a cryptorepublication of Lichtenberger. In 1523, it presupposed an awareness (strongly anchored in the compiler's mind) that the prophet had in fact appeared in the person of Luther. It is interesting to note, what is more, that the text is cut so as to reverse the sense of Lichtenberger's prediction. Lichtenberger stated that the prophet who was to come would indeed have an excellent mind and profound knowledge, "but will often speak lies and will have his knowledge cauterized; and will have poison closed up in his tail like a scorpion, where the [planetary] conjunction is made, and will be the cause of the spilling of much blood."[41] He was thus to be a false prophet (and we might well wonder at this point whether the passage was present in the minds of the anonymous anti-Lutheran polemicists discussed above who speak precisely of "a false prophet who will give new and false laws"). The omission of this passage in Alberto Napoletano's text indicates instead a radically different choice—the implicit affirmation that Luther was, to the contrary, a prophet as "true as St. Francis and St. Dominic were" rather than a pseudoprophet like Muhammad.[42] For this reason it seems to me that we can speak of Reform propaganda (hidden, to be sure) in connection with this pamphlet. The point of view and the purpose in repeating some of the most suggestive pages of the *Pronosticatio* are, in the last analysis, not far from Luther's own when he reprinted the same work in 1527 with a preface of his writing in which he recalls that much of what Lichtenberger had stated was erroneous, but that there was still truth in his pages, given that he had written "on the basis of the signs and the warnings of God."[43] When he offered only the pages of the German astrologer that

[41] Lichtenberger, *Pronosticatione in vulgare*, fol. f. ii*v*.

[42] Ibid., fol. f. i*r*; Alberto Napoletano, *Pronosticho*, fol. 3*v*, unnumbered.

[43] Johannes Lichtenberger, *Die weissagunge Johannis Lichtenbergs deudsch, zugericht mit uleys. Sampt einer nutzlichen vorrede und unterricht D. Martini Luthers* (Wittenberg: [Hans Lufft], 1527). Luther's preface is reprinted in Warburg, *La rinascita del paganesimo antico*, pp. 377–82, from which I quote.

appeared to be confirmed by being realized, Alberto Napoletano made a selection that Luther thought unnecessary.

The *Pronosticho de Maestro Alberto Neapolitano* seems to have fulfilled a need for some time, because it was reprinted without changes in 1529, except for retouching the date included in the title and the figures in the lunar calendar on the last page.[44] It is a shame that we cannot know the reactions of the readers of the two pamphlets, although we can reconstruct an echo of them: Fernando Colombo, who had bought the 1523 version of the work, hastened to purchase the 1529 edition (and probably was highly disappointed when he discovered that it was actually identical to the earlier edition). Thus we do not know whether this text aroused suspicion in Church circles. The most probable hypothesis is that this evocation of Luther the prophet—the only text to do so, since the others treated him as a pseudoprophet and a monster—either eluded unfriendly eyes or simply passed unobserved. The name of Luther does not appear in it, it is true, but, as Delio Cantimori wrote about another sixteenth-century episode involving prophecy for propaganda purposes, it is surer and less compromising to let people read between the lines than to say certain things out loud.[45]

[44] *Pronosticho de Maestro Alberto Neapolitano sopra lanno. Mille cinquecento vintinove. Con el Tacuin dela Luna Intitulato al Populo Christiano* (n.p., n.d.).

[45] Delio Cantimori, *Umanesimo e religione nel Rinascimento* (Turin: G. Einaudi, 1975), p. 173.

6

BETWEEN ASTROLOGY AND PROPHECY: THE FLOOD OF 1524

Astrology and Prophecy: The Flood *in piscibus*

AS WE have seen, in the early sixteenth century the divinatory arts, prophecy, and scrutiny of the signs that God had impressed upon nature or transmitted to men through visions seemed to form a complex cultural nucleus somehow perceived as a unit by the *popolari* who participated in that culture. The next problem concerns the relationship between this cultural phenomenon and the astrological science of the time (including areas of possible overlap), which is in turn connected to the broader problem raised some time ago by Eugenio Garin of the diffusion and utilization of astrology outside the confines of the universities and the courts that were its designated seats.[1]

How city dwellers reacted to the flood predicted for February 1524 provides an interesting case in point and throws light on both aspects of the question.[2] The debate was launched by the publication in 1499 of the *Ephemerides* of Johann Stöffler (reprinted in Venice in 1522),[3] which predicted that, due to multiple planetary conjunctions that year in the sign of Pisces, a large number of catastrophes would take place in 1524. As has been observed, the quarrel soon took a nonprofessional turn and involved not only astrologers but also physicians, theologians, and philosophers, all of whom would of course have encountered astrology during the course of their uni-

[1] Eugenio Garin, *Lo zodiaco della vita. La polemica sull'astrologia dal Trecento al Cinquecento* (Rome and Bari: Laterza, 1976), p. 146; available in English as *Astrology in the Renaissance: The Zodiac of Life*, tr. Carolyn Jackson and June Allen, revised by Clare Robertson (London and Boston: Routledge and Kegan Paul, 1983), p. 93.

[2] For the quarrel over the flood, see the ample discussion in Paola Zambelli, "Fine del mondo o inizio della propaganda? Astrologia, filosofia della storia e propaganda politico-religiosa nel dibattito sulla congiunzione del 1524," in *Science, credenze occulte, livelli di cultura. Convegno internazionale di studi (Firenze, 26–30 giugno 1980)* (Florence: L. S. Olschki, 1982), pp. 291–368; Zambelli, "Da Giulio II a Paolo III. Come l'astrologo provocatore Luca Gaurico divenne vescovo," in Fabio Troncarelli, ed., *La città dei segreti. Magia, astrologia e cultura esoterica a Roma (XV–XVIII secolo)*, Convegno Roma ermetica (1983: Rome, Italy) (Milan: Franco Angeli, 1985).

[3] Johann Stöffler, *Almanach nova plurimis annis venturis inservientia* (Venice: Lucantonio Giunta, 1522).

versity studies. What interests us is not so much—or not only—to weigh these people's contributions to the question but rather to measure and characterize, insofar as possible, the involvement in this affair of various social levels and different social circles. This may furnish a first round of data helpful in evaluating the extent to which astrology had penetrated the culture of the urban lower classes, how it was regarded, and, in this specific case, to what extent it was connected with the prophetic tensions that, as we have seen, played such a vital role among these segments of society at the time.

A Case of Collective Panic

Prediction of the flood *in piscibus* had a vast and far-reaching resonance. The sources seem to agree in insisting, albeit in generic terms, on the breadth and universality of the fear it generated. In the Marches the terrifying rumor spread that Mount Conero, which rises by the Adriatic south of Ancona, would be submerged, as would the Guasco hill, the site of the city's cathedral, San Ciriaco.[4] Tommasino Lancellotti wrote that in Modena "everyone is fearful," adding, "there has been great terror in people and perhaps some have died of fear."[5] Marin Sanudo, noting news that he had received from the *terraferma*, states, "The whole land is inclined to devotion for fear of these floods. . . . The entire mainland is in great fear."[6] The astrologer Silvestro Lucarelli reported that in Rome most people, if

[4] See Alessandro Pastore, "Un corrispondente sconosciuto di Pietro Pomponazzi. Il medico Giacomo Tiburzi da Pergola e le sue lettere," *Quaderni per la storia dell'Università di Padova* 17 (1984): 67–88, esp. p. 77, which stresses the widespread expectation of the flood in the region around Ancona. On the same subject, see Carlo Piancastelli, *Pronostici ed almanacchi. Studio di bibliografia romagnola* (Rome: D. Ripamonti, 1913), p. 32. For another example, see *Pronostico di Maestro Constantino de S. Maria in Georgio phisico excellentissimo sopra la significatione de li Eclipsi de la Luna e convento e congregatione de li pianeti nel signo di Pesce*: "Impresso in Ancona: per maestro Bernardino Guiraldo da Vercelli. Anno D.ni MDXXIII a di primo del Mese de Agosto." On this publication and on the efforts of the printer Bernardino Guerralda to publicize the flood, see Filippo M. Giochi and Alessandro Mordenti, *Annali della tipografia in Ancona 1512–1799* (Rome: Edizioni di storia e letteratura, 1980), pp. xxx–xxxvi, 20–22, 30, 32–33.

[5] Tommasino Lancellotti, *Cronica modenese*, Biblioteca Estense di Modena, MS α T1 2, fols. 176*v*–177*v*. In this chapter I have preferred to cite the manuscript version of this work rather than the printed edition cited elsewhere because the latter has a number of elisions and omissions concerning the very events under consideration. For example, Lancellotti's sense of alarm also came from the careful meteorological notes that he kept day by day for the entire month of February, which he subsequently amended in a more optimistic direction. These notations were all omitted from the printed edition.

[6] Marino Sanuto, *Diarii*, 58 vols. (Venice: R. Deputazione veneta di storia patria, 1879–1903), vol. 35, cols. 332 and 341.

not everyone, and people of all social conditions feared the flood: "Plurimos, ne dicam omnes, ac cuiusque conditionis homines, diluvium valde pertimescere."[7]

We shall soon see to what extent we can accept Lucarelli's statement at face value and apply it outside Rome. For now, it is important to note that the channels of communication concerning the expected flood were not the same for all social classes. In descending order of the social and cultural hierarchy, we find Latin treatises, epistolary communications, annual works of prognostication in Latin, brief works and annual prognostications in the vernacular, and, finally, oral transmission. All these means of transmission except the last, which remains hypothetical, can be documented.

We shall return, however, to preaching, an important and ascertainable oral means of communication. Giacomo Tiburzi, a physician in Pergola, in the duchy of Urbino, wrote in November 1523 that in earlier years the flood had been "ab astrologis praenunciato, a circulatoribus in foro decantato, ac a viris religiosis in rostris universo audiente populo divulgato."[8] Astrologers, *cantastorie*, and preachers all contributed to oral communication and to the extremely broad diffusion of diluvial predictions. Tiburzi, on the other hand, stresses the special role of preaching as a "mass medium" ("universo audiente populo"). This special role is confirmed in the journals of Andrea Pietramellara, son of the astrologer Giacomo Pietramellara. According to another source, Giovanni Cambi's *Istorie*, the Conventual Franciscans played a particularly prominent role in preaching about the flood, but "the Observant friars of St. Dominic laughed at the idea."[9] Whether people believed in it or no, the flood had become a commonplace. As early as May 1521, Niccolò Machiavelli included "the flood that is to come . . . and similar stories for tavern benches" in a listing of banal topics of conversation. When Francesco Guicciardini mentions the promised flood in a letter dated 25 January 1524 addressed to Cesare Colombo, his Roman correspondent for matters relating to the governance of Modena, his tone is light and he gives no explanations, taking it for granted that Colombo will understand what he is alluding to: "everything is asleep here; I dearly hope that either the deluge or some explosion in Lombardy will soon wake us up."[10]

[7] Silvestro Lucarelli, *Prognosticon anni MDXXIV quo opiniones pseudoastrologorum diluvium et siccitatem praesentis anni falso praedicentium improbantur* (Rome: [Francesco Minizio Calvo], 1524), fol. A i*v*.

[8] Cited in Pastore, "Un corrispondente sconosciuto," p. 77.

[9] Nerio Malvezzi, "Il diario metereologico di Andrea Pietramellara per l'anno 1524," in *Atti e memorie della R. Deputazione di storia patria per le provincie di Romagna*, ser. 3, no. 2 (1884): p. 445; Giovanni Cambi, *Istorie*, in Fr. Ildefonso di San Luigi, ed., *Delizie degli eruditi toscani*, 24 vols. (Florence: Gaetano Cambiagi, 1770–1789), vol. 23, p. 254.

[10] Niccolò Machiavelli, *Lettere*, ed. Franco Gaeta (Milan: Feltrinelli, 1961), p. 409; avail-

Not only had this particular flood become a commonplace; the very idea of a flood was part of the patrimony of widely held notions and clichés in fifteenth- and sixteenth-century Italy. There was a specific reason for this. *Diluvio*, "deluge," could be, and indeed in this period was, used as a synonym for *alluvione*, "flood,"[11] and, taken in this sense, "deluges" had occurred with unheard-of frequency in recent decades. Toward the end of the fifteenth century the effects of the deforestation practiced in Italy between the Trecento and the Quattrocento began to be felt, and they were disastrous. Data on the Po basin and water courses in Lombardy show that whereas between 1400 and 1450 there had been only two floods and one occasion on which high water broke through the embankments, between 1450 and 1500 there were seven floods and four breakthroughs, and from 1500 to 1550 six floods and three breakthroughs. According to other data, the Modena countryside suffered more than thirty floods, inundations, and washouts between 1493 and 1550.[12] We can find an echo of these disasters in the verse compositions addressed to a general public (and full of prophetic allusions) that were recited by the *cantambanchi* and published in low-cost, broadly distributed fugitive print pieces. Such works brandished the terrifying word in their titles: *Del diluvio di Roma del MCCCCLXXXXV*; *Diluvio successo in Cesena del 1525*; *Diluvio di Roma che fu a dì sette di ottobre lanno del mille cinquecento e trenta.*[13]

This literary genre, mixing poetry, prophecy, and chronicle, undoubtedly had a certain vogue and a sizable circulation, as reflected in Francesco Berni's burlesque imitation of the genre in his *Capitolo del diluvio*, which described the inundations that followed when in 1521 a brook in the Mugello, the Muccione, and the Sieve, a tributary of the Arno, overflowed

---

able in English as *The Letters of Machiavelli*, tr. and ed. Allan Gilbert (New York: Capricorn Books, 1961), p. 201; Francesco Guicciardini, *Carteggi*, ed. Roberto Palmarocchi, 17 vols. (Bologna: Nicola Zanichelli, 1938–), vol. 7, p. 59.

11 Paul of Middelburg even expressed irritation at the confusion of the two terms: Paulus Middelburgensis, *Prognosticon R.p.d. Pauli de Middelburgo episcopi Forosemproniensis ostendens anno MDXXIV nullum neque universale neque provinciale diluvium futurum* (n.p., n.d. [Venice, 1523]), fol. A. iv*r*.

12 *Vie d'acqua da Milano al mare. L'avvenire della navigazione interna padana*, catalogue ed. Aldo Giobbio (Ospiate/Bollate: Tip. I.G.A., 1963), p. 66; Gian Luigi Basini, *L'uomo e il pane. Risorse, consumi e carenze alimentari nella popolazione modenese nel Cinque e Seicento* (Milan: A. Giuffrè, 1970), pp. 127–30.

13 Giuliano Dati, *Del diluvio di Roma del MCCCCLXXXXV adi iiii di dicembre et daltre cose di gran meraviglia* (n.p., n.d.); Cornelio Guasconi, *Diluvio successo in Cesena del 1525 adi 10 de luglio* (Venice: Nicolò di Aristotele detto il Zoppino, 1526); *Diluvio di Roma che fu a dì sette di ottobre lanno del mille cinquecento e trenta* (Venice: "ad instantia de Zoanmaria Lirico Venetiano"). Information on other popular print pieces with verse descriptions of floods can be found in Robert Weiss, "Cesena e il suo diluvio del 1525 in un poemetto poco noto," in *Contributi alla storia del libro italiano. Miscellanea in onore di Lamberto Donati* (Florence: L. S. Olschki, 1969), pp. 359–69.

their banks.[14] Berni used the narrative techniques and the cadences of deluge literature to parody it. Addressing an imaginary audience, he employs buffoonery to evoke the aura of holy terror of inundations that pervaded such compositions. Because floods and inundations—God's castigation par excellence—recalled the Universal Flood of Genesis, they served as warnings and fitted into the complex systems of signs of divine wrath. On occasion they even acquired a prophetic significance. Leandro Alberti, speaking of the Tiber in his *Descrittione di tutta Italia*, calls the river a "true and religious prophet and diviner," and notes that "clearly, never has it been seen to come out of its bed and inundate Rome that it was not followed by some great destruction, war, pestilence, or famine."[15] Thus a flood might be but the first of many tremendous catastrophes sent by God, and this was precisely how the *cantastorie* presented them.

All this helps us to understand what lay behind a fear of floods. I might note that although Stöffler speaks of many calamities, he says not a word about floods. Only gradually did astrological literature begin to predict floods, which were never presented as coming alone, but were given as the first of many disasters. That the planetary conjunction prompting the current danger was to take place in Pisces, the water sign, undoubtedly shaped predictions. Still, we should not forget that floods, whether *diluvio* or *alluvione*, had recently become a more urgent problem and that they had acquired a strong prophetic and divinatory meaning familiar to a vast public. Thus out of the vague congeries of disasters predicted by Stöffler and his imitators the flood came to predominate. We find little echo in the popular consciousness of the forecasts of earthquakes and religious upheavals that took up so much space in the astrologers' predictions.[16]

Awaiting Divine Castigation

In reality, then, the flood of 1524 was viewed less as an exceptional astral catastrophe than as an aggravated version of a situation that was already all

[14] Francesco Berni, *Rime*, ed., Giorgio Barberi Squarotti (Turin: G. Einaudi, 1969), pp. 9–12.

[15] Leandro Alberti, *Descrittione di tutta Italia* (Venice: Domenico de' Farri, 1557), fol. 77*r*. This was a familiar commonplace. Pietro Martire d'Anghiera, writing to Pomponio Leto on 12 May 1499, states that it originated in the tradition of classical antiquity, for which see *Opus epistolarum Petri Martyris Anglerii* (Amsterdam: typis Elzevirianis, 1670), p. 118. Luis Gómez, *De prodigiosis Tyberis inundationibus* (Rome, 1531), reiterates the theme. In a letter sent 22 October 1530 to the marchese Federico II Gonzaga of Mantua, the recent flood in Rome is treated not only as a "judgment of God" but also as "prodigious and indicative of most terrible effects": Sanuto, *Diarii*, vol. 52, cols. 74–76.

[16] See, for example, Lodovico Vitali, *De terremotu* (Bologna: Giovanni Antonio Benedetti, 1508), fol. B ii *v*.

too familiar and that recalled hardships everyone had experienced. Any severe thunderstorm might be a signal and forewarning of its coming. On 17 October 1523, Lunardo Anselmi, consul for the Serenissima in Naples, sent word to the authorities in Venice of disastrous downpours that had inundated Naples four days before, "carrying away along via de san Zenaro [Via San Gennaro] trees [and] houses, with death of males and females, [and] all the mills ruined." Returning to the topic several days later, he drew a connection between the end of the rainfall and some people's opinion that the "prediction of the future deluge known in all the world" had turned out to be false.[17] Consul Anselmi and his circle had thus believed that the deluge *in piscibus* had already begun, and a contingent improvement in meteorological conditions was enough to prompt their disbelief in the astrologers' predictions.

Ways of dealing with the coming flood necessarily included expedients that had already been tried. Giuliano Dati describes in his *Diluvio di Roma* people procuring boats or moving to the upper stories of their houses or to the rooftops. Analogous preparations and systems of defense were put into operation to escape the effects of the sixteen terrible planetary conjunctions. As Eustachio Celebrino, a polygraph and engraver from Udine, stated,

> con victuaglie in cima agli alti monti
> ciascun s'asconde, se rinchiude e serra.
>
> (with victuals on top of the high mountains everyone hides himself, closes himself up, and locks the doors.)[18]

This was not mere poetic exaggeration. Evidence related to the event is so abundant and detailed that it leaves little room for doubt. In Rome and Florence great stores of grain were laid up. Anton Francesco Doni later wrote that in Rome "all fled into the highest rooms of the houses . . . and many left the city, retreating to the mountains." The astrologer Lucarelli, who arrived in Rome from the provincial city of Camerino in December 1523, totally unaware of the excitement, reports that alarm was general, and that in particular many nobles so feared that the Tiber would flood that they used hunting trips as an excuse to take to the hills.[19] Similar behavior was noted in other parts of Italy as well. In Sicily, many people

[17] Sanuto, *Diarii*, vol. 35, col. 171.

[18] Eustachio Celebrino, *La dechiaratione per che non è venuto il diluvio del 1524* (Venice: Francesco Bindoni e Matteo Pasini compagni, n.d. [1524]), fol. D. 2*r*.

[19] Francisco Delicado, *La Lozana andaluza*, ed. L. Orioli (Milan: Adelphi, 1970), p. 222; in English, *Portrait of Lozana: The Lusty Andalusian Woman*, tr. Bruno M. Damiani (Potomac, Md.: Scripta Humanistica, 1987), p. 285; Cambi, *Istorie*, p. 255; [Anton Francesco Doni], *Mondo piccolo dell'Accademia peregrina* (Venice: Francesco Marcolini, 1552), fol. 11*r*; Lucarelli, *Prognosticon*, fol. A i*v*.

fortified the doors of their houses; in Friuli and the Vicenza area, Sanudo reports, people "prepared wooden houses in the mountains with provisions"; elsewhere, houseboats or skiffs were built to ride out the flood.[20]

In short, the rich fled to the country much as they had done in times of pestilence—at least, the social selection involved was much the same. Those who were unable to amass provisions in mountain areas or rent space on upper floors reacted differently. Isidoro Isolani put it quite explicitly: "talia quidem excogitare ad principes spectat, perficere nobilium est. Plebs nempe . . . divinae pietatis opus arbitramur."[21] Thus great collective and civic religious rites were needed, and indeed did take place. There were public recitations of the litany to the Virgin, mass communions, and alms offered "for the community"; in Naples there were spontaneous penitential processions of "many young girls . . . with their hair in disarray and bare feet." More often, such processions were organized by the diocesan authorities, as was the case in France in Besançon or in Italy in Modena and Brescia, where representatives of all segments of associative civic life, "schools and arts [guilds], friars, priests," made their way through the city for three days in a row.[22] Two points need to be stressed. First, these were urban and communitarian patterns of behavior representing a specific contrast to the more private actions of those who moved to higher ground or took to the hills. Second, these collective efforts to ward off the catastrophe were immediately taken over by the ecclesiastical hierarchy, who established rigorous control over them. In theory, religious life should not have been affected by the results of a planetary conjunction that had been predicted on the basis of astrological science. In this case, however, the minute astrology left the inner circle of the specialists, prophecy was superimposed on it. The deluge *in piscibus* appeared to be a catastrophe sent by divine wrath, and as such it was an easy substitute for the Turkish peril in the schemes of the literary genre of prophetic preaching that we have already examined. We have no direct evidence, but it is certainly highly probable that the preachers who gave sermons predicting the flood in Florence, Bo-

[20] Francesco Maurolico, *Sicanarum rerum compendium* (Messina: Petrus Spira, 1562), fol. 200*v*; Sanuto, *Diarii*, vol. 35, col. 341; Agostino Nifo, *De falsa diluvii prognosticatione* (Bologna: Girolamo Benedetti, 1520), fol. a. ii*r*; Isidoro Isolani O.P., *Ex humana divinaque sapientia tractatus de futura nova mundi mutatione* (Bologna: Girolamo Benedetti, 1523), fol. 17*r*.

[21] Isolani, *Ex humana divinaque sapientia tractatus*, fol. 17*r*.

[22] Sanuto, *Diarii*, vol. 35, cols. 163 and 340–41; *Letters and Papers, Foreign and Domestic of the Reign of Henry VIII*, 21 vols. (London: Longman & Co., 1862–1932), vol. 6 (1870), pt. 1, p. 10. Brescia had been braced for the deluge for years: On 20 August 1519 the Brescian notary Girolamo Stella wrote to his brother Antonio that a tornado had devastated the countryside to such an extent that people "thought that all the land would be destroyed and submerged. I think that the deluge that is supposed to come in 1524 is trying to come this year": Sanuto, *Diarii*, vol. 27, col. 591. On Modena, see below.

logna, and the duchy of Urbino followed an outline much like the one in Agostino Nifo's *De falsa diluvii pronosticatione*. Nifo argued that if Noah's flood had been caused by human evil, certainly there should come a flood *now*, when the sins of humankind have never been so great: "futurum diluvium non vi illius contentus tamen, sed vi humani sceleris . . . sit diiudicandum."[23] It was in fact precisely in January 1524, when discussions were at their most heated and fear at its peak, that a series of letters was sent from the Holy See to ecclesiastical authorities in a number of Italian cities to remind them of the decrees concerning preaching established by the Fifth Lateran Council.[24] Why should it have been felt necessary to tighten control over preaching at just this moment? One possible answer is that this was simply a repressive norm from the beginnings of the Reformation, but the timing is so perfect as to suggest that the Church was attempting to control a recrudescence of apocalyptical thought, the prelude to which certainly existed, and probably concrete signs of it as well.

Furthermore, it is significant that in 1523 when Isolani proclaimed an "immutatio futura in omni vivente," basing his argument on the stars, he felt it necessary to confirm this prediction by citing prophecies of the blessed Veronica of Binasco and to conclude that prayer was the only effective way of warding off the flood. In 1524 Paulus Angelus—a well-known star in the prophetic constellation of the sixteenth century—stated his opposition to the "confuse sonans nomen illud praeteritum iam diluvii pro coniunctionibus planetarum" that had been revealed to him personally by means of visions warning that the sword of divine wrath was ready to strike the Christian world.[25]

Thus the idea that divine castigation was imminent in the concrete form of a flood, not because of the planetary conjunction but because of the sins of humankind, was present on different cultural levels. It was a commonplace, but in the specific circumstances it lent itself well to being used as an efficacious instrument of propaganda. During the course of the month of February an epistolary *Avviso* in vernacular, dated from Trent, 6 February, circulated in Italy and was sent through his ambassador to the doge by the marchese of Mantua, Federico II Gonzaga. (Sanudo commented, "non fo creto," "it was not believed.")[26] The letter told of floods and terrible inundations of the Danube and the Rhine that had submerged villages and towns in Germany, "opened and destroyed mountains, and covered many

[23] Nifo, *De falsa diluvii prognosticatione*, fol. a. iiiir.

[24] See above, p. 113.

[25] Isolani, *Ex humana divinaque sapientia tractatus*, fols. 15*r–v*; *Epistola Pauli Angeli . . . in Sathan ruinam tyranidis . . . item prefatio eiusdem P.A. . . . cum enucleata veraci apertiorique declaratione perfecta detegendo quid generis diluviorum coniunctio planetarum in anno MDXXIV significare voluerit* (n.p., n.d. [1524]), fols. 3*v*–4*r*.

[26] Sanuto, *Diarii*, vol. 35, col. 450.

villas and castles." The writer then recalled, in a seemingly abrupt shift of topic, that "the Lutheran opinion perseveres and grows" in precisely those regions, and he concludes with a warning that "the lord God will punish this crime with his scourge, *as he has already begun to do*." The thread of his argument is shown by where it leads: The flood, which he posits as already having taken place, thus served as a divine weapon offered to the Catholics for an easy victory over the arrogant Lutherans. The anti-Reformation slant of the sheet is obvious, and it becomes even more so in light of the deliberate falsity of the news given.

The relationship between the flood and the Reformation was not always understood in that key. In Rome, people seemed to allege some sort of connection between Luther and the catastrophe of the flood, seen as God's chastisement of the Church. Iacopo Lopis Stunica (in Spanish, Jaime López de Zúñiga) took the trouble, in an *Epistula . . . super significationibus XVI coniunctionum in signo piscium* addressed to Paul of Middelburg and dated from Rome, 8 January 1524, to counter the hypothesis that Luther was the prophet created by the sixteen great conjunctions, which he attributes to Giannotti. According to Lopis Stunica, this figure was a pseudoprophet who came from the south, not from the north as did the Saxon monk. He seems so intent on denying this hypothesis that we sense an interest in avoiding the image of Luther as a prophet that we have traced earlier. The following day, 9 January, Marino da Pozzo, secretary to Cardinal Francesco Pisani, wrote from Rome to Francesco Spinelli concerning the excitement in the city over Luther. After noting that "it is said that the pope will make him a cardinal so as to silence him," Da Pozzo gives a glimpse of his own opinions: "and I believe that this will be the deluge of the Church, but God will not want to see such destruction of the Church."[27]

"This" refers to Luther, not to the high waters expected in February. Here the deluge is not only divine castigation for the sins of humankind but also the destruction and submersion of the Church, its definitive ruin without hope of correction or ultimate salvation. Isidoro Isolani, reiterating the saving virtues of prayer to combat the flood, added, in like fashion,

[27] [Jaime López de Zúñiga], *Epistola Stunicae ad R.P. Episcopum Forosempronien. super significationibus XVI coniunctionum in signo piscium que future sunt mense Februario huius anni MDXXIIII* (n.p., n.d. [Rome: Marcello Silber, 1524]). See Alberto Tinto, *Gli annali tipografici di Eucario e Marcello Silber (1501–1527)* (Florence: L. S. Olschki, 1968), p. 186; Sanuto, *Diarii*, vol. 35, col. 334. The elector of Saxony was also aware of the rumor that Luther had been offered a cardinalcy: Hartmann Grisar, *Martin Luthers Leben und sein Werk* (Freiburg im Breisgau: B. Herder, 1926), available in English as *Martin Luther, His Life and Work*, adapted from the 2nd German edition by Frank J. Eble, ed. Arthur Preuss (Westminster, Md.: Newman Press, 1950), p. 141. It was reported a few decades later by Cosme de Aldana, *Discorso contro il volgo in cui con buone ragioni si reprovano molte sue false opinioni* (Florence: G. Marescotti, 1578), p. 193.

that only prayer was capable of saving the seat of Peter "ab incursibus tot adversantium, et magis forte internis quam externis."[28] Fear of the Lutherans, of the fragmentation of Christianity, and of the dismantling of ecclesiastical institutions was thus intimately connected with fear of the flood, through which it took on more concrete form. Albrecht Dürer's famous dream can perhaps be interpreted in a similar manner: Several years later (30 May 1525), he dreamed of the universal deluge fifteen days after the defeat of the peasants in the battle of Frankenhausen and four days after the decapitation of Thomas Münzer, and he illustrated his nightmare in a watercolor now in Vienna.[29] The deluge could be elevated to a symbol and provide a focus for the genuine anxiety prompted by the weakening of social structures and of religious unity in Europe at the beginning of the modern era; it could also be proposed as an awe-inspiring phantasm that obligatorily called forth a penitential *animus* and behavior (this is the sense in which processions and other collective rites should be understood) and made it necessary to tighten the reins on traditional orthodox religion.

The Deluge and Church Reform: Jean Albertin

A spiritual and prophetic reading of the deluge as the submersion of the Church can also be found in the work of a singular and isolated figure, Jean Albertin or Albertini, a priest from the Valais. We know little about him except that he was still living in 1542 and served as the administrator of the hospital in Sion.[30] Of his several remaining writings, one is of particular interest for our purposes, the *De mirabili temporis mutatione ac terrene potestatis a loco in locum translatione*, published by the Geneva printer Wygand Köln in 1524. In this brief work, Jean Albertin, who proclaims himself a prophet and doctor of theology, predicts the renewal of the universal Church and the imminent end of time. The Church, Albertin says, was once a precious edifice of sapphires and gems, but with the passage of time useless stones had been added to it. "In presenti mutatione, que est ecclesie reformatio." Those useless stones will be torn down, he continues, and, thanks to the abuses of the Roman curia, the power of Peter will be taken away from Rome and be transferred to the Church of Sion.[31] We might well wonder how Albertin could possibly have reached such a singular con-

[28] Isolani, *Ex humana divinaque sapientia tractatus*, fol. 17*r*.

[29] See A. Rosenthal, "Dürer's Dream of 1525," *Burlington Magazine* 69 (1936): 82–85.

[30] Henri Naef, *Les Origines de la Réforme à Genève: La cité des évêques, l'humanisme, les signes précurseurs* (Geneva: E. Droz, 1936), p. 427. On Albertin in general, see pp. 427–35. To my knowledge, publications in Geneva relating to the flood have not yet been studied.

[31] Johannes Albertinus, *De mirabili temporis mutatione ac terrene potestatis a loco in locum translatione* (Geneva: Wygand Köln, 1524), fols a. iv*r* and a. ii*r*–*v*.

clusion, and it is tempting to conjecture that he had somehow come to know (in whole or in part) the "book" that had appeared eight years earlier in Rome in which a monk named Bonaventura proclaimed the decadence of the Roman See and predicted "se . . . translaturum imperium ecclesiae ad ecclesiam in Syon"—that is, Zion, or Jerusalem.[32] If so, Albertin would have to have interpreted this passage in a highly personal, idiosyncratic manner, which was not impossible in the early decades of the sixteenth century.

In any event, Albertin declares in *De mirabili temporis mutatione* that even the stars show that great turmoil is nigh. The age of Noah has returned, he says, and a deluge (more spiritual than meteorological, however) is approaching: "omnium viciorum suprema inundatio, exorta ex partibus inferioribus" was about to submerge even the highest places (that is, the ecclesiastical hierarchy). As in the age of Noah when only those closed within the ark were saved, so now only those who take refuge in the spiritual ark of the "renewed Holy Mother Church" will be saved. Two signs were given to confirm this transformation of the Church, both taken from 4 Esdras (an apocryphal text that would, incidentally, repay study of its prophetic function at the beginning of the early modern period). The first passage, it seems to me, gives truly singular evidence of the profound impression that the invention of print made on contemporaries, to the point that, like the discovery of America, it acquired eschatological significance. Citing Esdras, Albertin writes that before the end "libri aperientur ante faciem firmamenti, et omnes videbunt simul. Libri per magna parte fuerunt aperti per artem impressoriam: per quam infiniti libri qui fuerent absconditi venerunt ad lucem." The second sign proclaimed in Esdras was that women would be delivered prematurely and the aborted fetus would live. Indeed, Albertin says, this is precisely what has begun to happen in the church of the Virgin "in villa Blise" (Blitzingen), where stillborn infants resuscitate—a detail that tells us that the church in Blitzingen was one of the hundreds of *sanctuaires à répit* that held out hope for the salvation of unbaptized dead infants by arranging for their momentary resurrection. Finally, Jean Albertin concludes, universal peace must be established and a general council must be convoked "propter ecclesiastici status reformationem."[33]

Even in the somewhat confused pages of Albertin's treatise, then, the image of the expected flood played a central role and was inextricably min-

[32] *Exemplum literarum Domini Stephani Rosin Caesareae Majestatis apud S. Sedem sollicitatoris ad Reverendum Principem D. Carolum Gurcensem* in Constantin Höfler, "Analecten zur Geschichte Deutschlands und Italiens," *Abhandlungen der Historischen Klasse der königlich Bayerischen Akademie der Wissenschaften* 4, no. 3 (1846): 56. On Bonaventura, see Giampaolo Tognetti, "Bonaventura," DBI, vol. 11, pp. 611–12.

[33] Albertinus, *De mirabili temporis mutatione*, fols. a. iv*r*; b. ii*v*; b. iii*r*; c. ii*r*.

gled with the notion of the renewal of the Church. Ecclesiastical society was to be profoundly transformed by the flood and would turn to new prophets and heed the prodigies that were omens revealing divine will. What makes the views of this Valais priest important is that they confirm the complexity of the meanings—the religious meanings, in particular—that contemporaries attributed to the diluvial catastrophe. The text is also interesting because it allows us to see that expectation of the deluge was widespread in the Valais and in Geneva. Indeed, in the *Annales de la cité de Genève* attributed to Jean Savion (but probably the work of his brother Jacques) we read that "in that year [1524] a certain fantasy-prone astrologer predicted in public by means of print that in that year a deluge would come like the one of Noah's time, which astonished many people, but events showed the contrary."[34] It is of course difficult, not to say impossible, to establish the identity of the "fantastique astrologue" to whom Savion refers. We might note, however, that in 1526 Wygand Köln, Jean Albertin's publisher, published comic prognostications under the title *Merveilles advenir en cestuy an vingt et sis*, a work structured as a response to predictions of the flood in Geneva. The text of this pamphlet refers to 1524 and not 1526, as is clear from the rhymes, which were distorted in order to update the original text:

> Je fais sçavoir que an moys de mars
> de cest an courant vingt et sit [quatre]
> plouviont nobles, douples ducas,
> ecus royaulx, quatre à quatre.
>
> (I tell you that in the month of March of this current year twenty-six [four] noble [coins], double ducats [and] royal *écus* will rain down hand over fist.)

The anonymous author turns prediction of the deluge upside down by listing Lenten foods:

> Puis tomberont aulx et oignons,
> pleura vinaygre, huille de noix,
> molles, aigrefins, estourions,
> ambles, anguilles, lavares.
>
> (Then there will fall garlics and onions, it will rain vinegar, walnut oil, mussels, haddock, sturgeon, perch, eels, whitefish.)

In the final hundred lines the poet assails the astrologers as mad perverters of the true faith ("those who fear floods [are] all insane and apostate").

[34] *Annales de la cité de Genève attribuées à Iean Savyon*, ed. Edouard Fick (Geneva, 1858), p. 113.

Who could have believed, he continues, "that magicians, mathematicians and necromancers could have such a wide hearing among us?" All they do is to spread "errors, lies, [and] heretical maxims" against the true faith. The author concludes with the fear that the erroneous calculations of those who had predicted "that we must die by a vast inundation of water" would in the end change the very motion of the great machine of the heavens:

> S'ilz continuent, vous verréz que les cieulx,
> la grant machine et tout le firmament,
> sera rieglé par l'erreur vicieulx
> de quoy ilz usent, d'ung veult ambicieulx,
> et changera l'antique mouvemant.
>
> (If they continue, you will see that the heavens, the great machine and the entire firmament will be regulated by the depraved error that they pursue with ambitious desire, and will alter the ancient motion.)[35]

We will find voices in Italy not too unlike this anonymous Genevan's, authors whose verse combined an impatient and burlesque parody of astrologers and their calculations with a more serious opposition between the true faith and the claims to decipher the heavens by means of a false and deceiving science.

Carnival Rites in Venice and Rome

The fear that gripped people in 1524 touched a good part of Italy and of Europe, extending from Brescia to Vicenza, Friuli, Trent, Mantua, Rome, Naples, Modena, and Ancona and including vast areas of France, Germany, Spain, and the duchy of Savoy.[36]

In Venice, however, Tommasino Lancellotti reported that "people are talking against the flood."[37] As we have seen, the dramatic announcement that the deluge had already taken place in Germany "was not believed" by the members of the Great Council, and it was only as a joke that Ruzante asked one of his ladyloves to prepare him a garret room in no less a struc-

[35] *Merveilles advenir en cestuy an vingt et sis. Prognostication satirique pour l'année 1526* ([Geneva: Wygand Köln] Geneva, 1893), pp. 27, 33–36.

[36] As discussed above. See also Pierre Bayle, s.v. "Stöffler," in his *Dictionnaire historique et critique*, 4th ed. rev., 4 vols. (Amsterdam: P. Brunel, 1730), vol. 4, pp. 285–87. For Spain, see Juan de Cazalla, bishop of Vera, "Escriptora contra los astrologos judiciarios," in Melquiades Andrés, "Un tratado teologico de Juan de Cazalla contra la astrologia judiciaria (1523)," *Burgense* 16 (1975): 583. Cazalla's brief tract is clearly based on the *Tractato contra li astrologi* of Girolamo Savonarola, though he does not mention the work (see below, n. 64).

[37] Lancellotti, *Cronica*, vol. 1, fol. 176*r*.

ture than the bell tower of St. Mark's.[38] That this was a broad joke (based, however, on farcical exaggeration of an accepted reality) is confirmed by the fact that on the very day of 4 February—the day on which the planetary conjunction was to have reached its most threatening point—Ruzante joined the buffoon Zuan Polo and other friends from the Compagnia degli Ortolani in a masquerade. The revelers were all

> dressed in costumes of crimson velvet with large sleeves of shimmering multicolored silk and with satin and velvet hats on their heads [and] face masks with noses. And each of them had two servants before him, each one with a torch in his hand, dressed as a peasant. One of them had a golden costume and they had great skill: first [came the] buffoons Zuan Polo and others, along with Ruzante of Padua, others dressed as peasants who jumped about and danced very well, and six disguised as young peasants who sang *villote*, and they all had various rustic things in their hands such as hoes, shovels, stakes, spades, rakes, etc., as well as trumpets, pipes, flutes, and deafening horns. And they went around the square of San Marco, then in the evening with their torches lit they went about the [city], and at one o'clock in the evening [7 P.M.] they came to the Palace of the Doge, in the courtyard, to show off their skill.[39]

The fact of the matter was that 4 February was not only "el dì del gran deslubio," as the *Alfabeto dei villani* called it, confusing it with the Day of Judgment,[40] but also *la zobia giota*—Fat Thursday—hence Carnival season. Carnival, which was just as much a collective rite as the religious processions that took place in Brescia, Modena, and Besançon, furnished the second great antidote to fear of the flood. The object of people's terror was transformed into an object of laughter; its real meaning was turned upside down by obscene double meanings; the stars and the planetary conjunctions were brought down to the level of bodily and genital functions. When Carnival, following its normal function, turned the deluge *in piscibus* into a *diluvio d'unto e grasso*, laughter gave it the power to conjure away the looming peril. This was precisely what happened during the first week of February 1524. The flood was chosen as the theme for Carnival floats and masquerades. In Rome, for example, there was a float "that was Noah's ark, on which there was a musical group that sang to signify that the flood had passed, and they loosed birds from the ark, a very lovely idea invented

38 "Lettera qual scrive Ruzante a una so morosa," in *Le lettere di messer Andrea Calmo riprodotte sulle stampe migliori*, ed. Vittorio Rossi (Turin: E. Loescher, 1888), p. cxx and n. pp. cxix–cxxi.

39 Sanuto, *Diarii*, vol. 35, col. 393.

40 Emilio Lovarini, *Studi sul Ruzzante e la letteratura pavana*, ed. Gianfranco Folena (Padua: Antenore, 1965), p. 429.

for Cardinal Cesarino."[41] On another float, the creation of Archbishop Marco Corner, "which was a boat being prepared to flee the deluge, and inside there was a very good musical group with lutes and viols," singers performed a song composed by Agostino Bevazzano that was a tissue of allusions and double meanings, respecting the prescribed patterns of the literary genre of Carnival songs. The singers sang of their flight from the deluge and invited the ladies to join them:

Belle donne, vi exortamo
a congiongervi con noi
perché quel che non possiamo
soli far, farem con voi;
non perdete il tempo poi,
ché il diluvio è per venire.
Noi portiam certi instrumenti
da allegrarvi il cor nel petto:
che li usiate siam contenti
per magior vostro diletto.

(Lovely women, we exhort you to join with us, because what we cannot do alone, we will do with you; waste no time, for the flood is about to come. We bear certain implements to cheer your hearts in your breasts: we will be happy if you use them for your greater delight.)[42]

Obscene double meanings were expected of Carnival language not only at the popular level but also at the level of the archbishop's *invenzioni*. In Florence, parading hermits invited Florentine women to take to the hills with them

imperò che ogni astrolago e indovino
v'han tutti sbigottiti
(secondo che da molti inteso abbiano)
che un tempo orrendo e strano
minaccia a ogni terra
peste, diluvio e guerra,
fulgur, tempeste, tremuoti, rovine,
come se già del monde fussi fine.
E voglion soprattutto che le stelle
influssin con tant'acque

[41] Sanuto, *Diarii*, vol. 35, col. 422.

[42] Ibid., col. 423. On Agostino Bevazzano or Beazano, secretary to Cardinal Marco Corner and, later, to Pietro Bembo, see Francesco Tateo, "Beaziano (Beazzano, Bevazzano), Agostino," in DBI, vol. 7, pp. 390–93, and the notes in Baldassare Castiglione, *Il Cortegiano del conte Baldesar Castiglione*, ed. Vittorio Cian (Florence: G. C. Sansoni, 1929), p. 249.

che 'l mondo tutto quanto si ricuopra.
Per questo, donne graziose e belle,
se mai servir vi piacque
alcuna cosa che vi sia di sopra,
. . .
venitene con noi
sopra la cima de nostri alti sassi.

(because all the astrologers and diviners have bewildered you, according to what many have understood, [by saying] that horrible and strange weather threatens all lands [with] plague, flood, and war, lightning, storms, earthquakes, [and] destruction, as if it were already the end of the world, and they all insist that the stars will overflow with so much water that the whole world will be covered. Thus, graceful and beautiful women, if ever you were pleased to make use of something on top of you . . . come away with us to the top of our high rocks.)[43]

This verse is Machiavelli's, though it is certainly not among his best. Delio Cantimori refers to it, but he fails to grasp fully the specific nature of the song as Carnival poetry or to emphasize its direct connection with the expected flood.[44] This "Canto de' romiti" does indeed contain an echo of the quarrel with prophets and hermits that Machiavelli pursued elsewhere with a good deal more acerbity, but it should also be noted that "hermits" were one of the most frequent Carnival disguises in Florence.[45]

As we have seen, cardinals and famous (and less famous) men of letters suggested themes for such Carnival parades and composed verse for them. We should also remember that verse had a secondary role in this sort of festivity, in the main being used to back up the music, lights, "machines" (floats and special effects mechanisms), and costumes. Nonetheless, Carnival provided an effective means of communication at a moment when people of many social levels rubbed elbows. This was true in general, and it was true in this specific instance. In Rome, where the festivities described took place, fear of the flood gripped people of every social condition, at least according to the astrologer Lucarelli, even if he speaks most about the

[43] Niccolò Machiavelli, *Opere*, ed. Ezio Raimondi (Milan: Mursia, 1976), pp. 958–59.

[44] Delio Cantimori, "Niccolò Machiavelli: il politico e lo storico," *Storia della letteratura italiana*, ed. Emilio Cecchi and Natalino Sapegno, 9 vols. (Milan: Garzanti, 1965–), vol. 4, *Il Cinquecento*, pp. 7–53, esp. p. 32; Cantimori, *Umanesimo e religione nel Rinascimento* (Turin: G. Einaudi, 1975), p. 251.

[45] See Charles Southward Singleton, *Nuovi canti carnascialeschi del rinascimento con un'appendice; Tavola generale dei canti carnascialeschi editi e inediti* (Modena: Società tipografica modenese, 1940).

terror of the nobility. The message may have passed down from high places, but the medium chosen involved lower social strata as well. Elsewhere, as we shall see, this movement was inverted, which means that the message was not the same.

If Rome and Florence chose the deluge as a theme for their Carnival celebrations without rejecting or denying the flood itself, in fact accepting it as logical (in Rome at least; Machiavelli is another affair), in other cities Carnival served as a satirical antidote to panic. This was true of an extraordinary celebration organized on Carnival Sunday by the Venetian "nation" in Constantinople. The Venetian colony passed the night watching "very lascivious" dances by Turkish and Epirote women and nibbling on "cakes and sweetmeats and elaborate dishes," and when their revels had gone "from songs to dances, from one treat to another, the sun rose [showing] its rays before they left the theater." This description comes from a letter from the vice-bailiff of Venice in that city, Carlo Zen, to Giacomo Corner. His description ends with a warning:

> You can pass the word to those most consummate philosophers and astrologers that these provisions were taken against their predictions of the deluge. . . . From here I do not know what may have happened among you; for the love we bear you, we are in the greatest fear that you have not been able to make like provisions.[46]

Thus Carnival and celebration functioned as antidotes to, and as *provisioni* against, astrology, the deluge, and fear. If among the Roman nobility and the cardinals the flood was the object of fear and was evoked in basically respectful terms, even in a Carnival mood, these Venetian merchants viewed both the flood and astrological science with antagonism and treated them with sarcasm. It is difficult to evaluate accurately whether this attitude was owing to their civic allegiance or to their social group—that is, whether it came from their being Venetians or merchants (remembering that where the flood is concerned, Venice was something of an island of indifference and incredulity unique in Italy). All categories of Venetian society seem to have shared this attitude, from the doge, who reacted with disbelief to the false news of the flood in Germany transmitted from Mantua by Federico II Gonzaga, down to the young nobles of the Company of the Ortolani, who, on the day that the flood was supposed to strike, paraded about Piazza San Marco by torchlight, led by the great Ruzante and dressed as peasants, singing and dancing. All Venice, down to the merchants in far-off Constantinople, rejected both astrology and fear. This attitude might well be compared to another, better-known reaction of the political establishment in Venice, when it long held out against panic dur-

[46] Sanuto, *Diarii*, vol. 36, col. 121.

ing periods of epidemic plague and widely shared fear of plague spreaders. We might well wonder whether this reaction to the promised flood was not also a deliberate political choice on the part of the Venetian Republic.

This question is not easy to answer. It is true that response to the flood was strikingly concordant in Venice, whether it came from high culture or street culture. In these same days of Carnival a *cantastorie*, perhaps from the Po valley, who called himself Master Pegasus Neptune was declaiming one of his compositions in a Venetian square (presumably Piazza San Marco) in which the coming flood and the astrologers who had predicted it were subjected to sarcasm a good deal more pointed and language a lot stronger than had been used in Rome or Florence. After the usual invocation to the "Lord whom all the stars obey," the tale singer promised his "benigni auditori" that he would give the lie to the "castronazi" and "frappadori" (gutless, deceiving) astrologers

> che volendo nel ciel troppo mirare
> caschan in gran precepitio d'errori
>
> . . .
>
> un gran diluvio dicono sti tali
> nel anno vintiquattro è per venire,
> e verranno per l'aque tanti mali
> che l'human sesso si haverà a stremire.
>
> (who, looking up at the sky too much fall over a great precipice of errors. . . . They say [that] a great deluge is to come in the year twenty-four and so many evils will come by the waters that humankind will be exhausted.)[47]

Every day during the month of February Pegaso Neptunio discredited such predictions by spouting mocking prophecies about the next Carnival season, the struggle between Carnival and Lent, and the death of Carnival, thus reducing the deluge *in piscibus* to a flood of food and wine. Carnival, as we know from Piero Camporesi's studies, was, by antonomasia, *il diluviante*,[48] an ambiguous epithet that finds its most telling expression and an excellent definition in this fine example of the Carnival genre. Pegaso Neptunio states:

[47] *Pronostico: over diluvio consolatorio composto per lo eximio Dottore Maestro Pegaso Neptunio: el qual dechiara de giorno in giorno quel che sarà nel mese de febraro: Cosa belissima & molto da ridere* (n.p., n.d. [Venice? 1524]), fol. 2*r*. We can suppose that Pegaso Neptunio worked the crowd in Piazza San Marco on the basis of what we know about the habits of charlatans and *cantambanchi*: See Peter Burke, *Popular Culture in Early Modern Europe* (New York: New York University Press, 1978), p. 98.

[48] Piero Camporesi, *La maschera di Bertoldo. G. C. Croce e la letterature carnevalesca* (Turin: G. Einaudi, 1976), p. 144.

Serà un diluvio tra i pollami ancora
nel'acqua cotta dentro i calderoni
. . .
e serà gran diluvio ogni matino
de vin grecho, dalmaticho e latino
. . .
seran venti terribili et horrendi
che se traranno a guisa de bombarde
mandando d'ostro fetori stupendi.

(There will be a deluge of poultry still in the soup cauldrons . . . and there will be a great flood every morning of Greek, Dalmatian, and Latin wine . . . There will be terrible and horrendous winds shot off like bombards sending off stupendous stenches.)

In this transposition into a Carnival key, astral conjunctions become "conjunctions of cheese and lasagna" or, with obvious sexual connotations, "conjunctions of Venus and Mars," and the sign of Pisces is a warning of the monotony of the Lenten diet. The deluge is reduced to the level of bodily and genital functions; it is turned upside down; it is swallowed—hence defeated—by Carnival, personified as "Pazifacio compagnone francho." However, even that merry prankster and boon companion was destined to be defeated and killed by Lent in the person of the onion, the Lenten foodstuff par excellence:

Una regina verrà con gran gente
con la coa verde et con lo capo biancho,
e moverà gran guerra immantinente
a Pazifacio compagnone francho:
per le cevolle et schalogne mordente
el povero signor venirà a mancho.

(A queen will come with many followers, with a green tail and a white head, and she will make sudden war on Merry Prankster, boon companion: by means of stinging onions and shallots will the poor lord come to his end.)

The exceptional event of the flood had no place in a cycle of years in which the seasons decline only to rise again unchanged. The poem concludes by prophesying a series of obvious events, a familiar procedure in comic prognostication:

li gatti et cani inimici serano
meglio de ravi taglieran le spade
campagne et monti al scoperto sarano
et l'hostarie saran ben visitade.

(cats and dogs will be enemies; swords will cut better than radishes; fields and mountains will be out in the open; and the taverns will be well frequented.)

The world, that is, will remain as it always has been, immutably cyclical. Thus there is no reason to upset oneself with foolish fears; it is better to turn to the ongoing Carnival and "triumph" by giving oneself over to the pleasures of the table, of sex, and of laughter:

Voi compagnoni contenti restate
d'altra pioza n'habbiate paura;
et in questi pochi giorni triomphate,
ché ve concede la madre natura.
Questi astrologi matti bertezate
ché in dir cotal pazie pongon sua cura,
et se questo ch'io dico voi farette
in cielo e in terra contenti sarette.

(You, good companions, stay happy and have no fear of more rain; and in these few days you will triumph, since Mother Nature concedes them to you. Mock those mad astrologers who take such trouble to say such insane things, and if you do what I tell you, you will be content in heaven and on earth.)[49]

The Carnival of Modena versus the Flood, Astrology, and Power

Obviously, a composition like Pegaso Neptunio's poem could have been designed not only to invite listeners to join in the laughter of Carnival but also to calm a public opinion that was subject to panic. Not that a hypothesis of the sort can be proved in connection with this particular text. It is certain, however, that this was a problem that transcended the individual case of Venice, and that revelation of danger needed to be disciplined and fear kept under control. This was why the Bolognese astrologer Giacomo Pietramellara published (just a month apart, 12 November and 10 December 1523) both a short work in Latin promising terrible calamities, *Enunctiationes generales de concursu omnium errantium syderum in signo Piscium*, and a much more reassuring prognostication in the vernacular.[50] In this

[49] *Pronostico: over diluvio consolatorio*, respectively, fols. 2*v*, 3*r*, 3*v*, 3*r*, 4*r*.

[50] Giacomo Pietramellara, *Enunctiationes generales de concursu omnium errantium syderum in signo Piscium futuro mense februario 1524* (Bologna: "per dominum Magistrum Iacobum Petramellarium," 1523). Following the *Enunctiationes*, the colophon for which is dated 12 November (fol. a. iv *r*), there is a *Iacobi Petramellari pronosticon in futuris rerum eventibus anni*

manner, the learned could be advised of the danger, while the vast and heterogeneous public that bought the vernacular yearly prognostications was spared useless terror and fed only crumbs of a truth (or what was believed to be a truth) that was apportioned unevenly according to social level. In other words, fear itself was to be feared and constituted a problem for public order. To speak in still more general terms, the real problem was one of political management. When astrological debate descended to the city streets it became a complex system of opposing and contradictory forces involving fear, ritual, and mockery. These forces had to be channeled. They also lent themselves to being exploited in various ways on the political plane.

This was what happened in Modena, where all the various strands involved in the predicted flood of 1524 were woven into a complex and ongoing whole. The opposing camps of deluge and Carnival became polarized, producing a particularly emblematic expression of political tension in that city. But let us proceed in orderly fashion, following the story as Tommasino Lancellotti relates it. Fear reached Modena "by letters from Rome" on 21 December 1523:

> And on the said day by letters written from Rome we heard how they are afraid of the deluge that it is said there is to be in February of 1524, and that in this hour many persons have set up stocks of provisions up in the hills to flee the deluge.[51]

The papal court in Rome, especially during the Medici papacy, was certainly one of the principal centers of astrological culture in Italy, and this may perhaps be enough to explain why fear of the flood should have arrived in Modena from Rome. There is something else, though. Relations between Modena and Rome were particularly close at the time. After Julius II occupied the city in 1510, it was ceded to Emperor Maximilian, only to be sold back to the Church, which meant that Modena had been in the

---

1524 dated 10 December. The same text appeared in Italian under the same date and printed separately with the title *Pronostico de Maestro Iacomo Petramellara sopra lanno 1524 delle cose in esso accaderanno* (Bologna: "per dominum Magistrum Iacobum Petramellarium," 1523). In the interest of clarity, I must add that the words attributed to me and given between quotation marks in Paola Zambelli, "Fine del mondo," p. 334—"The deluge and astrology are identified . . . with the interests of the dominant classes and a double literature came to be created, alarmist for the learned, reassuring for those who did not know Latin"—are not taken from any published work of mine but from a typescript distributed in preparation for discussion among the participants in the conference "Scienze, credenze occulte, livelli di cultura" held in Florence 26–30 June 1980. I agree with Paola Zambelli that such an "interesting thesis" would "require qualification," which was precisely what I did both in my paper presented at those meetings and in the discussions connected with them.

[51] Lancellotti, *Cronica modenese*, vol 2, in Biblioteca Estense di Modena, MS α T1 3, fol. 85*r*.

papal dominions since 1514 and was to remain under the popes until 1527.[52] Thus channels of communication between the two cities remained open, and it was by that route rather than through the Veneto, Bologna, or Lombardy that word of the expected flood reached Modena. Alarm spread rapidly, and on 31 January, the feast day of St. Geminiano, patron saint of the city, "a great throng came to the pardon of the said saint . . . and many persons confessed and were given absolution, in order to be well with God for anything that might happen." Thus far, the reaction was spontaneous, but on the following day, 1 February, the episcopal authorities took over the organization of religious practices aimed at preventing the flood. Gian Domenico Sigibaldi, vicar to Bishop Ercole Rangoni, spoke out in alarm:

> He exhorted everyone to fast on this first day, which is Monday, [and on] Wednesday and Friday; and Wednesday three processions will take place to pray to God and his Mother and St. Geminiano to defend this city of Modena from the prodigies of the astrologers, who have prognosticated that in February 1524 there is to be the deluge because of the conjunction of the planets in the place they were found at the time of the Flood, when Noah made the ark by God's commandment.[53]

It is not difficult to identify the work to which Sigibaldi refers: *De la vera pronosticatione del diluvio del Mille et cinquecento e vintiquatro. Composta per lo excellentissimo Philosopho Tomaso da Ravenna.*[54] Even in its title, this text was intended as an attack on Agostino Nifo's *De falsa diluvii pronosticatione*, and one of its arguments in favor of the reality of the flood was based on the hypothesis that the planets would be aligned in the sign of Pisces in 1524 exactly as they had been in Noah's time in the sign of Aquarius. The author of this tract was the same Tommaso Giannotti whom we have already met addressing laudatory enigmas to Leo X in a caption for a broadsheet on the monster of Bologna. In 1524 Giannotti was the personal astrologer of Count Guido Rangoni "Il Piccolo," commander of the papal military forces in Modena and a man so passionately interested in astrology that on several occasions Giannotti cites his opinions and suggestions.[55]

52 Tommaso Sandonnini, *Modena sotto il governo dei papi* (Modena: t. Sociale, 1879).

53 Lancellotti, *Cronica*, vol. 2, fol. 88*r*; vol. 1, fol. 176*r*.

54 *De la vera pronosticatione del diluvio del Mille et cinquecento e vintiquatro. Composta per lo excellentissimo Philosopho Tomaso da Ravenna* (n.p., n.d. [Venice? 1522? certainly before the eclipse of the moon on 13 March 1523]). The allusion to Noah's Flood is on fols. 4*r*–*v*.

55 On Giannotti, see Carlo Malagola, "Tomaso Filologo da Ravenna, professore nello studio padovano e mecenate," *Nuovo archivio veneto*, n.s. 2 (1901): 249–53; pp. 252–53; Piancastelli, *Pronostici ed almanacchi*, pp. 26–30, 32–34; Andrea Corsini, *Medici ciarlatani e ciarlatani medici* (Bologna: N. Zanichelli, 1922), pp. 76–77; Max Sander, *Le livre à figures italien depuis 1467 jusqu'à 1530. Essai de sa bibliographie et de son histoire*, 6 vols. (New York: G. E. Stechert, 1941; Milan: Heopli, [1942]), vol. 2, pp. 547–48. On Rangoni, see Luigi Rangoni

Giannotti's work thus represents one more link between the deluge and fear of the deluge, on the one hand, and papal power, on the other. Conversely, the bishop's vicar, Sigibaldi, entrusted defense of the city to a series of collective celebrations addressed to God, the Virgin, and St. Geminiano. The role of the city's patron saint, which has no parallel in antidiluvial rites in other cities, is easily explained when we realize that the saint's cult had recently been reinforced by a miracle that took place in 1511 when the French were besieging the city, and that Geminiano had in some manner become emblematic of the city's autonomy.[56]

Using the saint to oppose the astrological predictions might thus imply another source of tension between the city's freedoms and the central power. The following day, 2 February, opposition took an explosive turn when exorcising the flood took the form of Carnival rites and became explicit satire of procedures to enforce papal domination of the city. In the evening after vespers, the municipal trumpeters sounded a call, as if to announce a papal brief, and the people gathered in the main square.

> And when they had sounded, ser Zan Martino di Vechi opened the brief, which went thus: "On the part of the magnificent podestà of Modena. Banish misser Deluge from [this] land and place under pain of rebellion; and all the astrologers who will astrologize the flood in the future are not to be given credence; and may no one print or put forth anything whatsoever concerning the deluge, under pain of rebellion; and banish misser Thomaxo, astrologer of the lord Count Guido Rangon, for having fled to the mountains for fear of the flood," plus certain other things said to mock the said podestà who plays the astrologer, who bears the name misser Paulo di Brunori da Corezo, and also the astrologer of Count Guido.[57]

The joke was aimed, through Giannotti, at Count Rangoni, commander of the papal troops who, I might add, had also fled from Modena when danger seemed imminent. The other person mentioned was Paolo Brunori of Correggio, podestà of Modena from January 1522 to February 1525 and also a man fond of astrology. According to the city statutes, the General Council had the power to elect the podestà, but in reality this post was often filled by the central power, as was the case during the years 1514 to 1527.[58] The tension that this situation produced was so intense that when

Machiavelli, *Piccolo sunto storico della famiglia Rangoni di Modena* (Rome: Befani, 1908), pp. 30–42.

[56] Susanna Peyronel Rambaldi, *Speranze e crisi nel Cinquecento modenese. Tensioni religiose e vita cittadina ai tempi di Giovanni Morone* (Milan: Franco Angeli, 1979), pp. 34–36.

[57] Lancellotti, *Cronica*, vol. 1, fols. 176*v* and 177*r*.

[58] On Paolo Brunori, see Emilio Paolo Vicini, *I podestà di Modena. Serie cronologica 1336–1796* (Modena: Società tipografica modenese–Antica tipografia Soliani, 1918), pp. 189–90; on election procedures for the post of podestà, see Vicini, *I podestà di Modena, 1156–1796, Parte Ia (1156–1336)* (Rome: Giornale araldico-storico-genealogico, 1913), p. 14.

Brunori's immediate predecessor, Guerrino Garisendi, was made podestà, as Lancellotti tells us, "despite the Magnificent Community and the citizens," he was killed (in January 1522), and although his assassins were known, they were not brought to justice.[59] Brunori's successor, Angelo Tagliaferri of Parma, also died in office of a violent death (perhaps masked as an accident) on 5 June 1526.[60] All these events make it clear why astrology was linked with power in the eyes of the citizens of Modena, why it was epitomized in the unwelcome figure of Brunori, and why past events gave a further political tint to the Carnival derision aimed at astrologers. On the same day, 2 February,

> certain writings have been attached to the columns against the deluge making fun of the astrologers, saying that they have put a shrimp up in the heavens, a bow, a set of scales, a goat, and other signs; and who knows if they have not put up an owl and a hoot owl, crazy as they are, and other such things in vituperation of astrologers.[61]

The "scrite" to which Lancellotti rather vaguely alludes can be identified as three *sonetti caudati* also mentioned in a chronicle in Cremona.[62] The connection is clear from a passage in the first of these satirical extended sonnets. Paraphrasing Stöffler, it begins "O erigite caput, viri christiani" and continues:

> Ponete in ciel dui gambari, un montone,
> un becco, un'urna, un arco, una saetta,
> una bilancia, un luccio, uno scorpione;
>
> perché non li agiongiete una civetta
> e un barbagiani, pazzi da bastone,
> anzi da ceppi, da catena et cetta?
>
> (Put in the heavens two shrimp, a ram, a billy goat, an urn, a bow, an arrow, scales, a pike, a scorpion; why not add to them an owl and a hoot owl, mad enough to be beaten with a stick, or, better, to be put in logs or in chains, etc.?)

We do not know whether the three sonnets, which must have circulated fairly widely, were written in Modena, Cremona, or elsewhere. In any event, the cultural coordinates of these texts that show through the Carnival mask, particularly in the third sonnet and to some extent in the second, are more interesting to our purposes. The first sonnet expresses the au-

[59] Lancellotti, *Cronica*, vol. 1, fol. 137*v*.

[60] Vicini, *I podestà di Modena. Serie cronologica 1336–1796*, pp. 190–91.

[61] Lancellotti, *Cronica*, vol. 1, fol. 177*r*.

[62] Francesco Novati, "Il diluvio universale profetizzato per il 1524," *Archivio storico lombardo* 29, no. 2 (1902): 191–94.

thor's indignation at the "thieving" astrologers who have dethroned Christ from the heavens and substituted figures from classical antiquity for his "high and divine kingdom" by reading the imaginary figures of the zodiac into the stars. The second sonnet presents the planets as the source of life and as a symbol of cosmic harmony, whereas astrologers, "intent . . . on avarice, on gold," stress their supposed malignant influences. "You are astrologers, not prophets," the poet comments sarcastically, inverting the usual order of terms.

The third sonnet (which begins: "Cazzo! questo è il diluvio universale") is couched in strictly Carnival terms, transforming the astrologer's instruments into pots and pans and other kitchen equipment:

> Questi vostri astrolabi son patelle,
> le sfere balle da far magatelle,
> il quadrante è una pentola, un bochale;
> le tavole son mense apparecchiate
> ove voi vi calcati i buon bocconi.
> . . .
> Cuius, cuia, coioni,
> havete del profeta e del divino
> quando havete bevuto ben del vino.
> Ite col Tacuino
> nelle cocine, nelle stuffe, in chiasso,
> ove è sempre il diluvio d'unto e grasso.
>
> (These astrolabes of yours are frying pans, your spheres are juggling balls, the quadrant is a pot, a jar; your tables are [dining] tables set, where you put good things to eat. [*Nonsense conjugation*], you are part prophet and part diviner when you have drunk well of wine. Go with your Almanac into the kitchens, to the stoves in the back alley, where there is always a flood of grease and fat.)

The first thing to note is that although the author is obviously an educated man, he knows the forms of Carnival literature and uses them to perfection, which shows how difficult it is to evaluate accurately the social circle in which texts of this sort arose and just how ambiguous the term "popular" can be.[63] In any event, along with Carnival elements and blended with them, we see elements of a very different type that seem to have come from a specific source, the *Tractato contra li astrologi* of Girolamo Savonarola.[64] As is known, in this brief work Savonarola took argu-

[63] For analogous observations, see Burke, *Popular Culture in Early Modern Europe*, pp. 23–25.

[64] Girolamo Savonarola, *Tractato contra li astrologi* (Florence: Bartolomeo de' Libri, 1497),

ments that Giovanni Pico had already used, summarized them, organizing them differently and shifting their meaning, and mixed them with others to adapt them to the specific public of his followers, both among the lower classes and the governing class in Florence, with the aim of urging them to "castigate and punish" astrologers, as he says on the last page of his book. The work contains a good many themes that we have now encountered in the three sonnets. It criticizes the astrologers' greed, it contrasts astrology and prophecy, it affirms Christ's unique sovereignty over the heavens, and, in particular, it satirizes the zodiac, which men have created but which they have ended up by believing to be real. Savonarola declares that "such figures are fictitious" and that

> there is no man who, in such a multitude of stars, coupling them in various manners, cannot imagine whatever figures he wants. . . . Just as men have imagined animal figures, they could have imagined houses, or castles, or trees, or other similar things . . . but to believe that God and nature have drawn in the sky lions, dragons, dogs, scorpions, vases, archers, and monsters is a ridiculous thing.[65]

The verses I have cited as having been paraphrased by Lancellotti seem in turn to derive directly from these lines. Furthermore, it is interesting to note that in order to attack the idea of the deluge, in Modena and Spain alike, people turned to Savonarola when they sought a figure emblematic of the struggle between prophecy and astrology. But let us return to Lancellotti's account of the doings in Modena, which culminated on Fat Thursday, 4 February:

> Two men, masked, were amusing themselves dressed as philosophers. As misser Francesco Guizardino and misser Paulo di Brunori, podestà of Modena, passed along the Canalchiare [Corso Canal Chiaro] in Modena, taking a stroll, they encountered the said two philosophers. One had a sextant, a pencil, and an [armillary] sphere, and went about astrologizing; and in that instant the other astrologer lifted up his robe and showed him his rear, and his companion astrologized his rear with the sextant, and he accomplished this task with such grace that the lord governor and all the others took great pleasure in it, except for misser podestà, because the joke was made on purpose to mock the astrologers and the said podestà, whom they had astrologized on the rear end; and the lord governor took great pleasure in this, but misser Paulo no. You who read [this], do not marvel at what I write because I tell you a timely truth.[66]

Once more, denial of the flood and of astrology was mixed with mockery of the representatives of papal power. This was Lancellotti's reason for sug-

---

now in Savonarola, *Scritti filosofici*, ed. Giancarlo Garfagnini and Eugenio Garin (Rome: A. Belardetti, 1982), pp. 273–370.

[65] Ibid., pp. 370 and 339–40.

[66] Lancellotti, *Cronica*, vol. 1, fols. 177*r* and *v*.

gesting that the reader not be surprised at the vulgarity of his anecdote because it came "a bono proposito." It was not solely out of fondness for a coarse gag that the chronicler lingered over his description of two masked revelers representing the celestial sphere with the aid of a rotundity of a very different sort; it was also because Lancellotti understood and wanted to have his readers understand that a more general symbol was concealed behind that first, crude one—the refusal of the citizens of Modena to tolerate Rome's dual abuse of its power when it deprived the city of its political autonomy and imposed an ideology, astrology, that was both unwelcome and a source of fear.

Prophecy versus Astrology

This raucous scene provides an emblematic ending to our tale, as only a few final considerations remain. At the beginning of this chapter, two problems were posed: What was the relationship between prophecy and astrology, and how broadly distributed and how strong was belief in astrological science outside learned circles, in particular among the urban lower classes. On the first point, we can say that the affair of the deluge expected in 1524 is a good example of how prophetic culture could absorb, envelop, and to some extent annul astrological culture. There is no doubt that announcement of the deluge resounded far and wide, building on a tragically frequent series of inundations in recent years and on a specific tradition placing floods in a prophetic context. Above all, preaching gave prediction of the flood a vast audience (Giacomo Tiburzi deplored the "universo audiente populo") and placed it within an apocalyptical homiletic tradition that had long enjoyed broad popularity and had only recently been reined in by the ecclesiastical authorities (but not snuffed out, if in precisely those years the Church felt the need to remind local ecclesiastics of the decrees for its repression.) The flood was thus accepted and believed in more as a castigation from God for the corruption of the Church or, in another view, for the Lutheran rebellion, than as the effect of an inauspicious planetary conjunction (which in fact swept away the very foundations of astrological science). In confirmation of this hypothesis I might observe that when Carnival ritual merriment reigned and ecclesiastical and penitential rites lost their intensity and their effectiveness, manifestations of disbelief and derision not only became more frequent than displays of fear but overwhelmed and ultimately destroyed them. Two cities fail to fit this pattern: Rome, where panic seems to have been widespread, and Venice, where announcements of the flood, although widely known, were by no means accepted. Modena, finally, which fully conforms to the pattern indicated, indirectly confirms the strong connections that people perceived to exist between astrology and political power, in particular Roman political power. When astrology was mocked, power too was denied.

In short, at least as far as the specific instance examined here is concerned, we seem to be able to say that urban populations were fully aware of astrology, but that they gave it little credit. Popular divination used other means. The failure of the predictions of the flood and their comic inversion in a Carnival key thus had an enormous negative effect on the figure of the astrologer, but not on the image of the preacher, even though preachers had shared fully in that failure. In the end, the figure of the astrologer emerged much diminished by the way popular culture had received the supposed deluge. In the culture of the mass of urban folk, the astrological arts were reduced to the level of a juggler's bag of tricks, and astrological science is denied, derided, and seems ineffectual. As Celebrino said, "vedo dispersa gir l'astrologia."[67]

[67] Celebrino, *La dechiaratione per che non è venuto il diluvio*, fol. D. 2*r*.

7

AWAITING A NEW OCTAVIAN

A Case of Possession and of Propaganda

IN ROME in April 1519 a woman possessed by spirits ("she speaks Latin, predicts things to come, reveals people's secret sins") was taken to the basilica of St. Peter "to the column where they say Christ was bound" and subjected to procedures designed to liberate her.[1] The basilica did indeed boast a "column that casts out spirits," as one pilgrim from Brescia wrote when he was in Rome for the Jubilee of 1475 and had visited it among the other *mirabilia Urbis*.[2] The exorcist began by asking the spirit oppressing the woman to tell his name; it answered that it was not a demon—as it surely would have been some decades later—but a certain messer Agamennone Marescotti, formerly a Roman senator in the pay of the Venetians. He then offered a number of predictions, these among them, according to Marcantonio Michiel, writing to Nicolò Tiepolo:

> The Turk will come this year to Rome, and as victor will fodder his horse on top of the altar of Peter, and [the horse] not eating it, by miracle he will become a Christian. He also says that the king of France will be elected emperor, specifying the electors who will give him their votes and for what reason they will do so.[3]

Ostensibly, these two predictions were unconnected. In reality, the woman possessed by spirits juxtaposed a pro-French political viewpoint of the current struggle over the choice of a successor for Emperor Maximilian I with a specific reminiscence taken from a prophecy in verse that we have already encountered, the title of which, *La vera prophetia . . . la quale declara la venuta de uno imperatore*, clarifies the connection with the imminent

[1] Marino Sanuto, *Diarii*, 58 vols. (Venice: R. Deputazione Veneta di storia patria, 1879–1903), vol. 27, col. 224.

[2] "Cronaca di Corradino Palazzo," in *Le cronache bresciane inedite dei secoli XV–XIX*, ed. Paolo Guerrini, 5 vols. (Brescia: Editrice Brixia Sacra, 1922–1932), vol. 1, p. 220. This column was reputed to have come from the temple of Solomon, and Christ was supposed to have stood beside it. It is also mentioned by Bernardo Portinari in the dedication to Leo X of his *Disputationes II de daemonibus*, the manuscript of which is conserved in the Biblioteca Medicea Laurenziana di Firenze, Pluteo 84, 22. See also Lynn Thorndike, *A History of Magic and Experimental Science*, 8 vols. (New York: Columbia University Press, 1923–1958), vol. 5, p. 85.

[3] Sanuto, *Diarii*, vol. 27, col. 224.

election. The miraculous conversion reported above figures in that prophecy in these terms:

Poi vigniranno i Turchi
dentro a la cità de Roma;
li romani serano spurchi
per l'alpestra e grave soma.
La scrittura così noma
che 'l Turcho farà manzare
el cavalo sopra l'altare
quale è del primo pastore.

La gloriosa nostra Donna
un miracolo mostrarà,
quel caval in hora bona
presto si inzenochiarà.
Quando el Turcho vederà
tal miracolo per Dio mandato
presto sarà baptezato
e pentuto del so errore.

(Then the Turks will come into the city of Rome; the Romans will be bled dry by the rude and heavy burden. The writing thus says that the Turk will have his horse eat on top of the altar that is the first shepherd's. Our glorious Lady will show a miracle: the horse, now meek, will immediately kneel. When the Turk sees this miracle sent by God he will immediately be baptized and will repent of his error.)[4]

This must have been a well-known prophecy. A number of years later, in 1530, Marcantonio Magno, who translated Juan de Valdés's *Alphabeto Cristiano* into Italian, expressed fear that the Turk would come "all the way to Rome . . . so that we shall see him, in our days, fulfill the prophecy told so many times before, that he will have his horse feed on the altar of St. Peter's."[5] The poem contained another important element, however. Its refrain promised, "There will come an emperor who will put all the world in peace," which means that the possessed woman identified the promised peace-making emperor with Francis I, thus connecting the prophecy to a specific political content. This is not explicit in Michiel's letter, as he is

[4] *La vera prophetia prophetizata dal glorioso Santo Anselmo la quale declara la venuta de uno imperatore: el qual mettera pace tra li christiani et conquistara infideli trovata in Roma* (Collicuti: Francesco da Udine), fols. 2*r*–*v*. On the various editions of this prophecy, see chap. 1, nn. 10 and 46.

[5] Sanuto, *Diarii*, vol. 53, col. 425.

more interested in other, more comic aspects of the episode, but it seems obvious, considering that although Leo X's policies were usually ambiguous, he favored the Most Christian king of France over the Most Catholic Spanish. Many aspects of this episode arouse our curiosity to know more. Not only does it confirm the broad propagandistic use made of cases of possession, which have already been studied;[6] it also shows the broad distribution of prophecies in verse. We cannot help wondering whether the possessed woman had gotten her hands on the printed text or whether she had simply heard it declaimed or mentioned. Finally, we see here yet another example of prophecy concerning the emperor, a topic that is certainly well known. It is a singular example, however. Not only was it manifested orally but by a woman in a state of psychological turmoil who quite unconsciously organized into one statement both the rumors that were circulating concerning the elections in course and her reminiscences of a widely distributed text accessible even to the lower levels of the Roman population.

The Emperor of Peace in Popular Print

A good deal of study has been devoted to the vast place that medieval and Renaissance prophecy, from Dante on, reserved for a holy imperial figure who would bring peace and on whose saintliness a beneficent renewal of the papacy in the person of an angelic pope would depend.[7] What is not yet fully understood is the circulation of these themes among the "lower" levels of society, nor in what form and by what paths they were connected with the changing scene in Italian and European history, to which they adapted by shifting the emphasis of their varied parts.

Both in their physical existence and in their utilization, "popular" print pieces on prophecy doubtlessly represent one of the chief signs of and principal media for the "lower" circulation of imperial themes. Indeed, such themes were among the topics most frequent in popular print literature; compared with the medieval tradition of Church reform under an "angelic pope," they represented a current of extraordinary sticking power. It is probable that the crisis in imperial power, by then irreversible, encouraged

[6] See Daniel Pickering Walker, *Unclean Spirits: Possession and Exorcism in France and England in the late Sixteenth and early Seventeenth Centuries* (Philadelphia: University of Pennsylvania Press, 1981). For northern Italy, see Ottavio Franceschini, "L'esorcista," in *Medicina, erbe e magia* (Bologna: Federazione delle Casse di Risparmio e delle Banche del Monte dell'Emilia Romagna, 1981), pp. 99–115.

[7] As an absolute minimum, see Friedrich von Bezold, "Zur deutschen Kaiserage," *Vortrag von Sitzungberichte der Philolosophisch-Philologischen und historischen Klasse der königlich Bayerischen Akademie der Wissenschaften* (1884): 560–606; Marjorie Reeves, *The Influence of Prophecy in the Late Middle Ages: A Study in Joachimism* (Oxford: Clarendon Press, 1969), pp. 347–74.

such publications by contributing to expectations of peace and prosperity projected onto the figure of a *deus ex machina* that was in reality nonexistent but was predicted for a near but indeterminate future. Thus we read, in a random sampling of prophetic print pieces, that an "emperor . . . of the lineage of David will lead all the people back to justice . . . returning the clergy to the way of the apostles."[8] Similarly, we read that

> Farassi un sancto e digno imperatore
> che 'l mondo tenerà sotto a sua alla
> con bona divotione e bono amore.
> *Rex regum* serà lui che già non falla,
> di casa David, dil mondo signore,
> pien di possanza il suo vigor non calla;
> adunarà la christianità tutta
> contro l'infidel, con magna condutta.

> (A saintly and worthy emperor will be made who will hold the world under his wing with good devotion and good love. *Rex regum* will he be who will not fail; of the house of David, lord of the world, full of power, his strength will not decline; he will gather together all Christianity against the infidel with mighty deeds.)[9]

These are fairly generic indications, which do not lend themselves particularly well to association with specific persons or political situations. The same was true of the *Vera prophetia . . . de uno imperatore*, the first edition of which is undated but has been placed at around 1510. Certainly anyone who listened to these lines being declaimed to the sound of a viol in the public square or who acquired for a half *quattrino* the two- or four-page printed version asked nothing better than to find in them the reassuring effigy of a real person, but in order for the connection to be made, some concrete historical connection had to be provided. Thus when in 1512 Emperor Maximilian, who was admittedly gifted with inventiveness but had little charisma, joined the Holy League against the French, the prophetic books opened their pages to him.

> Non convien più dubitare
> nel venir de Maximiano
> che in Italia a mano a mano
> sue bandiere vol spiegare.
> Non convien più dubitare.
> Gli è adempiuto quel ch'àn ditto

[8] *Pronostico overo profecia delanno MCCCCCXCV fina alanno MCCCCCXXXII* (Stampata in Bologna del MCCCCCVII. Die XXIIII Decembris), fol. 3*r*.

[9] *Imminente flagello de Italia* (n.p., n.d.), fol. 6*r*.

le Sybille tutte quante,
quel che Brigida ha poi scritto
gli è finito ad questo instante,
et però gli è quivi astante
per la Italia trapassare.
Non convien più dubitare.

(There is no longer cause to doubt of the coming of Maximilian, who in Italy, bit by bit, intends to unfurl his banners. There is no longer cause to doubt. With him, what all the Sibyls said has been fulfilled; what Bridget later wrote has just ended in this instant, and yet he is here present in order to pass through Italy. There is no longer cause to doubt.)[10]

The Milanese chronicler Ambrogio da Paullo also recorded the prognostication that Maximilian would "make all the world obedient and reform the Church and make [a] new order."[11] These were expectations that went far beyond the person in question. Their deeper roots—the call for reform of the Church and for a new order in Christianity—emerge from even the most generic passages quoted above, but they sprang into operation attached to a real person whenever concrete historical events allowed.

Charles V, the Second Charlemagne

As we have seen, the new imperial election of 1519 was seen as the moment that would finally produce the emperor hailed in the prophecies. Steady pressure from the Turks in the Mediterranean basin probably contributed to this sentiment. Nearly three years had passed since Selim I had invaded Egypt, feeding the worst fears for the fate of Europe, Italy in particular. Conversely, it was part of Charles's electoral propaganda that he "promised to go against infidels,"[12] which was also one of the principal characteristics of the emperor promised in the prophecies. This explains why the prophecy of the second Charlemagne was modified to apply to Charles V immediately after his election. This prophecy, formerly applied to Charles VIII of France, predicted a sovereign, victor over both Europe and Asia, who would end his life on the hill of Calvary, at last liberated from the infidel. Along with the earlier publications of a text beginning

[10] *Questa sie la venuta del Imperatore* (n.p., n.d.), fol. 1*r*. In a similar vein, see also *Questa sie la tregua fata con limperatore e san Marco e con tutti gli altri principi christiani novamente confirmata* (n.p., n.d. [1512]).

[11] *Cronaca milanese dall'anno 1476 al 1515 di Maestro Ambrogio da Paullo*, ed. Antonio Ceruti, *Miscellanea di storia italiana* 13 (1871): 91–353; p. 282.

[12] Sanuto, *Diarii*, vol. 27, col. 446.

"Charolo fiol de Charoli," an edition of the same prophecy now circulated, undated but presumably printed in 1519, entitled *Prophetia Caroli Imperatoris*, the first phrase of which was altered to read "Carolus Philippi filius" (Charles V was the son of Philip the Handsome). The text was in Latin, as if to show that the piece was addressed to the learned, but it also contained three prophecies in the vernacular, which would have guaranteed it a fairly large circulation.[13]

In the years that followed, the prophecy of the second Charlemagne, adapted in this fashion, circulated above all in manuscript, reemerging at crucial moments in Charles's imperial career. In this fashion, one member of the d'Arco family transcribed the prophecy at the time of the battle of Pavia, adding a commentary of his own on that memorable event, which seemed to him to fulfill certain aspects of the prophecy (he connected the many nations that were defeated by Charles at Pavia with the phrase in the prophecy, "educet bella subjugans anglos, gallos, hispanos et longobardos").[14] Later, in January 1527, Tommasino Lancellotti transcribed the same text into his chronicle, stating that he had received it four years earlier but had lost it, finding it again at that time "by God's will" (since the prophecy, according to Lancellotti, was fulfilled precisely in those days).[15] However, during those same months of the battle of Pavia, presumably toward the end of 1524, another publication connected Charles with the great medieval prophetic tradition. This work was a broadsheet from Piedmont entitled *Hystorie nove: dove se contiene la venuta de lo imperatore per incoronarsi: et de le grande cose che hano ad essere*, the text of which reads:

Fugeti et non aspetando el gran furore
ché vene un novo Xerze et novo Marte;
questo he dil vero Cesar sucessore

che vinse il mondo con la sacra mano
facendosi sol primo imperatore;
questo he quel divo e sacro Carlo Mano

13 *Prophetia Caroli Imperatoris con altre Prophetie di diversi santi huomini* (n.p., n.d.). The hypothesis that this edition of the prophecy was printed in 1519 is based on the text that follows the *Prophetia Caroli Imperatoris*, here given the title *Prophetia stampata nel mille quatrocento nonantaotto: che tratta de la cose passate et che debbeno venire*, the first two lines of which read: "El se movera un gato / anni sete diece e quatro." If we add up the date given in the title with the years indicated in the first lines, we get 1498 + 7 + 10 + 4 = 1519, the presumed year of publication. The compiler undoubtedly had this calculation in mind and would have changed his numbers if he had realized that the date for the fulfillment of the prophecy had passed.

14 Antonio Medin, "La battaglia di Pavia. Profeti e poeti italiani," *Archivio storico lombardo* 52 (1925): 252–90; p. 254.

15 Tommasino Lancellotti, *Cronaca modenese*, ed. Carlo Borghi, 12 vols. (Parma: P. Fiaccadori, 1863), vol. 2, p. 170.

qual Brigida predisse in le sue carte
che extinguerebe il furore galicano.
Merlin comprese anchor con la sua arte

che l'ucel di Iove volarebe a tondo,
regnabit ubique, et disse: "in ogni parte
tutte le profetie d'alto e da fondo

volto he rivolto, finalmento trovo
che ha essere sol costui signor dil mondo."
. . .

Per questo tornaran l'aride piante
et reverdire, dicho per ogni deserto
naseran fiori più che mai galante.

Il ciel per soa clementia ne l'hano offerto,
sol per cavarne da le man de Faraone:
ut implent scripture ab experto.

Surget rex magnus a septentrione
qui destruet potentiam omnem Galorum,
nec redibunt in Italia regione

per infinita secula seculorum.
Amen.

(Flee without awaiting the great furor because a new Xerxes and a new Mars is coming; this one is truly the successor of Caesar who won the world with sacred hand, making himself the only first emperor; this one is that divine and holy Charles the Great of whom Bridget predicted in her papers that he would extinguish the Gallican fury. Merlin still understood by his art that Jove's bird would fly back, "he will reign everywhere," and he said, "everywhere, all prophecies high and low has he turned inside out, finally I find that he alone is to be the lord of the world." . . . For this one the dry plants will revive and turn green again, I say, in every desert flowers will be born more beautiful than ever. The heavens have offered him to us out of their clemency, simply to remove him from the hands of the Pharaoh: "So that Scripture may be fulfilled in experience." A great king will rise in the north who will destroy the power of all Frenchmen, and they will never return to Italian lands for all eternity, Amen.)[16]

[16] *Hystorie nove: dove se contiene la venuta de lo imperatore per incoronarsi: et de le grande cose che hano ad essere* (n.p., n.d. [Turin: 1524?]), fols. 1*r*–*v*.

Thus Bridget and Merlin had already predicted the victory of the imperial forces over the French and the imminent descent of Charles into the Italian peninsula. This tissue of prophecies gradually defined Charles by placing his persona in the sacred and providential context discussed by Frances A. Yates.[17] Elements of the current political scene (the Turkish question, the Lutheran problem) came to be combined with others that belonged to the prophetic realm (the image of the emperor who would come to bring peace to all Christendom when the Church had been reformed and the Holy Sepulchre liberated) and with the portrait of the universal sovereign that Charles was gradually coming to resemble for objective cultural and dynastic reasons. The result of all these combinations was an extraordinarily sturdy image, well adapted to the demands of imperial propaganda, that could be circulated and received with great ease by means of pamphlets and broadsheets, which in turn contributed much to keeping alive hope and expectation.

Prophecies of the Sack of Rome

When on 27 January 1527 Tommasino Lancellotti once again got his hands on a copy of the prophecy of the second Charlemagne, which he had seen four years earlier under the title of *Pronostico dela Maestà delo Imperatore Carolo* and subsequently lost, he thought that this had happened "by God's will"—that is, that God himself had presented him with the best key for understanding and interpreting the present and foreseeing the future.

It was generally true in 1517 and the years immediately following that known prophecies were read again and meditated anew. When Rome was sacked, it was as if a veil had been rent and prophecies that had been obscure had found definitive clarification in events. This sort of attitude is evident in one passage of the *Dialogo di Lattantio et di uno Archidiacono* in which Alfonso de Valdés speaks of the many prophecies that had circulated in Rome during the years preceding the sack:

> LATTANTIO: Oh! Lord help me! I remember that when I was in Rome many prophecies were found there that spoke of this persecution of the clergy that was to come in the time of this emperor.
>
> THE ARCHDEACON: That is the truth. A thousand times have we read them there for our comfort and amusement.[18]

[17] Frances A. Yates, *Astraea: The Imperial Theme in the Sixteenth Century* (London and Boston: Routledge & Kegan Paul, 1975), pp. 20–28. See also Reeves, *The Influence of Prophecy*, pp. 359–74, and (concerning Antonio Arquato in particular) Delio Cantimori, *Umanesimo e religione nel Rinascimento* (Turin: G. Einaudi, 1975), pp. 164–74, 182–92.

[18] Alfonso de Valdés, *Due dialoghi. Traduzione italiana del sec. XVI*, ed. Giuseppe de Gennaro (Naples: Istituto universitario orientale, 1968), p. 396.

Tommasino Lancellotti reread the *Profezia di santa Brigida* in much the same spirit and he reports that it "tells of the widespread death in Rome just as they now say it happened." In fact, Lancellotti was still reflecting on the question several months after the sack of Rome (which seemed to him a well-deserved punishment of Rome, the pope, and the Church), observing that "all these things were predicted many years ago by the preachers and no one believed them."[19] With hindsight and in light of the sack of Rome, the typical themes of apocalyptical preaching—denunciation of the failings of the ecclesiastical hierarchy, warning of divine wrath, prediction of terrible punishment—seemed to have been proved valid.[20]

Prophecies were not only reread but reprinted. Around 1530 or slightly earlier a very short work of four leaves was published without indication of place or date. The title page reads: *Profetie cavate duno opuscolo stampato gia trentanni passati il quale si chiama pronosticatione vera et piu non udita: et io ho tratto fora quelle cose le qual par che ocorra al presente acio che ognun senza comprar el libro possi saciar lapetito suo circha aquesta materia. Laus Deo*. Thus the work was a reprinting (or a partial reprinting) of Lichtenberger's *Pronosticatio*, which it cited only by its title, however, without mention of the author's name. Better, it was an anthology of extracts chosen according to both economic and historical criteria.[21] Thus this brief work offered, at the lowest possible cost, the predictions from the *Pronosticatio* "that seem necessary in the present"—that is, that seemed to have just come true. The statement that thirty years had passed since the publication of the original together with the type of selections made bring the publication without question to the time of the sack of Rome. It reads:

> Here St. Bridget in the book of her Revelations says, "the Church of God will be placed under the great eagle. . . . The eagle will leave the rock of la Magna [Germany] accompanied by many griffins who, coming swiftly into the orchard, will chase away the shepherd of the fifth terrestrial zone into the seventh. . . . O holy mother Church, weep. . . . Thus the root of sin will arise again out of the scorpionists, worse than Antiochus, who overturned the vases of the Temple; worse than Joab, most full of deceit; worse than Ahab who made gardens of sweet-smelling herbs of the vineyard of the Lord Sabaoth; even worse than Appollonius who despoiled the temple of the Lord. . . . He

[19] Lancellotti, *Cronaca modenese*, vol. 2, p. 271.

[20] I do not intend to go into prophecy of the sack of Rome here. See P. Picca, "Il sacco di Roma del 1527. Profezie, previsioni, prodigi," *Nuova Antologia* 345 (1929): 120–25 and, of course, André Chastel, *The Sack of Rome, 1527*, tr. Beth Archer (Princeton: Princeton University Press, 1983), pp. 78–90.

[21] Following the order of the *Profetie cavate duno opuscolo*, these extracts were taken from Lichtenberger, *Pronosticatione*, pt. 1, chap. 3; pt. 2, chaps. 4, 9, 35, 36; and pt. 2, chap. 14, respectively.

will not be ashamed to smash the holy places, nor will he be ashamed to commit sacrilege . . . thus as the root of sin, you will be punished by God.

The anonymous compiler thus performed the editorial tasks of rereading, selecting, collating, and rethinking prophecies that were already known, just as others were doing on that tragic occasion. Other predictions followed, not concerning the sack. Unlike the earlier ones, they no longer respected the internal order of Lichtenberger's book, thus seeming to shift their main focus to the spread of the Reformation:

> Until such time as the Church is renewed, God will permit a great schism to arise in the Church. . . . Three names of blasphemers preaching heresy will incite the people against the clergy. . . . Take care, you religious from Trier, and you, philosophers from Cologne, that the rapacious wolves do not enter your sheepcote: . . . for in your time will unheard-of woes arise in your churches (which God forbid). Finis.[22]

Even in Lichtenberger's *Pronosticatio*, then, one could find references to the sins of the Church and its punishment, to the religious schism in Germany, and to the "great eagle"—the emperor—whose winged vortex would bring chastisement and renewal to the ecclesiastical hierarchy. If we compare this reading of Lichtenberger to Alberto Napolitano's, we see that by their very nature prophecies had an ambiguous and contradictory life of their own. They could acquire specific meaning (which might change from age to age) only in contact with both the selective eye of a reader and the historical event that somehow guided that eye to locating a continuous and meaningful line in what to an indifferent bystander would seem a vast confusion of vague and superimposed signs. Nor is that all; such a selection could be made directly by the reader, but it could also be the work of others aware of the need for short, easy-to-read, low-cost texts aimed at a mass public. Compilers distilled only a few elements out of the original prophecy—different ones every time—and offered readers passages from Lichtenberger that seemed to speak of Luther as a new prophet or of the sack of Rome and the ambiguous (because both sacrilegious and regenerative) role of the emperor. Naturally, this facilitated all sorts of propagandistic operations.

Leonello Beliardi and His Collection of Predictions

This use of predictions clearly shows how prophecy could construct a charismatic halo around real persons. As we have seen, the medieval image of the emperor of peace that reemerged in support of Maximilian contributed

[22] Ibid., fols A. i*v*, A. ii*r*, A. ii*v*, A. iii*r*–*v*, A. iv*r*.

to the creation of broad-scale expectations concerning the imperial election of 1519 that reached so far down in society that they could even appear in the incoherent statements of a possessed woman. Furthermore, the political status and personal positions of Charles himself (not to mention the ideology fashioned for him by his counselors) created an appealing correspondence between that image and the person of the young emperor. Finally, the sack of Rome led people of a variety of cultural and social levels (Alfonso de Valdés and Tommasino Lancellotti, but also the anonymous purchasers of the *Profetie cavate duno opuscolo*) to reread and rethink prophecies, both the written ones and those transmitted orally by preachers, that spoke of punishments inflicted on the Church for its failings by an emperor sent by God. It seemed strikingly evident that this emperor was Charles.

This mental process is well illustrated by a group of six prophecies appended to the *Cronaca della città di Modena* of Leonello Beliardi, a man of law of that city.[23] The events that Beliardi chronicled occurred from 1512 to 1518, but this corpus of prophetic texts gives the impression that it could have been compiled separately, after the text of the chronicle had been written, hence that it parallels the manuscript collections of prophecies that have already been discussed. The text of the chronicle has not come down to us in an autograph version but through a transcription (apparently a fairly accurate one) that Tiraboschi made in 1785 from the original, then in the hands of Ireneo Affò,[24] and it is plausible to suppose that the texts collected at the end of the chronicle were written in a separate notebook. In fact the first of them, the verse prophecy *Più volte nella mente so' exforzato*, lacks its beginning, indicating that the first page of the notebook of prophecies may have been lost.[25]

These texts are quite varied. They include *Più volte nella mente so' exforzato* without a first page; a *Pronosticon Diaboli D.ni Caroli Suxenae, 1441*; the prophecy, mentioned several times earlier, *Gallorum levitas*, here under the title *Carmina Romae inventa in marmore sculpta apud sanctum Pancratium*; a *Pronosticum* dated "Ex Urbe X Iulij 1511" and attributed to one Panfilo Morano or Moreni, a prophecy known as early as the late thirteenth century; the *Bononia Studium perdet*; and, finally, a *Scriptura quaedam tabula aenea sculpta, quae fuit inventa in partibus Angliae in vetustissimo quodam sepulcro, anno 1456*. Some of these texts are long, some short; their age varies; some of their authors are known, others unknown; they are in

[23] Leonello Beliardi, *Cronaca della città di Modena (1512–1518)*, ed. Albano Biondi and Michele Oppi (Modena: Parini, 1981), pp. 144–55. See also the "Nota al testo" of Albano Biondi, pp. 166–68.

[24] Ibid., pp. 159–60.

[25] On this prophecy, see Roberto Rusconi, *L'attesa della fine. Crisi della società, profezia ed Apocalisse in Italia al tempo del grande scisma d'Occidente (1378–1417)* (Rome: Istituto storico italiano per il Medio Evo, 1979), pp. 156–58.

verse and in prose, in Latin and in the vernacular. Rather than investigating the origin of these texts, it is probably more worthwhile to speculate on the overall interpretation that Leonello Beliardi might have given them and on the meaning they may have had for him as a set of texts.

The poet Girolamo Casio de' Medici sheds light on the question. Immediately after the sack of Rome he composed a "Canzon ove si narra la Strage e il Sacco di Roma diritiva al Catholico re di Spagna & de Romani Carlo Quinto eletto imperatore."[26] Like Lattantio and the Archdeacon in Alfonso de Valdés's dialogue and like Tommasino Lancellotti and so many others of their age, Casio went back to ancient prophecies and attempted to read into them the meaning dictated by current events. One of the prophecies that Casio summarized in verse was the *Scriptura quaedam tabula aenea sculpta*, which proclaimed:

> in varie profetie
> trovassi, e legge iscritto
> e sculto in una tavola di rame
> . . .
> nel Mille e Quatrocento Cinquantasei
> in Anglia trovata
> fu in uno avel.
>
> (in various prophecies there is found and there reads, inscribed and sculpted on a brass tablet. . . . in 1456 it was found in a tomb in England.)

For Casio this prophecy represented both an explanation of the horrors of the sack of Rome and a program for the emperor: "Victory over Rome accomplished, to the Holy Land is he called." Indeed, the sack, which Casio interprets as a purification for the "nefarious sins" of Christians, should be followed by a crusade with Charles V as its predestined hero. Once Charles VIII of France had seemed to embody the prophecy:

> volò la fama, e il disse esser quel Carlo.
> Ma tu quel sei, di cui scrivendo parlo.
>
> (the rumor flew and the saying that it was that Charles. But you are the one, [you] of whom I speak as I write.)

This provides a key for reading at least one of the texts collected by Beliardi. In reality, however, even in their variety, these texts show a singular consonance of themes, which can be reduced, in substance, to impatience

26 Girolamo Casio de' Medici, *Vita et morte di Giesu Christo* (n.p., n.d. [1527/1528]), fols. +1*r*–+4*v*.

before the arrogance of the clergy ("vana gloria cleri")[27] and, above all, the expectation of the "great eagle,"[28] mentioned in several texts, who "superbos corriget, domabit et affliget,"[29] will bring the Turks to heel, and will vanquish the French[30]—in short, to expectation of the emperor "promised in the law and prophesied":

> poi che saranno distrutti li tiranni
> et li preti cattiati con lor danni
> verrà quellui ch'enfra Lamandi
> serà alevato.
> . . .
> Custui serà singnore de tuto el mondo
> . . .
> Costui farà pace in ogni lato.
>
> (after the tyrants are destroyed and the priests chased away with their evil deeds, there will come one who will be raised in Germany. . . . He will be lord of the entire world. . . . He will make peace everywhere.)[31]

He was also to assure the regeneration of the Roman church:

> li santi preti de novello stato
> predecarano
> . . .
> or te ralegra populo romano.
>
> (the holy priests of the new state will preach. . . . Now will you be happy, people of Rome.)[32]

In Italy, and above all in Rome, there would be "tot clades, tot subversiones, tot suspensiones, decapitationes, depopulationes, depredationes, rapinas, ruinas et incendia . . . usque ad annum 1529." Then, however, there would come a "monarcha nomine Carolus Imperator toto orbi, cujus imperio etiam Christi hostes parebunt et prostrati succumbent."[33]

It seems difficult to deny the sense that underlies these juxtaposed texts,

[27] *Carmina Romae inventa in marmore sculpta apud sanctum Pancratium*, in Beliardi, *Cronaca della città di Modena*, p. 150.

[28] *Pronosticon Diaboli D.ni Caroli Suxenae, 1441*, in ibid., p. 149; *Carmina Romae inventa*, in ibid, p. 150; *Pronosticum*, in ibid., p. 153.

[29] *Pronosticon Diaboli*, in ibid., p. 149.

[30] *Più volte nella mente so' exforzato*, in ibid., p. 147; *Pronosticon Diaboli*, in ibid., p. 150; *Carmina Romae inventa*, in ibid., p. 150.

[31] *Più volte nella mente so' exforzato*, in ibid., pp. 146–47.

[32] Ibid., p. 147.

[33] *Scriptura quaedam tabula aenea sculpta, quae fuit inventa in partibus Angliae in vetustissimo quodam sepulcro, anno 1456*, in ibid., pp. 154–55.

which immediately evoke a precise political and cultural climate in which confounding the evil prelates and heralding the advent of a universal emperor seemed one and the same thing. In that Beliardi died on 24 February 1528,[34] it hardly seems risky to suppose that these prophecies were collected and transcribed during the months immediately following the sack of Rome, when "a monarch of the name of Charles" seemed an instrument for the purification of the Church and even in Modena people were returning to the old prophecies that predicted, in Lancellotti's words, "la mortalità di Roma."

Prognostications and Prophecies for the Congress of Bologna

In this fashion, an atmosphere of prophetic expectation gradually developed to welcome Charles when he finally arrived at the Congress of Bologna in 1529. A generous harvest of print pieces appealing to a broad audience expressed Italy's hope that the emperor and the peace he would make with the pope would bring relief from the wars that had tormented the land until then. One *Historia nova quale trata de la venuta del lo Imperatore* began with these words:

> Italia dati piacere,
> da ti leva ogni gravezza
> convertir sa in alegrezza
> il pasato dispiacere.
> . . .
> Italia dati piacere.
> Bona pace he ordinata
> tanto in mare quanto in terra.
>
> (Italy, take pleasure, chase away all care, may you convert past displeasure into joy. . . . Italy, take pleasure. Good peace is commanded both on the seas and on land.)[35]

Other compositions placed the same ideas in a more strictly prophetic framework:

> Questo è il sacro Imperatore,
> questo è quel profetizato,
> questo è quel vero signore
> che ci harà pacificato.

[34] Lancellotti, *Cronaca modenese*, vol. 2, p. 341.

[35] *Historia nova quale trata de la venuta del lo Imperatore a laude de Italia de Genova et del nobille Andrea Doria* (n.p., n.d. [Savona, J. Berruerio, 1530?]), fols. 1*r*–*v*.

Or sia donque laudato
questa sua bona arivata.

(This is the holy Emperor, this is the one prophesied, this is that true lord who will bring us peace. Thus may his fortunate arrival be praised.)

Italy herself spoke these words, personified in a pamphlet of four unnumbered leaves and entitled *Alegreza de Italia per la venuta del Sacro Imperatore*.[36] Thus Charles V was the emperor of peace, "quel profetizato." The same idea appears in another anonymous composition of the same year (1530), entitled *Il gran susidio el qual domanda tutta Italia al Imperatore*:

Cercato ò santa Scriptura quasi tuta,
di molte profetie son adimpito,
del suo bell'arbor tolt'ò ciò che fruta:
io trovo esser tu quello sì gradito
che tanti fati farà sua conduta,
che l'alle extenderai in ogni sito,
e sbigottir farai el turco tale
tra lor seguendo d'infiniti male.

(I have searched nearly all of holy Scripture, I am filled with many prophecies, from its fine tree I have taken what was productive: I find that you are the one so welcome that many acts will smooth his way, who will extend your wings in every place and so confound the Turk, infinite afflictions following among them.)[37]

It is understandable, then, that there was no dearth of astrologers and prophets of all sorts in Bologna, all of whom took care to accommodate events and predictions in the form most appropriate to the interests of one party or another. A Latin prophecy that had been known for at least twenty years by its first line, "Veniet de occidente rex magnus et ferus," was particularly popular. It predicted that after a period of suffering and destruction, the sovereign to which its title referred would be crowned in Bologna, followed by a period of joy and universal abundance. Moreover, the prophecy was adjusted to the advantage of the municipality in the sense that in the version distributed on 14 February the phrase "et postea erit civitas imperialis," absent in the original, was added to the phrase "et Bononiae

[36] *Alegreza de Italia per la venuta del Sacro Imperatore con la exortatione. Soneto per Pietro Venetiano* (n.p., n.d. [Venice, 1530?]).

[37] *Il gran susidio el qual domanda tutta Italia al Imperatore cognoscendo che quello è inspirato da Dio e venuto in Italia per liberarla* (n.p., n.d.).

coronabitur."[38] In that way, the city hoped to get something in return for the expense and trouble of welcoming the pontifical and imperial parties and their troops.

The emperor himself was the principal topic of the prophecies, however. Girolamo Balbi published a work entitled *De futuris Caroli Augusti successibus vaticinium* in honor of Charles's arrival in Bologna in November 1529.[39] The work was a pure and simple panegyric in Latin hexameters forecasting the return of the eagles of victory to the Campidoglio and the recuperation of the sacred sites in the Holy Land thanks to Charles. It is nevertheless significant that Balbi's ultra-Ciceronian praises should have been expressed in the form of a prophecy. Astrological prognostication was another sort of prophecy that lent itself well to the praise of political power during these same years. The astrologer had to take into account his debts toward the ruler when he made up his annual *iuditium*, and that gratitude was often part of the logic of simple dependence and patronage is common knowledge and has been clearly demonstrated for astrologers in Ferrara.[40] Furthermore, when the astrologer failed to respect such courtesies he had to suffer the consequences. This is what happened to Luca Gaurico when he predicted "una gran iattura" (a hex cast) on Giovanni Bentivoglio. Gaurico was subjected to torture (he was stretched on the ropes), then turned over to the inquisitor "as an invoker of demons and heretic," and his writings and prognostications were burned in the city square.[41] Another astrologer, Alfonso Pisano, was imprisoned by Pope Clement VII when he predicted the pope's death in 1533. He was kept in jail on bread and water for six months and then exiled.[42]

Relations between the astrologer and the ruler were further complicated when the astrologer took not only his prince's requirements into account as he compiled his predictions but also the needs of the general reading public. He then had to combine praise with propaganda and exhortation,

[38] Matteo Dandolo to Lorenzo Priuli, 25 February 1530, in Sanuto, *Diarii*, vol. 52, col. 638. The text of the prophecy, transcribed during March 1510, is also given in its entirety in Tommaso di Silvestro, *Diario*, ed. Luigi Fumi, in RIS 15, pt. 5 (Bologna: Nicola Zanichelli, 1923), vol. 2, p. 425.

[39] Girolamo Balbi, *De futuris Caroli Augusti successibus vaticinium* (Bologna: Giovan Battista Faelli, November 1529). Balbi published another work as well: *Ad Carolum V imperatorem De coronatione* (Bologna: Giovan Battista Faelli, 1530). On this work and on the symbolism of the coronation in general, see Tiziana Bernardi, "Analisi di una cerimonia pubblica. L'incoronazione di Carlo V a Bologna," *Quaderni storici* 61 (1986): 171–99.

[40] By Cesare Vasoli, *La cultura delle corti* (Bologna: Cappelli, 1980), pp. 129–58.

[41] Cherubino Ghirardacci, *Della historia di Bologna, parte terza*, ed. Albano Sorbelli, RIS 33, pt. 1 (Città di Castello: S. Lapi, 1912–1932), p. 342; Giuliano Fantaguzzi, *Caos. Cronache cesenati del sec. XV*, ed. Dino Bazzocchi (Cesena: Tip. Arturo Bettini, 1915), p. 231.

[42] The episode is narrated in the *Pronostico de lanno del 1538 per lo excellente maistro Alphonso Pisano: in laude del sumo Pontifice papa Paulo terzo vicario de Christo et de tutta la Christianitate* (n.p., n.d. [1538]), fol. 1*v*.

which was precisely what happened during the Congress of Bologna. Luca Gaurico was among the astrologers present,[43] but he does not seem to have written prognostications, nor did he take an active part in setting the date for the coronation (which, as is known, was chosen by Charles himself because it was both his birthday and the anniversary of the battle of Pavia). Still, we can in some fashion hear the voice of the man who was considered the prince of astrologers of his time through the person and pen of one Gasparo Crivelli from Milan, Gaurico's self-proclaimed disciple (to the point that Crivelli joined Gaurico's name to his own twice on the title page of the vernacular prognostications that he compiled and had printed in Bologna on 10 November 1529).[44] The prognostication (during the course of which Guarico's works are cited repeatedly) alternates between predictions of peace and prosperity for Italy, for the pope, and particularly for the emperor, and other more negative predictions concerning Süleyman and the city of Florence. The sultan was to be struck by the plague and every sort of disaster, to the point of losing his state "for the conjunctions of all the planets in Pisces that took place in 1524" (which means that when the sixteen terrible conjunctions had failed to bring on a flood, they were recycled to augur harm to the Turks). As for the Florentines, they were to have a change of government and to suffer "all sorts of misfortunes and so many shipwrecks that they will not know what to do." The predictions aimed at Francis I of France and for the Venetians were more ambiguous. Both were promised, though in equivocal terms, an encounter with the pope and with the emperor, "and thus they will treat of difficult things."[45]

As is evident, these predictions were suffused with propaganda and with adulatory intent, in particular where Charles V was concerned. The imperial fortunes were associated with the fortunes of all those (and only those) who accepted alliance with the emperor and fell in with his aims; when all was said and done, Charles was the sole fixed point of reference in peace or for a just war and the center of a cosmos that was harmonious and content because it revolved around him. Crivelli also repeatedly exhorts the emperor to lead a crusade "against the enemies of and rebels to the Christian name," an expression that apparently covered both the Turks and the Lutherans. In another passage, one might argue, exhortation is concealed as

[43] Sanuto, *Diarii*, vol. 52, col. 503.

[44] *Pronostico De lo Anno M.D.XXX. de Gasparo Crivello Milanese Discipulo di M. Luca gaurico*, "Datum Bononiae die decimo novembris 1529." The title page bears an architectonic framework with cupids, candelabras, and griffins enclosing the title. At the bottom, an oval shield bears the words "Lucae Gaurici Neapoli." My observation is based on the copy conserved in the library of the Archiginnasio di Bologna.

[45] Ibid., fols. 3*r* and 4*r*.

prediction: Crivelli interprets two eclipses to mean "that before the end of four years the Church will be very well reformed."[46]

In predictions of this sort, reform of the Church, the crusade, and punishment of heretics and rebels were lumped together and founded on the idea of empire. They also contributed to that idea, enriching it and giving it added complexity. The vehicle of the annual prognostication in the vernacular guaranteed this ideology a broad distribution and lent it conviction. The prophetic possibilities inherent in the figure of Charles V could easily be made explicit, particularly since his coming to an agreement with the pope seemed likely to generate a solution to the problems that tormented Italy and Christendom.

Three Suns for a New Octavian

The religious and prophetic reading of the encounter between the pope and the emperor in Bologna is demonstrated by another episode as well. On 22 April 1531, Tommasino Lancellotti described in his chronicle a prodigious phenomenon that had appeared in the sky:

> And all the persons who were in the piazza of Modena said that there were three suns; every person marveled much at such a signal in the sky in this age, saying that in the time of Emperor Octavian three suns had appeared, [and] at that time universal peace was made for the entire world. God grant that this be so in the present, because for forty-nine years now there has been no peace in Italy, and never in the days of men who are living in the world has there been greater dearth than there is at present.[47]

The phenomenon of refraction alluded to here, known as parhelion (here triple parhelia), was commonly taken as "a fearful sign," and between 1485 and 1514 we find it noted in contemporary chronicles at least four times, always accompanied by expressions of terror. In 1536 it was called "most cruelly out of nature" in the *Gran prodigio di tre soli apparsi in Franza*.[48] Only in 1531 were the three suns considered an omen of "universal peace for all men" as "in the time of the Emperor Octavian." Tommasino Lancellotti was referring here to what a widespread medieval tra-

[46] Ibid., fols. 2*r* and *v*.

[47] Lancellotti, *Cronaca modenese*, vol. 3, pp. 238–39.

[48] Leone Cobelli, *Cronache forlivesi*, ed. Giosuè Carducci and Enrico Frati (Bologna: Regia tipografia, 1874), pp. 284–85; Andrea Bernardi, *Cronache forlivesi . . . dal 1476 al 1517*, ed. Giuseppe Mazzatinti, 2 vols. (Bologna: R. Deputazione di storia patria, 1895–1897), vol. 1, p. 159; Tommaso di Silvestro, *Diario*, p. 11, Stefano Infessura, *Diario della città di Roma di Stefano Infessura scriba-senato*, ed. Oreste Tommasini (Rome: Forzani, 1890), p. 280. The phrase "un segno spaventoso" comes from Tommaso di Silvestro in the passage cited.

dition, publicized through preaching, considered to be one of the prophetic signs of the coming of Christ.[49] Vincent de Beauvais described it in the thirteenth century in these terms:

> The day after [the death of Caesar] there appeared three suns in the East, which gradually united again into one sun, foretelling that the triumvirate of Lucius Antonius, Mark Antony, and Augustus would be transformed into a monarchy; and above all that the knowledge of a God one and three was then imminent in all the world.[50]

The three suns that appeared after the death of Caesar were thus considered both an imperial sign and a religious sign, the interpretation of which went back to the providential reading of the empire of Augustus given in the Middle Ages as a necessary background of peace for the birth of Christ. That the parhelia could be interpreted as an "imperial" sign explains why they were considered an omen of peace by those who gathered in the main square of Modena. The passage of the new Caesar Augustus and his coronation in Bologna, which had taken place only a few months earlier, seemed to have launched a new Golden Age. That made it necessary to read positively a sign that in all other instances was considered inauspicious.

This interpretation can only be hypothetical, but it is clarified and confirmed by a passage on the three suns that had appeared the year before written by Friedrich Nausea, bishop of Vienna, in his *Libri mirabilium septem* in 1532. Among the many prodigies that had occurred in 1531, Nausea writes, paraphrasing Vincent de Beauvais without mentioning him, the parhelia, or three suns, were of particular interest, because they recalled the suns that appeared after the death of Caesar and that foretold both the advent of a universal monarchy after the triumvirate and the cult of a three-in-one God. Nausea continues:

> And may the heavens grant that in the present circumstances as well the three suns signify that the same cult will become established, even among the Turks, under the most invincible and most Christian princes, Charles V, emperor and Ferdinando, most glorious king of the Romans, God be their highest guide!

Nausea had a few doubts about this. He remembered that in other circumstances the three suns were an inauspicious prodigy. Thus he states

[49] Carlo Delcorno, *Giordano da Pisa e l'antica predicazione volgare* (Florence: L. S. Olschki, 1975), pp. 264–66, demonstrates that the prodigy of the three suns was part of the repertory of *exempla* of late medieval preaching. See also Bernardino da Siena, *Le prediche volgari*, ed. Ciro Cannarozzi, 7 vols. (Pistoia: Alberto Pacinotti, 1934–), vol. 2, p. 278.

[50] Vincentius Bellovacensis, *Bibliotheca Mundi. Tomus qui Speculum Historiale inscribitur* (Douai, 1644), bk. 6, chap. 41, p. 187: "Die sequenti apparuerunt tres soles in oriente, qui paulatim in unum corpus solis redacti sunt, significantes quod dominium Lucii Antonii et Marci Antonii et Augusti in Monarchiam rediret. Vel potius quod notitia trini Dei et unius toti orbi futura imminebat."

(and we thank him for it) that in furnishing these suggestions, he is by no means basing his thought on the canonical laws of augury and astrology ("haud quaquam sim sequuturus leges nec Prophetarum, nec Astronomorum, nec Astrologorum, nec Augurum, nec Auspicum") but only on the traditions handed down by his elders, founded on the oral transmission of certain rules:

> Rather will I follow the criteria of those old men with white hair who, basing themselves on long experience and attentive comparison and reciprocal confrontation of many events past and present, predict future [events] with great certainty and finesse, and evaluate in substantially accurate manner what the greater part of the celestial and terrestrial signs signify and foretell.[51]

Thus we see a hint of the "popular divination" that we have already seen and that was the common fodder of the city dwellers who gathered in the squares to compare the *mirabilia* that appeared in the heavens, or that they were shown for a few pennies at the fairs and the taverns, with the marvels pictured on the broadsheets or described by the *cantastorie*. The very term, "popular divination"—*genus divinationum . . . populare vel plebeium*—was used in this same sense by Kaspar Peucer, Melanchthon's son-in-law. According to Peucer, this was divination that did not look deeply into the cause of events or into the profound relationship between omens and the events they signified, but rather recalled and compared past omens and events, arriving at the establishment of divinatory rules that give foreknowledge of the future "satis foeliciter."[52]

Although Nausea was a bishop and a humanist, then, he was aware of and could manipulate criteria of "common" and "popular" divination. He soon abandoned this terrain, however, to return to the atmosphere of a different and higher culture, citing an epigram of the Neapolitan poet Girolamo Borgia on the three suns. Among the works of Borgia, who lived from 1475 to about 1550, there were an unpublished *Historia de bellis italicis*, a poem with a divinatory background entitled *Incendium ad Avernum Lacum nocte intempesta exortum*, and a number of verse compositions in praise of Charles V.[53] In his epigram on the three suns, Borgia outdid himself, however. After evoking the prodigy of Augustus's days, as tradition dictated, he continues:

[51] Friedrich Nausea, *Libri mirabilium septem* (Cologne: apud P. Quentell, 1532), fols. 33*v* and 30*r*: "Atque utinam ii nostra quoque tempestate tres soles subsinnent eundem vel apud Turcas cultum, sub invictissimis et christianissimis principibus Carolo Imp. V et Ferdinando Rhomanorum [*sic*] rege gloriosissimo, duce Deo rediturum!"; "Sim sequuturus . . . dumtaxat normas canorum senum, qui longo usu et diligenti rerum praeteritarum et praesentium comparatione mutuaque collatione freti nonnunquam certius exquisitiusque presagiunt et signa plerumque caeli et terrae quid haec ipsa nobis velint et portendant non impie diiudicant."

[52] Kaspar Peucer, *Commentarius de praecipuis divinationum generibus* (Wittenberg: Johannes Crato, 1553), fols. 40*r* and *v*.

[53] See Gianni Ballistreri, "Borgia (Borgio), Girolamo," DBI, vol. 12, pp. 721–24.

Pandite, mortales, oculos in caligine mersos
numen et in terris cernite esse novum.

Charles V was thus not only the new Augustus but also a new divinity, and his holy and imperial vocation, his *numen*, was proclaimed to the ends of the earth:

Caesar numen habet radios a margine mundi
victores mittens; omnia iura domat.

Charles V's device, with two columns and the motto *Plus oultre*, expressed a notion similar to the one implied in these hexameters. Furthermore, the discovery and Christianization of new worlds had very clearly defined prophetic implications.[54] It is certain, however, that one of the missions Providence had set the Sun God was to extend his rays to the confines of the world and bring back within the *res publica christiana* the savages of the new Indies, whom Borgia defines as "genus ille ferum." No one could withstand him, because it was God's will that he come, god himself:

Hic est ille deus demissus Numine terris;
longo expectatus tempore Caesar adest,
omnes qui terras teneat ditione sub una,
qui domitet Turcas ac genus ille ferum.
Caesaris imperio populi parete volentes,
caesaris imperium credite iussa Dei.[55]

Thus an exceptional harvest of prophecies common to men of learning and to popular literature (with evident reciprocal influences) accompanied the start of a new Golden Age. The medieval image of the emperor of peace had dissolved into that of the new Caesar Augustus, a transformation, incidentally, that was due not only to reasons of general historical evolution or the mere triumph of classical tradition over the medieval tradition but also to the need to express, albeit in encomiastic form, an urgent and real need for peace and political and economic stability, clearly identifiable through the realization of a concrete model "of Octavian, emperor."[56]

[54] See Adriano Prosperi, "America e Apocalisse. Note sulla 'conquista spirituale' del Nuovo Mondo," *Critica storica* 13 (1976): 1–61 and the bibliography contained in that article; Yates, *Astraea*, p. 31.

[55] Nausea, *Libri mirabilium septem*, fol. 34*r*.

[56] One excellent indication of this attitude is the title of a brief work of four leaves, *Il priegho d'Italia detto su'l Pater Nostro fatto al sommo iddio nel quale il priegha voglia liberarla dalle longhe guerre, miserie et affanni, de i quali per longho tempo e stata afflitta et gli piaccia renderli quella libertà che gia hebbe prima et darli pace universale come hebbe al tempo d'Augusto con altri capitoli. Cosa molto degna et bella di nuovo stampata* (n.p., n.d.).

EPILOGUE

1530: The End of Popular Prophecy: The End of Liberty in Italy

STRANGE TO SAY, after the Congress of Bologna the various forms of prophecy that until then had been so lively among the Italian urban populations died out almost simultaneously. The three years between 1527 and 1530 seem to signal the apex of street-corner prophecy and were soon followed by its collapse. This is particularly true of the forms of prophecy best adapted to oral transmission, which were less standardized and could seek a broader range of means of communication. Prophetic print pieces suddenly disappeared from the market; prophetic preaching from the pulpit had already virtually died out (we have seen the singular case of Zaccheria da Fivizzano); hermits continued to circulate, but with every-increasing difficulty, censured from on high and derided on all sides. It is also interesting to note that the decline of popular prophecy had no parallel in other parts of Europe; indeed, in France and England prophecy began to be established only after 1530 and lasted to the mid-seventeenth century.[1]

The "monsters," for their part, had a curious destiny. In Germany the Reformation saw to it that they continued to fulfill their ominous mission,[2] but in Italy they were gradually transformed into curiosities in museums

[1] See, in particular, Katharine R. Firth, *The Apocalyptic Tradition in Reformation Britain, 1530–1645* (Oxford and New York: Oxford University Press, 1979), pp. 10–13; and Elisabeth Labrousse, *L'Entrée de Saturne au lion. L'éclipse de soleil du 12 août 1654* (The Hague: M. Nijhoff, 1974). See also Anne Jacobson Schutte, " 'Such Monstrous Briths': A Neglected Aspect of the Antinomian Controversy," *Renaissance Quarterly* 38 (1985): 85–106.

[2] That Melanchthon in particular retained an interest in monsters is well known and especially applicable here. See Stefano Caroti, "Comete, portenti, causalità naturale e escatologia in Filippo Melantone," in *Scienze, credenze occulte, livelli di cultura. Convegno internazionale di studi (Firenze, 26–30 giugno 1980)* (Florence: L. S. Olschki, 1982), pp. 293–426. Another interesting case is the collection of *terata* that the Zurich canon Johann Jakob Wick inserted in his journals, at Bullinger's suggestion, precisely in order to reach a better understanding of the "catastrophic times" in which he lived. (The diaries, written between 1560 and 1588, are now conserved in the Zentralbibliothek of Zurich.) See Matthias Senn, *Johann Jakob Wick (1522–1588) und seine Sammlung von Nachrichten zur Zeitgeschichte* (Zurich: Leeman, 1974) and, for the print pieces on monsters under consideration here, Brigitte Schwarz, "Johann Jacob Wick e la sua raccolta di fogli volanti a soggetto mostruoso," tesi di laurea discussa presso l'Università di Bologna, a.a. 1985/86, relatrice Ottavia Niccoli. In general, see Robin Bruce Barnes, *Prophecy and Gnosis: Apocalypticism in the Wake of the Lutheran Reformation* (Stanford, Calif.: Stanford University Press, 1988).

or anatomical exhibits. When in 1550 in Modena a domestic cat gave birth to a deformed kitten, no one thought to draw prognostications from the event. However, one Geminiano de' Rossi, who found the dead kitten, had it embalmed and kept it as "a monstrous thing."[3] The exhibition of deformed creatures was of course no novelty, but here it seems to fit better in a *Wunderkammer* (admittedly of minimal size) than at a village fair. In any event, the divinatory function that abnormalities had once had no longer existed. That is not all. We have seen that between the fifteenth and the sixteenth centuries monsters in some fashion represented the finger of God pointed at the sins of humankind, but predominantly at their political sins and, to some extent, their social sins. They highlighted such matters as the corruption of the ecclesiastical hierarchy, the decline in civic virtue and religion in urban life, or cowardly vacillation before the Turkish menace. Somewhere between 1525 and 1550 an important transformation took place in this area, and around 1550 monsters once again became a sign of sin, but of a private sin—indeed the most private of all sins, because they were held to be clamorous proof of the parents' transgression of sexual taboos, in particular the mother's, whose fault was consenting to sexual relations during menstruation.[4] This was a highly significant shift in the ongoing process of the narrowing of sexual ethics during the latter half of the sixteenth century and an intensification of the negative conception of women and their bodies as a direct source of corruption. Thus monsters were still some sort of sign, but no longer were they to be deciphered by the criteria dictated by orally transmitted lore (as the *divinatio popularis* was transmitted by the elders of the community). They were a manifest result of improper conjugal behavior, visible to all eyes, and needed no help from divinatory science to be understood. Eventually physicians were called upon to decide whether the cause of a "monstrous" conception was this or another. The accent, however, had shifted from a relationship of sign and signified to one of cause and effect.

From Expectation of a New Age to the Age of Repression

Thus far I have sought to interpret a cultural phenomenon as a unified entity and global culture that aimed at encompassing nature, history, and the supernatural in a single act of comprehension. One might well wonder whether the nearly instantaneous end of a cultural phenomenon of this

[3] Tommasino Lancellotti, *Cronaca modenese,* ed. Carlo Borghi, 12 vols. (Parma: P. Fiaccadori, 1863), vol. 9, p. 210.

[4] See Ottavia Niccoli, " 'Menstruum quasi monstruum' parti mostruosi e tabù mestruale nel '500," *Quaderni storici* 44 (1980): 402–28.

importance was connected with a process of exhaustion within that culture, or whether it resulted predominantly from outside repression.

In all probability, the two hypotheses should be combined. I have sought to analyze, particularly in the first and last chapters of this book, the immediate and conscious relationships that operated within the minds of those who transmitted the cultural values of prophecy and linked it to the calamities of the Italian wars. The relationship was complex, but it was stated so explicitly and with so much insistence that it is impossible to doubt its existence. Andrea Bernardi, to pick one example, stated that there had been many forewarnings of the arrival of the French, chief among them "the many prophecies of many saints" that had circulated throughout Italy. He also comments:

> That does not mean that the said prophecies showed no celestial influence: but everyone everywhere among the peoples of Italy prognosticated and wanted to speak of [their] coming for the bad government and great rapine of our said Italian lords, for truly there was nothing left of us but bones, because they had taken the blood and the flesh.[5]

Urban prophecy was thus born of dissatisfaction with the present situation, and it encouraged an openness toward political novelties. These novelties in turn generated prophecies, in an apparently continual exchange of cause and effect. As Matarazzo wrote, "in those times there were found and newly published prophecies without end . . . because in those times Italy began to do new things everywhere."[6] As we have just seen, in one sense the tremendous increase in prophecy in 1529–1530 was a mirror image of the preceding fifty years. Where in the decades before the catastrophe, all prophecy focused on expectation of reform and renewal, afterward it expressed the triumphal fulfillment of those expectations. Prophecy was a language of medieval origin, even though it attempted to emphasize its total embodiment in one real political situation after another, and it is quite comprehensible that by 1530 it should have become somewhat threadbare. Even without considering the wearing out of a tradition, prophecy so to speak signed its own death warrant in 1530, for when all prophecies are fulfilled, prophecy itself has no further reason for being. For that reason widespread acceptance of the notion that Charles V's descent into Italy, his pact with the pope, and his coronation truly signaled fulfillment of the predictions of the advent of a sovereign of peace and the beginning of an era of renewal for both Christendom and the empire could not help but result in a lessening of prophetic tension. There is something

[5] Andrea Bernardi, *Cronache forlivesi . . . dal 1476 al 1517,* ed. Giuseppe Mazzatinti, 2 vols. (Bologna: R. Deputazione di storia patria, 1895–1897), vol. 1, pt. 2, p. 72.

[6] Francesco Matarazzo (detto Maturanzio), *Cronaca della città di Perugia dal 1492 al 1503,* ed. Ariodante Fabretti, *Archivio storico italiano* 16, pt. 2 (1851), p. 16.

else, however. These events seemed to signal the end of a catastrophic period of wars and disasters. To recall the words of Tommasino Lancellotti that have already been cited:

> In the time of Emperor Octavian . . . universal peace was made for the entire world. God grant that this be so in the present, because for forty-nine years now there has been no peace in Italy, and never in the days of men . . . has there been greater universal dearth.

These words go far to explain the sudden decline of public prophecy after 1530. Although armed combat did not cease entirely,[7] there was greater political and military stability in the Italian peninsula and the situation as a whole seemed radically changed. The phase of the "liberty of Italy" had ended, but continual harassment by the horrors of war slackened for people all over Italy. This was why prophecy had run its course. Conversely, the relation between war and prophecy seems confirmed by the fact that in other parts of Europe, where wars of religion still gripped the population, apocalyptical tensions continued to be strong until the end of the Thirty Years War, only to die out with the end of that conflict and the rise of a new balance of power in Europe.[8]

The coronation in Bologna also opened a new period in ecclesiastical life in Italy (and not only in Italy, to tell the truth). The urban prophecy examined here was doubtless an aspect of the strong expectations of a new age that permeated society from the latter half of the fifteenth century.[9] As we have seen, the relationship between novelty and prophecy is clear in both Bernardi and Matarazzo. After 1530 it is clear that pressures for renewal and reform (particularly reform of the Church) tended to peter out, giving way to a period in which the ecclesiastical hierarchy closed ranks and reorganized to combat the spread of heresy. All direct forms of relationship with the supernatural were judged to be dangerous and came under increasingly stringent control. A number of phenomena that had been characteristic of religious life in the fifty years between 1480 and 1530 thus either ground to a halt or were suffocated. We know, for example, that one specific model of female saintliness centering on charisma, with strong prophetic tendencies and demonstrably capable of attracting groups of followers, died out or was repressed precisely around the same time. Supernatural visions, which previously had been accepted as a singular but not anoma-

[7] See Bernardo Nobile, " 'Romiti' e vita religiosa nella cronachistica italiana fra '400 e '500," *Cristianesimo nella storia* 5 (1984): 303-40; p. 337.

[8] See above, note 1, and Josef V. Polisensky, *The Thirty Years War*, tr. Robert Evans (Berkeley: University of California Press, 1971), p. 76.

[9] See, in particular, the studies published in *L'attesa dell'età nuova nella spiritualità della fine del medioevo. Convegno del 16–19 ottobre 1960)* (Todi: Accademia tudertina, 1962); and Eugenio Garin, *"L'età nuova. Ricerche di storia della cultura del XII al XVI secolo* (Naples: Morano, 1969).

lous part of the life of piety and had been repeatedly documented, re-elaborated, and retold, met with constantly increasing mistrust and reprobation.[10]

The forms of prophecy that have been examined in these pages also came under increasingly rigid control, but something else happened as well. We have seen that on various occasions (with the "monsters" of Ravenna and Bologna and the apparitions at Verdello and in the letter of Giovanni Antonio Flaminio to Leo X) ecclesiastical "high" culture manipulated, re-elaborated, and turned to its own purposes elements that more properly belonged to the prophecy of "low" culture. Paradoxically, the classical and Ciceronian culture that flourished at the papal court and in the circles around it during the years of Leo X's papacy and the early years of Clement VII favored this habit. Interest in the world of classical antiquity brought with it a renewed fascination with the *monstra, prodigia,* and *portenta,* a fascination that popular divination, for its part, pursued indefatigably. During the decade between 1520 and 1530 these intense interchanges between high and low culture declined steadily, and after 1530 the elites rejected any sort of involvement with the world of folklore. Models of saintliness, visionary experience, and pious practices that had roots in folk traditions were defined as superstitious; divination in all its aspects, *divinatio popularis* in particular, was rejected more and more decisively. Such attitudes add up to what we would have to call the Counter-Reformation, a conventional but efficacious term.

Divination, An Iniquitous and Female Art

In 1578 a work was published in Florence entitled *Discorso contro il volgo in cui con buone ragioni si reprovano molte sue false opinioni*. It was the work of Cosme de Aldana, a Spaniard. Among other topics that he treated, Aldana reproved a number of popular beliefs (and in some cases, people's failure to believe), for example, that the common people derided astrologers and refused to believe in them, maintaining their own divinatory beliefs

> in which because a dog barks in a certain way . . . you say, if anyone is sick in the neighborhood, he will die. . . . You do not leave anything on earth to which you do not give some significance.[11]

[10] Ottavia Niccoli, "Visioni e racconti di visioni nell'Italia del primo Cinquecento," *Società e storia* 28 (1985): 253–79; Adriano Prosperi, "Dalle 'divine madri' ai 'padri spirituali,' " in *Women and Men in Spiritual Culture: XIV–XVIII Centuries,* ed. Elisja Schulte van Kessel (The Hague; Netherlands Govt. Pub. Office, 1986), pp. 71–90; Gabriella Zarri, "Le sante vive. Per una tipologia della santità femminile nel primo Cinquecento," *Annali dell'Istituto italo-germanico in Trento* 6 (1980): 371–445.

[11] Cosme de Aldana, *Discorso contro il volgo in cui con buone ragioni si reprovano molte sue false opinioni* (Florence: G. Marescotti, 1578), pp. 264-65. On astrology, see pp. 250–63.

The contrast between the learned science of astrology and popular divination was clearly defined, as is evident today and as contemporaries were well aware. It is interesting that Aldana went on to liken this contrast to the one between learned and popular medicine (as he says, between *medici* and *ciarlatani*), in which the physicians were scorned by the common people, who heeded only the charlatans.[12] Still, Aldana's total contempt for the low science of divination is singular; Leo X or Guicciardini, not to mention an artisan, a merchant, or a notary, would never have expressed such a thought fifty or sixty years earlier.

So *divinatio popularis* was rejected. It survived somewhat longer among the common people, however, in particular, as Aldana says, among "certain ignorant and silly old enchantresses and charm purveyors," women who went about "throwing flour on a polished table on St. John's Eve to forecast the husband their daughter would have." The same women, he continues, attempt to heal the sick "with their [spells], part conjuration, part old wives' sayings [*parole da veglia*] or comic expressions, [and] with certain measurements of the palm to be made (they say) with the heart hand."[13] Aldana's criticism reflects an ancient polemic against healers—*vetulae*—that began with Thomas Aquinas.[14] Nonetheless, these words show early traces of a more specific phenomenon that was to take shape during the second half of the sixteenth century and run its course by the end of the century. A work published in Venice in 1599, written by Giuseppe Passi and entitled *I donneschi diffetti* shows that we have returned to the climate of revived misogyny discussed earlier. Some passages of this work merit closer examination, however. Passi deplores the wicked arts—*"arti scellerate"*—proper to women that consist in "wanting to know things that are to come." It was not the learned science of astrology that he had in mind; for that he refers his readers to the *Disputationes contra astrologiam* of Giovanni Pico. He was alluding instead to the "thousand superstitions" of women, such as their custom of observing birds and heeding their cries,

> their casting spells with odd and even numbers, with letters, [and] with figures attributed to the celestial signs . . . like [their] casting straws of uneven length, considering the designs that show in molten lead, drawing points on a tablet or a stone with one's face turned to the moon, selecting beans [blindfolded], and similar folderol and vanities put to use by women. . . . Now it is clear, *madonne,* and there is no "maybe" about whether these spells that you use superstitiously are legitimate, for if you chance to lose as much as a penny,

[12] Ibid., p. 231.

[13] Ibid., pp. 266 and 232.

[14] See Jole Agrimi and Chiara Crisciani, "Medici e 'vetulae' dal Duecento al Quattrocento: problemi di una ricerca," in *Cultura popolare e cultura dotta nel Seicento: Atti del convegno di studi Genova, 23–25 novembre 1982* (Milan: Franco Angeli, 1983), pp. 144–59.

> immediately like a dog after a hare you run for the shears and the sieve to see if so-and-so stole it from you . . . with a thousand silly and vain words, thinking that the sieve will move when you pronounce your superstitious words.[15]

By reading between the lines of Passi's reproaches to women we can grasp a number of magic practices, which are corroborated in Inquisitorial trials of the sixteenth and seventeenth centuries. We also see traces of the *libri delle sorti* that were immensely popular during the sixteenth century.[16] Divination in these spell books was increasingly colored by a desire to entertain—though Passi seems not to have been amused. Finally, it is interesting to find the divinatory technique of the movement of a sieve suspended from the point of a pair of shears mentioned here. The procedure was already known to Pomponazzi, Tommaso Campanella had tried it personally, and it was known in England as well.[17]

Passi presents an interesting and varied array of divinatory practices and techniques, but it should be noted that he attributes them solely and in all circumstances to women, in opposition to astrology, which—by implication, to be sure—seems reserved to men. Pomponazzi, by contrast, speaks of the shears and the sieve as a technique practiced by charlatans and tale singers, thus as a predominantly male technique. From a sort of divination exclusive to the subalternate classes—to the *volgo,* to use Aldana's term—we have shifted over to a divination specific to another subalternate world, the world of women. With these women's procedures we have reached the last residue, the last shreds, of the prophetic culture that I have sought to reconstruct in these pages. They are scattered, however, and stripped of any coherence. Tied to purely private concerns, they are powerless to read the supernatural world, the world of nature, or human society (thus politics and history) in any sort of unified manner.

Indeed, the channels of diffusion for prophetic culture had been blocked once and for all. The element that perhaps had given them their greatest breadth—the swift and diversified circulation of cultural entities through a variety of social levels and circles—had stopped quite a while earlier. In all

[15] Guiseppe Passi, *I donneschi diffetti* (Venice: Iacobo Antonio Somascho, 1599), pp. 141–45. Scipione Mercurio, who wrote approximately at the same time, considered "this art . . . more exercised by women than by men": Scipione Mercurio, *De gli errori popolari d'Italia libri sette* (Padua: Matteo Cadorino, 1658), p. 311.

[16] See Ottavia Niccoli, "Gioco, divinazione, livelli di cultura. Il Triompho di Fortuna di Sigismondo Fanti," *Rivista storica italiana* 96 (1984): 591–99 and the bibliography contained therein.

[17] Pietro Pomponazzi, *De naturlium effectuum admirandorum causis, Et de incantationibus liber* (Basel: ex officina Henricpetrina, [1567]), p. 55; Tommaso Campanella, *Del senso delle cose e della magia,* ed. Antonio Bruers (Bari: G. Laterza & figli, 1925), p. 300. For England, see Keith Thomas, *Religion and the Decline of Magic* (New York: Scribner, 1971), pp. 213–14.

probability, prophecy did not totally die out, however. Further study could certainly discover remaining traces even in the late sixteenth century, for example, in the sect of "Benedetto corazzaro" (Benedetto the armorer) in Venice, or among the followers of Giorgio Siculo, or again among the nuns of the convent of San Lorenzo in Bologna.[18] But the political and public use of the prophetic and visionary experience—in short, its civic dimension—had certainly ended. What once took place in the city squares now retired behind closed doors in houses, in the confessional, and in the cloister, isolated and relegated to an exclusively private domain. Expectation of the new age had meant religious, political, and cultural palingenesis, but now there were no more new ages to forecast and await. The time for prophecy had ended; the time for utopias had not yet begun.

[18] Carlo Ginzburg, "Due note sul profetismo cinquecentesco," *Rivista storica italiana* 78 (1966): 184–227; Prosperi, "Dalle 'divine madri.' "

Index